MANAGER'S GUIDE TO SMALL COMPUTERS

MANAGER'S GUIDE TO SMALL COMPUTERS

Evaluating, Selecting, Financing,
and Installing a Business
Computer That Works

Charles W. Bradley

HOLT, RINEHART AND WINSTON
New York   Chicago   San Francisco   Philadelphia
Montreal   Toronto   London   Sydney   Tokyo
Mexico City   Rio de Janeiro   Madrid

TRADEMARKS:

Altos 586-10 - Altos Computers; Apple IIe, Apple Macintosh, Apple Lisa - Apple Computer; CompuPro 10 - CompuPro; CP/M-80, CP/M-86, CP/M Plus, Concurrent CP/M, MP/M-86, CP/Net - Digital Research, Inc.; dBase II, Friday! - Ashton Tate; DEC Rainbow - Digital Equipment Corporation; Diablo 630 - Diablo Systems, Inc.; Easywriter II, Easy Business Systems, SuperCalc - Sorcim/IUS Microsoftware; Epson FX-80 - Epson America, Inc.; General Accounting - BPI Systems Inc.; Hewlett-Packard 150 Personal Computer - Hewlett-Packard Company; IBM PC, IBM XT, IBM PC-DOS - International Business Machines Corporation; Intel 8088-Intel Corp.; Lotus 1-2-3—Lotus Development Corporation; Morrow Micro Decision - Morrow Computer Inc.; MS-DOS and Xenix Operating Systems, Multiplan - Microsoft Corporation; Multimate - Softword Systems, Inc.; NEC 3500 and 7700 Spinwriters - NEC Information Systems, Inc.; Okidata Microline - Okidata Corporation; Peachtree Accounting Software - Peachtree Software Incorporated; PFS:Write, PFS:File - Software Publishing Corporation; RealWorld Business Software - Micro Business Software, Inc.; Scotch DC 300 XL/P - 3M; Software Fitness Program - Open Systems, Inc.; Spellbinder - Lexisoft Corporation; TeleVideo 924 - TeleVideo Systems, Inc,; Texas Instruments Professional Computer - Texas Instruments; UCSD-p Operating System - SofTech Microsystems Inc.; Unix Operating System - American Telephone and Telegraph; VisiCalc, VisiFile - VisiCorp; WordStar, InfoStar - MicroPro International Corporation.

Library of Congress Cataloging in Publication Data
Bradley, Charles.
   Manager's guide to small computers.
   Includes index.
    1. Microcomputers—Purchasing.   2. Small business—
Data processing.   I. Title.
HF5548.2.B6775 1984   001.64   84-19222

ISBN 0-03-059538-X

Printed in the United States of America

Published simultaneously in Canada

4 5 6   039   9 8 7 6 5 4 3 2 1

CBS COLLEGE PUBLISHING
Holt, Rinehart and Winston
The Dryden Press
Saunders College Publishing

First distributed to the trade in 1984 by Holt, Rinehart and Winston general book division.

TO TWO GREAT KIDS,

BRIDGET
and
BRENDAN

Contents

16 INSTALLATION PREPARATION 297

17 SYSTEM INSTALLATION 319

GLOSSARY 335

INDEX 345

Preface

This book is about buying your first computer. It's for the business person who looks at the perplexing world of hardware and software products and thinks all small computers look alike.

Computers once cost more than most people could afford. Now they are within reach of most businesses, but many managers are holding off on buying this powerful tool to help them improve their business—mainly because they are confused and lack adequate buying information. Without proper guidance there is simply too much trial and error, resulting in less than successful installations.

While computers are now easier to use, little has been done to make them easier to buy. For most people, computers remain a complex issue. Yet no other innovation has so much potential for any organization, and no other technology will have as profound an impact on the way we handle information in our business. In response to these needs, I created this book to provide the necessary basic information and to simplify the buying process as much as possible.

This book is non-technical. It does not discuss the history of computers, binary math, computer electronics, or the joys and woes of programming. It does not contain chapters on how computers work, nor is it a survey of the latest computer hardware.

Instead, it takes a management point of view about evaluating, selecting, and installing a computer. The focus is on accounting, but the content also applies to many other business applications. It will help you make decisions based on sound business principles rather than technical features. It is designed to help create your own success story in using computer technology.

How is this book different from most others on the subject? First, it not only details the hardware *and* software considerations, but also covers working with people in the computer industry. It provides practical information on these key elements for anyone faced with buying a business computer. Second, this book offers you decision criteria. No two businesses are run alike, and no two computer installations are exactly the same. This text helps you decide what is best for your business based on your circumstances. Third, it answers the questions managers most frequently ask about small business computers:

◪ Do I need a computer?
◪ What size computer should I buy?
◪ How do I choose the software?
◪ How much will it cost?
◪ What kind of dealer should I buy it from?
◪ What are my risks?

Fourth, this book explains how to install the computer. These important steps include preparing the office staff and computer site, making the physical installation, and converting to the computer. These are also part of the purchase.

How to use this book. The first three chapters provide an introduction to the rest of the material. In them it is assumed that the reader has no previous exposure to computers. I expect, however, that advanced readers too will benefit from the remaining chapters. Thus, depending on your experience and your interest, you may want to read as follows:

◪ If "Do I need one?" or "What would I use it for?" are questions at the top of your list, read Chapters 2 and 3.

- ◪ If you have already decided to purchase a computer, or if you want an overview of the book, read Chapter 4.
- ◪ If you already have a computer and want to learn how to select an accounting package, read Chapters 5 and 6.
- ◪ If you have already chosen the software, Chapters 7 and 8 are devoted to the selection of hardware. (I have tried to make these chapters alone worth the price of the book.)
- ◪ If you want to know about costs before anything else, see Chapters 10 and 11.
- ◪ If you want to know how best to work with computer dealers and other industry suppliers, read Chapters 12, 13, and 14.

Acknowledgments.   A project like this is not done without some able help. I wish to thank Joyce Crain, Sharleen Fiddaman, and Tisha Kitchens for their assistance in preparing the manuscript. I am indebted to Patricia Jones, Brad Silva, and Patrick Wentworth for their reviews and constructive comments in helping make the text better than I could have done alone. Larry Norton, an attorney with a practice in Berkeley, California, contributed Chapter 15 on legal contracts. And, of course, Dennis Briskin, a pro at writing, worked with me through each chapter, tested the material, and not only patiently corrected my mistakes but also made many sound suggestions.

Charles W. Bradley
Palo Alto, California

CHAPTER

1

Computers in Perspective

Wouldn't it be nice if you could buy a computer the way you buy a toaster? Everything would come in one box—just unpack it, plug it in, and it does what you want. You wouldn't even need to read the instructions. Or wouldn't it be grand if you didn't have to know much about computers to use them? You just push a few buttons and out pops the solution to your problem. We hope that someday it will be this simple with computers.

Maybe you would like a close friend or associate to whisper, "_____ computer is the one to buy." Or maybe you would like all the answers you're looking for by the end of this chapter. The problem with computers is that quick solutions aren't really solutions at all.

Businesspeople get into trouble with computers simply because they don't know enough about them. Managers don't take the time to understand the essentials. When confronted with computers as a complex, intimidating issue, most managers try to avoid the necessary learning process. Others will postpone it, hoping that buying computers will become easier or that they will automatically get smarter about them.

Why is it so difficult? It needn't be. You need to recognize that buying a computer for your business is different from buying anything else. You need to know how to choose the correct path in your search, and protect yourself against the pitfalls. You need to know how to stay on the track to meet your goals. Approach the purchase of a computer the same as any other major business investment: In a nutshell, for best results buy your system VERY CAREFULLY. With the fundamental guidelines provided in this book, the process is almost painless.

Unfortunately, many buyers select computer systems irrationally, taking the wrong approach, even though they legitimately need a computer. Or

Figure 1-1   Small Business Computer (Courtesy of Compupro)

they find themselves in a mess even when they buy the right system for their purpose. To provide a perspective, we will look at several well-intentioned businesspeople who need a computer, but who go wrong in the buying process.

The Bargain Hunter.   The bargain hunter sees the lowest price as the best deal. After all, he or she can get the computer at a discount from one place, the printer through a friend, and software by mail order far below retail cost. Since the equipment has the same warranties as the system in the computer store showroom, how can he or she go wrong? Easily—especially with no experience in hooking up components from different manufacturers and making them work. Computer suppliers cannot provide specific instructions on how to integrate their equipment with every other manufacturer's attachments. The price-only bargain hunter overlooks some important services that many dealers normally provide as part of the retail selling price.

The Technician.   The technician spends hours making notes and comparison tables of computer equipment. He or she details all the technical hardware features, looking for strengths and weaknesses on which to decide. Why not? A stereo system was bought that way, and it worked out well. While hardware features alone are sometimes important, their real significance depends on the user's specific application. Often the technician overlooks computer software as part of the total picture. Application software (computer programs for word processing, financial planning, general accounting, etc.) is actually the most important part of the computer system. The technician ends up with a state-of-the-art system, but too often it is not the best solution to the problem.

The "Expert."   After a couple of computer programming courses in college and a few months of personal home computer experience, the "expert" has full confidence he or she she can set up a system for an uncle's business—in spare time. Although they have the right system and software for the job, months pass and nothing really productive comes out of the computer. In the meantime the owner pays on the system and continues to use outdated manual methods. Novice "experts" underestimate what they need to know about programming computers for business. A wise business owner seeks the level of help really needed to properly install the computer system.

The Delegator.   The delegator, a management person, picks an employee to select and install a computer for the company, then walks away. He or she does not want to know anything about computers. Often the employee is well-qualified to handle the project. The manager has full confidence in the employee and just occasionally checks that the costs are in line with the budget. Later, the system is installed and everything goes well for a few months, until someone discovers the computer cannot be expanded for some new but anticipated requirements. Since the manager was not directly involved in the buying process, he or she was not aware of the machine's limitations. Successful installations tend to occur when management understands enough about computers to ensure their effective use and a payoff on the investment.

The Student. The student strives to know everything needed to make an intelligent decision all on his or her own. The student has heard a few horror stories about computers in business and makes an all-out effort not to get caught in the same traps. The antithesis of the delegator, he or she starts by taking a programming class at a local community college, which helps in learning how to program a computer. Unfortunately, programming has little to do with buying one for your business. Further, the student soon learns that programming is labor-intensive and requires more time than can be spared. Then the student becomes disillusioned by the overwhelming amount of information that must be mastered to "know everything" about a computer. The student would have better spent his or her time picking a qualified computer professional.

Aside from irrational decision-making, the buyer's difficulties can come from several other sources as well. First, the large number of suppliers of computers and peripherals makes the choices difficult. Given the number of brand names, the differences in hardware features, and the complexities of software packages, choosing the right system can be a major undertaking. Second, no single computer is best for every business. Each firm has its unique characteristics, so that the computer needs to be tailored to the specific operation. Equipment brochures, magazines, and trade journals contain only general information and are rarely sufficient to guide the buyer. Third, the industry continues to confuse the consumer with its technical jargon. Most published material applauds the amazing capabilities of computers and explains how they work with technical discussions. While these publications are good in helping judge the technical merits, they have little to do with making business decisions.

Clearly, buying a small business computer is not a simple two-step process, like buying a desk calculator or an office copying machine. You do not, however, need to be a programmer or understand binary math. Nor must you make a career of computers. You do need enough information to decide where and when a computer is appropriate, and how to select a system. You also need enough information to make a decision based on sound business principles without wasting time. In short, you need decision criteria on how to buy a computer from a management point of view. That is the main purpose of this book.

SMALL BUSINESS COMPUTERS DEFINED

With the advent of the microcomputer about 1975, the terms "home computer" and "personal computer" became popular for describing the new small electronic machines. In the same way, a microcomputer used for

Figure 1-2   Personal Computer (Courtesy of Hewlett-Packard Company)

any business purpose, large or small, became a "business computer." Since the mid-1970s the distinction between the earlier small business computers (traditionally called minicomputers) and microcomputers has become blurred. (A number of microcomputers have equalled or surpassed the capabilities of some minicomputers made just a few years ago.) Therefore, the "small business computer" is now less clearly defined. In this book we will define a business computer by how it is used, rather than its physical size or price. Also, the process of selecting and purchasing a business system is significantly different from buying the home or personal computer.

A business system is distinct from both a home computer and a personal computer, although either in a limited fashion may be used in business. While it has many features in common with a business computer, a home computer is used primarily for games, education, and simple financial calculations. Home computers are often equipped with color video screens and "joysticks" to enhance their entertainment value. This type of computer differs from the others in not having, generally, the larger mass storage devices (disk drives) found in the personal and business systems.

Personal computers are a step up from the home computer, and they may have all the same features and capacities as a business computer.

While a personal computer may be used at home or at work, it differs from the others in that it is used almost exclusively by one individual. Its primary purpose is to improve one's productivity or enhance one's job. An employee, for example, uses a computer as a personal tool much as he uses a typewriter, a calculator, or a scientific instrument. Here personal computers are used for word processing, financial calculations, and information management tasks. The individual may purchase a system on his own or be assigned one by the company for his work.

A business computer, on the other hand, is used in the mainstream of the business. It supports the entire business operation by handling the primary accounting functions, and it may be used by any number of people.

Thus, as a matter of definition, a small business computer provides financial information for the operation, control, and planning of a business. Such systems typically process three or more accounting functions; for example: general ledger, accounts receivable, and inventory control. These systems cost from $5,000 to $35,000 (1984 figures) and usually can accept extra work stations to form what's called a "multi-user" system. However, even the smallest "single user" business computer has the following four basic components (a detailed discussion of these units can be found in Chapter 7):

1. **Main processor.**   This is the heart of the computer, also known as the central processing unit (CPU), which contains the microprocessor chip. The main processor can be housed in the same cabinet with the disk drives or video display, or it can be in a separate cabinet, depending on the manufacturer's design. It contains such items as the main memory of the computer system (expressed in "K," such as 64K), back panel connectors for the other components, and a front panel, which usually has the main On-Off switch and a reset button.

2. **Keyboard with video screen.**   The video screen and keyboard together are often called the "terminal" or work station. The unit is also sometimes called a "CRT" (for its Cathode Ray Tube, much like those found in television sets). The terminal is used to enter data, display it, and control computer operations. In some terminals the keyboard is contained in the same cabinet as the video screen; in others it is separate and attached only by a cable. Either way, they constitute one of the four basic units.

3. **Mass storage device.**   This is usually a disk drive for storing computer programs and data files. This device is sometimes referred to as "memory," but is not to be confused with the main memory in the main processor. The most popular medium is the floppy disk, which comes in two standard sizes, $5\frac{1}{4}$-inch (which resemble 45 rpm records in a square jacket) and 8-inch. Another mass storage device is the hard disk drive, which is larger and more expensive, but holds much more data than the floppy. Almost all business computers have two drive units side by side, called dual drives.

Figure 1-3 Components of Small Business Computer (Courtesy of IBM)

4. **Printer.** This device provides printed reports of accounting and other information, such as customer listings, invoices, and monthly statements. Printers come with a wide variety of features, but are generally of two kinds: dot matrix or full character. The first kind prints with a series of tiny dots to make a single character, and the second kind prints the character with an individually molded hammer-key much like a typewriter's. The dot matrix printers are good for most accounting reporting, while the full character printers are more appropriate for word processing.

Therefore, the definition of a small business computer is not determined by its physical shape or how much it costs, but rather by how it is used. A business computer functions at the heart of one's business and provides management with essential information for its operation and control. By contrast, home computers and personal computers are used for distinctly other purposes. Buying and installing a business computer for accounting is the focus of this book.

WHAT THE NEW TECHNOLOGY MEANS

Today's small business computer contains a microprocessor, a "computer on a chip," which is about one-quarter inch square, less than one-eighth inch thick, and contains the equivalent of more than 100,000 transistors. The original computer chip was developed in 1971 by Ted Hoff of Intel Corp., and it contained the equivalent of 2,250 transistors. Hoff's one-chip CPU, which could be held on a fingertip, greatly exceeded the computational capability of the ENIAC, the first true electronic computer, built in 1946. In fact, his microprocessor matched the power and performance of some early 1960s minicomputers that cost more than $40,000 and required a central processing unit the size of a large desk.

Since the microprocessor is "programmable" it can be supplied with a series of instructions to handle almost any number of tasks. Computer programs, of course, are what give the computer its versatility in performing different jobs. These tiny program chips are so small and inexpensive they can be fitted into almost any device that can be improved by adding some "thinking" power, such as typewriters and microwave ovens, but especially small computers.

Computers are now considerably less expensive than before. But if the cost is one source of amazement, the long term impact is even more profound. More people's work will involve computers than ever before, and they will be used in many more areas of business. Computers in business will no longer be restricted to financial and accounting applications consisting of tons of numerical data. Small computers now make sense for jobs like name and address lists, personal financial planning, data collection terminals, and manufacturing machine control. They will also be used more for graphics and other creative applications, which were previously difficult to do on large computers. Some industry experts have paralleled the impact of small computers to the versatility of electricity. Others have expounded the ability of computers to disseminate information at nearly the speed of light.

When you consider that the cost of computing is declining during a period of inflation and rising labor costs, the implications are even greater:

In 1970, a business computer equivalent in power to today's $18,000 small business system would have cost more than $100,000. Over the decade, the decline

Figure 1-4 Microprocessor Chip (Courtesy of Intel Corporation)

in computer prices has averaged about 16 per cent per year. Over the same time, the manpower resources required to do manually what a small business computer can do, have been increasing in cost at an annual rate of 7 per cent and today would cost more than $200,000.

(Source: Data General Corp.)

As a result of this technological phenomenon, businesses of all sizes will look to computers to offset rising labor costs while improving efficiency. The real significance will be in small businesses and industries where traditional computing was previously too expensive. For example, one-person law offices and writers who work at home can now afford word processing computers. Small retailers and insurance agents can now take advantage of computers. Many small businesses will find that computers are easy to buy when the annual cost of ownership is less than 1 or 2 percent of their gross revenues. The technology has changed so that small computers are affordable by nearly every small business.

ADVANTAGES OF SMALL COMPUTERS

Several advantages of small computers emerge when comparing them with the large, traditional computers. Before making comparisons, though, we need to dispose of a couple of misleading notions. A small computer is not a toy or a cheap imitation of the real thing. The small computers discussed in this book are powerful, true general purpose computing systems. They operate and perform functions in much the same way as the large machines. They are programmable, can store and manipulate data, and they are exceedingly fast, accurate, and reliable. The smallness relates more to their physical size and cost, which is the result of recent technological advances.

Small computers are not limited to running only simple programs. An estimated 80 percent of the jobs that run on large computers can now run on a small business system. In the past, many small jobs were run through the large mainframes because they were the only computers around. Without the miniaturization of today's electronic components and their great effect on reducing costs, the earlier technologies dictated that only large computers could be made. Due to their large-scale costs, these giants had to be designed to process hundreds of tasks simultaneously from a large number of users who "shared" the system. Now a small computer can process these jobs without the sharing. The advent of small systems brings individualized computing power to those previously confined to large systems.

Direct Data Entry

One strong advantage of the small computer is direct data entry, which is the step of entering the information you want the computer to store and manipulate. Because small computers accept data directly through the keyboard, information goes immediately into the computer memory to be processed or stored on the diskette. In the past, large systems accepted data only by groups or "batches" before they were processed. This method did not provide immediate feedback on errors and other processing conditions. As with the larger machines now, direct data entry with the small computer saves time and trouble by giving editing and verifying responses as the data is entered.

Inquiry Response

Another advantage is the immediate response on data file inquiries. A data file inquiry is roughly the equivalent of looking up something in an office filing cabinet. With a small computer you can key in certain identifying information, such as an account number, customer name, or vendor number, and immediately have flashed on the screen all the related data for the item. A common example using a large computer is an airline reservations system, in which entering the passenger's name and flight number displays everything about the trip. The speed of a small computer system allows the convenience of checking a customer's order while he waits on the telephone. Another dimension of immediate response is that small computers can also give quick turn-around in generating printed reports. Small computers enable you to run a report any time you like, without having to wait for things to shuffle through a large computer.

User-Oriented

Small computers are simpler to operate and thus more "user-oriented" than the big machines. Clerical-level people and office personnel can quickly be trained to operate the small machines. In other words, you do not need a high-powered computer programmer or systems analyst to attend your installation. Once your staff are experienced with the system, they can recover from errors and mistakes without undue effort. The experience in software design and development of large computers gathered over the years has allowed the more successful user-oriented software to be adapted to the small computer.

Dedicated Task

Another advantage is the dedicated task concept. Because of their new, dramatic low cost, small computers can be justified for only one purpose such as word processing, information retrieval, or special accounting functions. The high cost of large computers, by comparison, demands that they be used for a wide variety of tasks almost around-the-clock. A computer in a small business can easily be cost effective with less than full-time use. A number of small systems distributed through various departments of large organizations can also be economically justified. Thus, the concept changes from a large, centralized, shared computer resource to one that is localized and, if desired, devoted to one particular function.

The dedicated task concept also means the computer is closer to the person who benefits from its use. The machine is as available as a telephone or a copier. With large systems, executives are often two or three levels removed from the person who actually pushes the buttons and gets the data out. Small business systems give management more direct access and control. For example, the manager can walk out to the operator and say, "Who are our top five customers for the last six months?" or "Which is our longest overdue account?" and be able to get an answer fairly quickly. With a large system, a special request to the data processing manager might have to be made. Small computers eliminate these kinds of bottle-necks. Decision-makers thus can get more information on a more timely basis.

Reliable

Small business systems are built to work in normal office environments and have much greater tolerance for heat and humidity conditions. By being less sensitive, the small computer is more reliable. In contrast, large computers often require special environmentally controlled rooms. If something goes wrong with the air-conditioning unit, for example, the computer is affected. The small computer is also more reliable because of its simple design and solid-state electronics. With fewer moving parts, these systems are much easier to maintain than large computers, which have many peripheral devices attached to them. Naturally, the fewer and simpler the components, the greater the reliability.

Disadvantages of Small Computers

Obtaining a computer can create the feeling of taking "the big step" without knowing exactly how it will all turn out. The small business computer purchase usually requires spending considerable time and money before you reap any benefits. As with a custom house, you must first pay to have it planned and built before you can start using it. Computer vendors typically want up-front cash payments, although leasing is an alternative. Also, since each installation is customized to the business, it's difficult to arrange to "try it out" before making any commitment. The whole process of buying and using computers has all the risks of any other major investment. Lack of computer expertise, however, makes these risks greater in a small business than in a large corporation, where technical people are commonly available.

Computers have to be managed properly, which is an on-going effort. You don't simply install them and forget them. Since you are responsible for the operation of the system, no vendor will guarantee the success of any computer installation. So you and your staff must commit to being trained and making proper use of the computer.

Technical obsolescence comes much sooner for small computers than for large ones. Almost all manufacturers constantly race to produce products they think will sweep the market. Manufacturers of microcomputers can bring equipment and software to market much faster than manufacturers of large computers, which creates a high obsolescence factor. How do you know when to jump in and when it's worthwhile to wait? Sometimes this question is difficult to answer. (See "Buy Now or Later?" in Chapter 11.) In addition, this "technology spiral" creates low resale and salvage values for used equipment.

GETTING YOUR MONEY'S WORTH

What is the bottom-line advice of this book? The following chapters are designed to give you all the detailed advice you will need to purchase a computer for your business. They have been carefully prepared to save you time in your selection and assure a successful installation. If, however, you just can't wait to do the reading, here is a quick summary.

Plan and Prepare

Computers are not consumer impulse items or purchases to rush into. The time spent in looking, comparing, and making the final decision will have all the proportions of a major effort. Take the time to clarify and articulate your needs. Consider the time spent up front essential to a successful installation. Buying a computer is something like taking on a new partner in the business. The most important part of the process is defining what you want the computer to do. Thereafter it's finding the right combination of hardware and software for the problem you want to solve.

Start with Basic Applications

The computer applications that small businesses stand to benefit from most are the basic accounting functions. These include accounts receivable, accounts payable, inventory, payroll, and general ledger. More comprehensive, time-proven software packages are available for these applications than any others. Using canned packages is the quickest way to make effective use of your system. Also, timely, accurate computer-generated accounting information will lead to a faster return on your investment than any other application.

Buy Packaged Software

Off-the-shelf software packages offer the highest value for your dollar. Good software packages can be purchased for a fraction of their development cost. Software suppliers have devoted a vast amount of time and effort to producing packages that will succeed in the marketplace. Searching for packages to match your requirements will consume the major portion of your time. Avoid buying "futures"; ask to see a working version before you put your money down. If necessary, look for accounting software that can be modified, but keep the modifications to a minimum, since they can be costly. Buy only proven software that has a known track record, and if you're not sure ask for references.

Buy a Business Computer

Buy a business computer, not a home computer. At a cost of only a few hundred dollars, home computers may seem like a bargain. They are fine to have fun with and to learn some fundamentals about computers from, but they often have severe limitations for business. They don't have the disk storage capacities, they can't be expanded for future applications, and the software packages available generally are not adequate for business. Also, you may not find the level of support that business users require. Buy a general purpose business computer when you need to computerize your business, and always buy at the bottom or the middle of a manufacturer's line so the computer can grow with your business.

Buy an Established Brand

Purchasing a computer can be the beginning of a long-term relationship with your dealer. You need the best assurance that the computer manufacturer and your vendor are going to be around for as long as you need them. While you may want to make future purchases of disk drives, printers, and other equipment, you should also be certain that you have a reliable source of spare parts in time of repairs. Computerizing any business is a major first step, and you should make sure the manufacturer has a secure position in the industry.

Buy from a Reputable Dealer

Computers are sold through system houses, retail stores, office equipment dealers, original equipment manufacturers, and manufacturers' representatives—any of which may serve your purpose. Look for a dealer who is local to your business, who has the software and the hardware you need, and who can provide on-going support for your system. Buying all the components in one place is your guarantee they will work together properly. First-time buyers can well start with a computer retailer, since it offers a selection of low-cost computers from which to compare and choose. As you become more experienced in your search, you may want to go elsewhere, but the retailer will give you a quick entry into the world of small computers.

Small Business Computer Manufacturers

APF Electronics, Inc.
Advanced Information Design
Alpha Microsystems
Alspha Computers
Altos Computer Systems
Apple Computer, Inc.
Applied Data Communications
Applied Digital Data Systems, Inc.
Archives Incorporated
Basic Four Information Systems Div.
Blackhawk Computer Systems
Burroughs Corporation
CPT Corporation
Cado Incorporated
California Computer Systems
Campbell Scientific, Inc.
Canon USA, Inc.
Century Computer Corporation
Commodore Computer
Compal, Inc.
Compupro
Computhink Corporation
Consolidated Computer Industries
Control Data Corporation
Corvus Systems, Inc.
Cromemco, Inc.
Cyberdata
Data General Corporation
Data Wholesale (Technology)
Datamac Computer Systems
Datapoint
Delta Products
Digilog Business Systems, Inc.
Digital Equipment Corporation
Durango Systems, Inc.
Dynabyte Corporation
Eagle Computers
Epson America, Inc.
Fortune, Inc.
Four-Phase Systems
Fujitsu
Gimix, Inc.
Hewlett-Packard
Hitachi Sales Corp. of America
IBC/Integrated Business Computers
IBM
IMS International
Intelligent Systems
Intertec Data Systems Corporation
Lazor Systems, Inc.
Lexor Corporation

Logical Business Machines
Magnolia Microsystems, Inc.
Micro Computer Technology, Inc.
Micro Five Corporation
Micro Technology Unlimited
Microdasys, Inc.
Micromation, Inc.
Mitsubishi
Molecular Systems, Inc.
Monroe Systems for Business
Morrow Designs, Inc.
NEC Home Electronics USA
NEC Information Systems, Inc.
Nestar Systems Incorporated
Nixdorf
NNC Electronics
North Star Computer, Inc.
Novell Data Systems, Inc.
Ohio Scientific, Inc.
Olivetti
Onyx Systems
OSM Computer Corporation
Panasonic
Perkin-Elmer
Polymorphic Systems
Printer Terminal Communications Corp.
Professional Data Systems
Quantel/Mohawk Data Sciences
Quasar Company
Quay Corporation
R2E of America
STC Systems, Inc.
Sanyo
Scientific Data Systems
Sentinel Computer Corporation
Sharp Electronics Corporation
Sperry Univac
Sycor
Systems Group
Tandy Corporation
Techtran Systems
Telcon Industries, Inc.
TeleVideo Systems, Inc.
Terak Corporation
Texas Instruments
Three Rivers Computer Corp.
Toshiba Information Systems
Vector Graphic, Inc.
Wang
Xerox
Zenith Data Systems, Inc.

Figure 1-5   Small Business Computer Manufacturers

Get the On-Going Support

The on-going support is all the "after-sale" services you'll need to keep things running smoothly. These include everything from delivery and installation, training, and field maintenance, to answering questions by phone. In short, your dealer becomes your standby data processing department. Make sure your vendor is equipped with a technical staff to provide these important services, and that more than one person is involved with your installation. The on-going support is as important to your success as buying the right computer system.

CHAPTER

2

Why Buy a Computer?

As you consider buying a computer, you need to have a rational idea of how the computer can improve your firm's operation. People buy computers to help monitor and control their business, to improve performance, and to complete jobs that are impossible manually. The most fundamental reason for computerizing is to increase profitability through a combination of lower costs and higher productivity. These are broad generalizations, of course. The ultimate purpose of a business computer differs little from the purpose of other kinds of investments: to help improve your business.

Almost all brochures for small business computers claim that they save time, money, and effort. The question remains: Just how does a computer system improve profitability? This chapter answers that question by identifying the four most common, legitimate reasons for considering a computer. If you have in mind other purposes than those outlined here, perhaps you need to rethink your desire for a computer.

A good reason for buying a computer becomes a benefit, tangible or intangible, once the computer is installed and working. For instance, a firm whose overall goal in buying is to minimize new staff hires, benefits specifically by reducing future labor costs. Probably you will not learn how much you may benefit from a computer until you progress further with your buying interest. Until you reach that point, the reasons outlined in this chapter will at least help assure that your approach is valid. You need to know early in the game if your desire matches the reality of what a computer can do for you. Chapter 10 provides specific examples from an investment viewpoint on your computer purchase.

To put rational reasons in perspective, first let us dispense with the most frequent irrational reasons for getting a computer.

"I want to try it for a while and see if it works."   You can sample many aspects of business at low risk or minimum cost. For example, you can install an office copying machine without having to tailor it to the business. Computers are different. A computer system is difficult to sample due to all the ramifications of its purchase, installation, and operation. Certainly you would not propose to buy only half the office space you need just to see what it's like. "Trying it out" is faulty reasoning because it shows less than full commitment. Better to save your money than to enter such an undertaking with the intent of only a curious experimenter. Computer installations are most successful when managers do their homework, have realistic expectations, and remain committed to making it pay off.

Maybe you mean, "I want to try a computer to see how it works," like a desk-top system or a word processor. That's fine. You probably will learn how to use one, but this will not show you much about the benefits of a computer installed in the mainstream of your business.

"My competition just bought one."   It's smart to know what the competition is doing, especially if they're getting a computer. For most people, this looks like a definite competitive advantage. Nonetheless, you should wonder if they're doing the right thing. Find out, if you can, under what circumstances they decided to buy a computer. Maybe a son-in-law offered to do some programming on the side. Or maybe they got a great deal on slightly used gear. It's prudent to be aware of your competitors' activities, but you have to run your business according to its own circumstances and what's good for you.

"Computers are fascinating."   Whirring sounds, blinking red lights, and keyboards with buttons begging to be pushed capture the child in many people. If you want a fascinating hobby, computers are terrific—as long as they remain a hobby. Studying a computer's inner complexities and writing programs can devour the time you need to spend on your business. If you're serious about your business, you know there is little time for this kind of personal interest at the office.

"I need a computer to save my business."   With this kind of rationale it's no wonder we hear the horror stories about computers in business. Computers don't solve business problems, they only execute a well-planned solution. Only in rare circumstances does a computer actually save a business from going under. For example, a computer will not correct your poorly implemented manual procedures. Normally, only the better-run organizations have the right environment to make optimal use of a computer system. In fact, in the wrong setting adding this new technology may only make things worse. As one wag put it: "There is no problem a computer cannot make truly hopeless."

These irrational reasons come from distorted perceptions of how to buy and use a computer. You need to set objectives that are realistic in terms of what a computer can and cannot do for your business. The remainder of this chapter discusses how a computer can help reduce operating costs, increase productivity, and improve management decision information based on sound business principles.

REDUCE OPERATING COSTS

A properly installed computer can result in tangible dollar savings in three areas: basic accounting functions, cost of outside services, and the expense of new employees. This section introduces the principles by which you achieve these savings. Chapter 10 provides specific examples applying these principles to a total cost/benefit analysis.

Savings in Accounting Functions

Applying a computer to even one area of your business may provide sufficient benefits. You may justify the entire cost of the computer with a single accounting application, such as inventory control. However, you are more likely to use the computer for a combination of applications, making it easier to recover your investment sooner. Here's how a computer can save money in four accounting functions.

Accounts Receivable.   Accounts receivable is the first area where you can save money, through improved, more timely billing methods. You save money when you reduce your outstanding receivables. For example, the computer easily generates accurate aged-accounts reports whenever needed, which is often difficult under a manual system. With more accurate reporting you can quickly identify slow payers and take action to collect. Improved collections provides more working capital and saves interest on funds you might otherwise have to borrow.

Consider Stanford Distributors, a hypothetical company with annual sales of $4.5 million and average outstanding receivables of $1.5 million. Until it installed a computer, Stanford took an average of 105 days to collect its receivables. The annual cost of borrowing $1.5 million at 15 percent simple interest is $225,000. With a computer to speed up invoicing and provide better control over past-due accounts, Stanford reduced its average collection time by eight days. This reduction of eight days saves pre-tax annual interest charges of $17,100 ($\frac{8}{105}$ = 7.6% @ $225,000).

Accounts Payable.   The second area of potential savings is accounts payable, although many business people ignore this as a potential source of savings. Computerized payables tells you precisely how much you owe your suppliers. Payable-aging reports help you decide who to pay, when, and how much, based on your particular cash flow. You can thus avoid over- and under-borrowing, or even save money by taking full advantage of payment discounts, which might be difficult to schedule in a manual system. Suppose your total monthly payables are $35,000 and half offer payment discounts of 2 percent, resulting in a potential savings of $4,200 a year. If you elect to take the discount you save $350 per month.

Inventory Control.   The computer helps here in several ways. In a large inventory it can pinpoint slow-moving items and help eliminate unnecessary stock. The savings come from not having to borrow money to maintain idle inventory, let alone the shelf space and insurance premium costs. You save even more in labor costs by not restocking the slow-moving items once they are known. For many companies the inventory carrying costs are 25 to 40 percent of its value. In short, you save by knowing better what not to buy.

The computer also helps increase sales by better tracking of profitable, high-turnover items. You can more accurately identify your best-selling products. In addition, the computer helps avoid lost sales by identifying good-selling but frequently-depleted inventory items that should be restocked. Many businesses estimate losing between 5 and 30 percent of annual sales due to inventory shortages.

With all this, you can have accurate information on who buys what, by customer and type of product. The benefits here are increased gross profits through increased sales. With all these factors combined, an annual savings of even 4 percent on an inventory of $400,000 amounts to $16,000.

These inventory savings are only part of the total benefit picture. The computer can tell you upon entry if an order is above a customer's preset credit limit for all outstanding orders. Some inventory packages allow you to allocate inventory for orders already placed, so you know how much you have on hand for future orders. And the computer can maintain all billing and shipping addresses, the salesperson's name, price extensions, sales tax, freight codes, discount terms, and other account information. All this means more business by bringing better service to your customers.

General Ledger. Computers can generate monthly income and expense reports, balance sheets, and trial balance statements much faster than your staff can do them manually. Further, you benefit from information in the reports that often could not even be generated from manual accounting systems, such as actual-to-budget expense comparisons, or current year-to-date figures, or comparisons for the same period last year. A quicker, broader range of accurate reports gives you a more realistic view of financial developments and helps you prevent serious problems. The benefits here are real but not easy to calculate. How do you measure the amount saved because a crisis never happened?

Reduce Outside Services Cost

Chances are if you use an outside computer service, you can save money by having your own computer, since the price for outside services is usually much higher per unit of information processed. Most small businesses using such a service spend from $300 to $2000 a month for only a few accounting functions. Depending on current interest rates, you can lease an $11,000 computer system on a five-year term for approximately $300 per month, and run all the accounting functions you need.

Three cost considerations appear when comparing an in-house computer with an outside service:

1. With your own computer you pay a one-time license fee to use application software packages such as accounts receivable or inventory control. You can use the software as often as you like at no extra cost. Many computer services charge a royalty or run-time fee every time you use their software. A software license fee for your own computer requires a larger initial investment, but amortized over the life of the computer, it becomes much less expensive.

2. Many computer services charge for additional processing, such as extra reports showing your data in a different format. Like an electric utility, they typically charge more when your usage increases, or for each additional service they provide. On your own system, you pay virtually nothing more to run an extra report already built into your software package. The exception is if you have to pay for software modifications for a report that was not originally included.

3. Money spent on an outside service is like paying rent: You pay for use without any form of ownership. When you borrow money to buy

a computer, you have equity build-up during ownership and some salvage value at the end of its useful life. You also save money through tax benefits such as expensed items, depreciation, and investment tax credits. With all of the money-saving advantages of an in-house computer system, why would anyone use an outside service?

Briefly, an outside service offers a good way to evaluate a particular software package before buying. It allows the user to focus on the features of the package without contending with the operation of the computer. For a few months' rental charges you can find out the real value of the software to your organization and thus reduce the risk in your decision. Also, an outside service provides the advantages of data processing over a manual system for a low initial investment. Thus, for the organization lacking the financial means for an in-house computer, outside services are a good temporary solution.

Eliminating outside computer services is not the only potential savings for your firm. You can eliminate other services, like a part-time bookkeeper or a CPA, especially if the person handles routine transactions to keep the business from falling behind in the accounting workload. Some full-charge CPA services, such as generating income statements or profit-and-loss statements, can be computerized. You can retain your CPA just for advice on accounting practices and general auditing, at a much lower cost. Still other kinds of service costs can be cut, for example, if you use temporary manpower services for peak or annual accounting workloads. In one case a wholesale distributor stopped using outside help for the

Computer Ownership and Outside Computer Services Comparison		
	Your Own Computer	*Outside Services*
Intangible Considerations		
Report Turnaround	Immediate	Hours/Days
Control of Processing	Complete	None
Access to Computer	24 Hrs/7 Days	Limited
Data Confidentiality	Low Risk	Moderate Risk
Software Evaluation	Moderate Risk	Low Risk
Tangible Considerations		
Application Software	One-time Fee	Royalties
Additional Reporting	Minor Costs	Charged Extra
Initial Investment	High	Low
Equity Build-up	Yes	None
Investment Tax Credit	Yes	None

Figure 2-1 Computer Ownership and Outside Computer Services Comparison

physical inventory when it installed a computer that provided cycle accounting, a method for routinely matching the shelf inventory with the quantities entered in the computer memory.

Minimize New Staff Expense

It is a myth that computers save overhead costs by displacing existing employees. Very likely your business will need these employees to enter the daily transactions and operate the equipment. Effective use of a computer, however, does help prevent new hires by allowing the present staff to take on workloads that otherwise would require more people. By minimizing the need for new hires you reduce payroll, benefit costs, and other employee related expenses. Furthermore, since an installation is a fixed cost compared with the rising cost of future labor, the computer is a good hedge against inflation.

A side benefit of holding down new staff hires is that managers find their jobs easier when they have fewer employees to supervise. Here a computer keeps the operating staff small but efficient, and thus easier to manage.

Managers typically face the choice of either hiring clerical level people, say at $15,000 each per year, or buying a computer. At today's bargain prices that $15,000 buys a lot of workpower when applied toward the purchase and annual maintenance of a computer system.

INCREASE PRODUCTIVITY

You may have heard the claim that computers can make your job easier and your time more productive. True, computers can do all that. With a computer you can complete more with less effort than ever before. You can finish complex tasks and time-consuming projects in a fraction of the time they would otherwise take.

Let's look at how computers save time spent on routine office procedures. The computer is good at doing repetitive tasks. When a clerk prepares an invoice and types in the account number, the computer can automatically fill in the bill-to and ship-to addresses, along with all other required information, saving the clerk several minutes on each invoice. This time saved readily accumulates into hours and days over an accounting period.

Or, an accounting manager for a small manufacturing firm might use a computer to quickly and easily prepare sales projections each month. He obtains the figures from the product sales summary and spends ten to fifteen minutes entering them into the computer. With a program designed to process the information, the job is done as soon as the current sales figures are entered. Within minutes, the report showing the new projections is printed out.

Word processing also saves a great deal of time by eliminating the redundant typing often found in offices. Form letters, price lists, quotations, contracts, and proposals require much repetitive typing. The texts for all these documents can be stored in the computer. The operator can generate a new proposal after only a few minutes of making changes to update it. The computer can even be set up to generate form letters automatically while the operator does something else. The time the operator saves can be passed on to other levels of the organization. In one case, after sophisticated word processing systems were installed, a company manager started delegating 10 percent of the work to a secretary.

The actual amount of increased productivity by a computer may be hard to measure, but the effects are obvious to management. This is because improved productivity is often found as a result of improved staff morale, a reduction in the paperwork, and more useful information.

More Useful Information

The computer, with its speed and accuracy, provides more useful information. For example, up-to-the-minute inquiries on the video screen or

Figure 2-2 Word Processor (Courtesy of Xerox Corporation)

immediate hard copy reports enable you to do things you could not even imagine with a slower, less reliable manual reporting system. Or by capturing the sales information as a by-product of invoicing you can increase the productivity of the sales staff. They can monitor sales and know immediately what products are selling and which customers are buying. This kind of information is highly useful in boosting sales.

This sales example illustrates an important concept in using computers. In the absence of timely and accurate information, management has always used some amount of guesswork in making decisions. In order to provide more useful information when using computers, you must first capture the detailed information somewhere along the way. In a computerized accounting system, for example, the information comes from day-to-day transactions such as inventory, order entry, general ledger, payroll, accounts receivable, and so on. This information, when fed into the computer, becomes the raw material from which to make calculations and comparisons for decisions. Once you begin gathering the information up front, the computer can return information to you in just about any combination you desire: histories, comparisons, details, and summaries, to name only a few, all helping your productivity through better decisions.

Reduce Paper Work

Anyone using a manual accounting system knows the repetitive nature of the operation. Many pieces of information, such as dates, invoice numbers, account numbers, and part numbers, are rewritten manually several times throughout each accounting period. Some estimates suggest the same piece of information may be re-recorded from eight to fifteen times in a manual accounting system. With that kind of repetition any clerk is prone to making errors. Typically, management attempts to hold down errors by using two people for the same job, one clerk to verify what the other clerk does. The complexity of your billing may justify such redundancy, but if the computer can calculate the original bill, then only one clerk is needed to review and verify it. With a computer you enter the information only once and therefore minimize costly duplication and reduce the supporting paperwork.

The video screen component, often referred to as "the terminal," can also greatly reduce the amount of paperwork in the office, while saving time and effort. The video screen is like an electronic blackboard; it easily and quickly displays detailed accounting information such as customer history, inventory status, and general ledger account balances. With an easy-to-use interactive terminal, your employees can enter, store, access, and update file records without generating any excess paperwork.

While the computer helps eliminate some office paper shuffling, certain basic documents, such as contracts, letters, invoices, and orders, may still be held in a filing cabinet as before. Thus, these paper files serve as backup sources of information to the computer system.

As mentioned before, once the detailed information is stored in the computer, you can organize it almost any way you wish. This includes consolidating and summarizing different kinds of reports. For example, a computer can easily summarize four sales territories into one for an overall report. In the same way, it can summarize various expense categories in the chart of accounts for general ledger reporting. With specific instructions, this detailed information is gathered internally in the computer, which has the ability to sort and merge files of information. Generating consolidated reports is no more difficult for the computer than running off a detailed list of all the journal entries for a particular period. Thus, the computer's built-in capabilities are a source of productivity.

Improve Staff Morale

One important aspect to consider in your proposed computer installation is the computer's effect on your office staff. Computers are usually brought

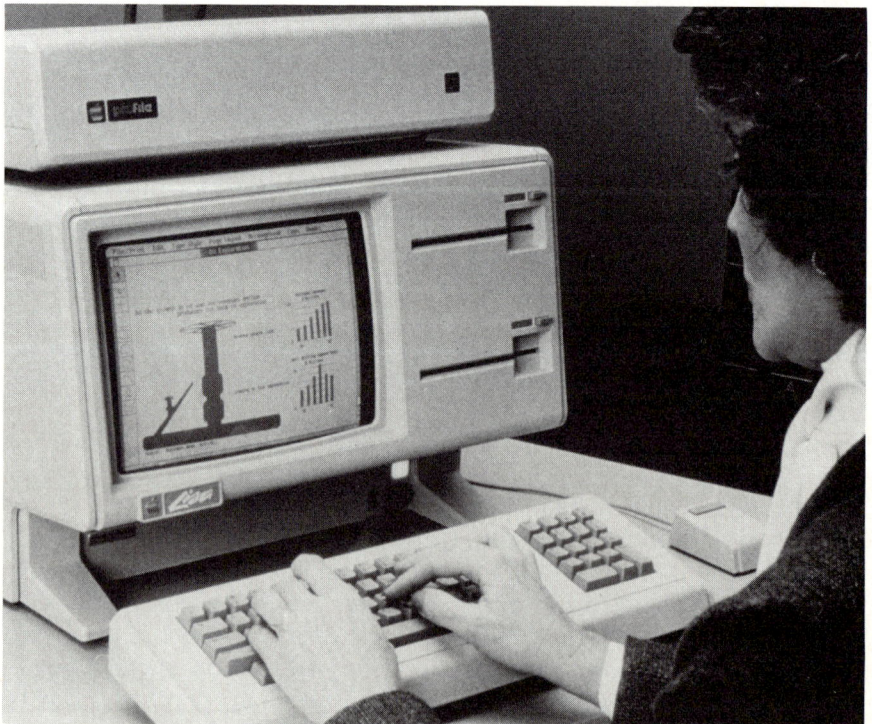

Figure 2-3 Video Display: The Electronic Blackboard (Courtesy of Apple Computer, Inc.)

in because people are overworked. As the computer reduces or removes the most tedious, repetitive work, people enjoy their jobs more. The worst of the work has been delegated to the machine, while the discretionary parts of the job remain with the worker. Morale improves as people feel more human about what they do. Improved morale also brings better overall performance for the entire organization.

Most employees become enthusiastic about the computer once they begin to use it. In the transition from a manual to an automated system, they soon develop the new skills that are becoming increasingly important in an information-oriented business world. Once a person's job becomes both easier and more personally valuable, he or she may feel a greater sense of importance to the company. These added skills and improved attitudes tend to lower the risk of employee turnover. Here the side effects of placing a computer in your organization add to productivity.

IMPROVE DECISION INFORMATION

How often have you wished you could say, "Get me a list of all the projects that are over budget by more than 10 percent. And show me the expenses causing these overruns"? Too often this kind of request goes unmet in a manual system because of workloads or the time needed to gather the details. Good management functions best with accurate and timely information.

One sound reason for considering a computer is to improve the quality of management decision information. A manual system too often gives stale, incomplete information. Computers are the best way to provide current, accurate information on the firm's situation quickly enough to allow decisive responses. A computer's electronic speed can provide details or summaries immediately after the data are entered into the machine. This means critical accounting or financial information can be monitored bi-monthly, weekly, or even daily if necessary. It also means important projects can be tracked for progress and controlled for expenses before the limits are exceeded.

Here are some examples of how computers provide more precise information for management decisions:

- ◢ Determine performance of individual profit centers
- ◢ Identify which products are consistently back-ordered
- ◢ Determine which projects are on schedule
- ◢ Identify the best-performing sales people
- ◢ Assess financial conditions for major expenditures

Since computers give meaningful information more quickly than any other method, they can help avert a crisis. For example, if a particular project is losing money, a computer can red flag it quickly enough for management to minimize the loss by changing its direction or scrapping it. Or the computer can quickly compare raw materials on hand with current orders and show when to replenish the supply to meet new orders. Also, computers are great for monitoring receivables and payables, thus avoiding cash shortages. Improved decision information can give management a large advantage over earlier methods, but, of course, this information alone will not show any benefits unless it is acted upon.

Improve Information Creation and Flow

Using computers to improve decisions means more than just capturing the detailed information and storing it on the disk. As mentioned earlier, data entry becomes the main activity in using the computer throughout the accounting period. Almost all information falls into categories that the computer can check or verify. You can program the computer to validate data as it is entered, immediately catching erroneous codes or data and allowing on-the-spot correction. For example, if the operator enters numeric information where alphabetic should go, the computer can stop and display an error message. (This is called "on-line editing," and is discussed further in Chapter 5.) This kind of control eliminates costly follow-up errors, while achieving two important objectives.

First, the data is entered only once, while copies or derivatives of it are automatically posted to related accounts. For example, a sales order number is stored in the customer open item and inventory files and is maintained through the system until the invoice is created. Payroll withholding amounts are posted to the general ledger while the individual totals are carried forward until the end of the tax year. Avoiding redundant entries simplifies creating the information and helps maintain data integrity.

Second, entries and postings affect all computer files using the same information. If the original entry is correct, then all related entries are also correct. If the original entry is in error, then all related records are equally incorrect. Changing all of them, however, is no more difficult than changing the original entry because almost all accounting packages are designed to reverse errors by automatically backing them out of their associated records. (The change is recorded in a special computer log as an audit trail.) This system of single entry posting improves the quality of information created throughout the accounting period.

When accounting information is entered, it goes into the disk storage, which holds all the data of the firm's operation in files. Almost all of the firm's data is available electronically through any of the video screens or terminals connected to it. This centralized data base is a great convenience simply because the data is not subject to the delays typically found in using In/Out baskets or other paper-oriented office procedures. Any authorized person can use the computer to get the information needed through a work station rather than having to go to a filing cabinet. Thus, with the data to be found in one place the computer makes it easy to search for information and virtually eliminates the frustration of looking for lost files.

Consistent Accounting Discipline

One of the hallmarks of solid accounting is consistent procedures from year to year. Consider the problem for a small but profitable student newspaper at a prestigious university. Since the students running it serve only one-year terms, the organization suffered from widely different accounting practices each year. No one knew the exact status of the paper's income, expenses, or assets. When a computer was installed the problem went away because everyone was forced to use the methods structured by the accounting software package. Thus, as a positive consequence, computers impose a consistent accounting discipline, which helps a business run smoothly.

CONTROL A GROWING BUSINESS

Finally, computers allow managers to *manage* the company's growth. While growing sales is a healthy state, it brings many changes that can compound management problems. As accounts receivable and inventory transactions increase, larger orders take longer to arrive, and inventory shortages become more frequent. Most critical for survival during this period of rapid expansion is to maintain good service to existing customers while adding new ones. The key to controlling the growth is to install a computer just before the business begins to rapidly expand.

The beauty of using an expandable business computer is that it can be as flexible as you like, growing as your business grows. Some computers are modular and can add more processing power as you need it. As your volumes and needs change, you can add more terminals, more storage capacity, and more business software. A computer can help you both control and accelerate your business growth without suffering growing pains.

CHAPTER
3

Common Business Applications

I n New York, a hobbyist uses a $500 computer to turn on a coffee pot in the morning. In Texas, a burglar uses a microcomputer to keep track of stolen inventory. In California, a belly dancer uses a small business computer to prepare sales reports of Nefertiti symbols. Although unusual, these are all computer applications. The word "application" appears frequently throughout this book. In simple terms, a computer application means using the machine for a significant project or task. Figure 3-1 shows a composite list of applications used in business and industry.

Computers are best used where traditional methods of processing data have become too expensive, too complex, or too slow. The list in Figure

---

Business Applications

ABC Parts Analysis	Form Letters	Product Analysis
Accounts Payable	General Ledger	Production Scheduling
Accounts Receivable	Government Reports	Project Cost Control
Actuarial Analysis	Grade Reporting	Purchasing Orders
Asset Depreciation	Graphics	Receiving Control
Back Order Control	Information Retrieval	Sales Analysis
Bill of Materials	Inventory Control	Sales Commissions
Budgeting Expenses	Investment Analysis	Sales Lead Reports
Capacity Planning	Job Estimating	Sales Orders
Cash Flow Analysis	Label Generation	Savings Deposits
Cash Management	Labor Distribution	SEC Reporting
Census Statistics	License Accounting	Shipping Control
Circulation Accounts	Loan Accounting	Simulations
Client Billing	Machine Scheduling	Statistical Analysis
Communications	Mailing Lists	Stock Quotations
Controlling Devices	Maintenance Schedules	Student Scheduling
Cost Accounting	Management Reports	Subscriptions
Credit Accounting	Material Requirement	Supplies Accounting
Credit Verification	Modeling	Tax Accounting
Critical Path Models	Monitor Devices	Tax Assessments
Customer Analysis	On-Line Data Entry	Tax Planning
Data Base Files	Order Processing	Timecard Accounting
Data Collection	Patient Accounting	Trust Accounting
Demand Deposits	Payroll	Union Reporting
Dispatching	Pension Funds	Utility Billing
Fares/Ticketing	Personnel History	Vehicle Scheduling
Financial Planning	Personnel Skills	Vendor Analysis
Fixed Assets	Premium Billing	Warehouse Control
Forecasting	Price Lists	Word Processing

Figure 3-1 Business Applications

3-1 shows that computer applications address particular functional areas of a business. Choosing the hardware and software depends on the predominant application use of the computer. In some applications, such as inventory or accounts receivable, the data change constantly. Such applications, called "data entry intensive," require a computer with a fast processing speed. Other applications, such as census statistics or historical economic data, need vast amounts of information storage. For such "data base" applications a computer with expandable mass storage makes a better buy. Therefore, the type of application is a factor in choosing the right system.

TYPES OF APPLICATIONS

Computers can be used in almost as many different ways as electricity can, but this chapter outlines only the basic kinds of applications. When narrowed down to the uses commonly found in the business world, almost all applications fall into one of the classifications discussed below.

Accounting

Accounting is one of the most popular uses for a computer, since it can quickly provide vital financial information for the firm's operation. Common accounting applications are general ledger, accounts receivable, accounts payable, inventory, and payroll. The data entry activities for these functions consist of posting journal entries, sales orders, cash receipts, timecards, and so on. Accounting transactions are then gathered and processed in cycles or accounting periods, during which the information is sorted, totaled, and summarized for various management purposes. Accounting information changes frequently, yet the data flows or carries over from one period to another.

Planning

Computers assist planning functions in one of two ways. First, management makes projections or inferences from historical data already recorded in the accounting functions. In this case management uses factual data reported by the computer to make its own interpretations and projections. Second, the computer can be programmed to make the projections by optimizing a complex set of variables, such as those found in sales forecasting. The next section of this chapter, "Characteristics of Good Applications," shows how the success of this method depends on the programmer's ability to assess all the variables.

Modeling

In modeling, a computer manipulates programmed numerical representations of real life situations. Using a model typically involves a process called linear programming, which finds the best choice or optimal performance among a wide set of variables. For example, a manufacturer wants to find the lowest cost alternative for a given level of production. The model represents the production process and finds an optimal production level considering such variables as projected sales, fixed and variable costs, material availability, equipment resources, labor, and skill levels. Models can also be developed for much-larger-scale variables, such as those found in econometric models of all the production processes in the United States.

Financial modeling is common on microcomputers using a general purpose software program called an "electronic spreadsheet," which is described later in this chapter.

Estimating

Certain professionals, such as architects and building contractors, spend many hours plowing through detailed procedures to provide accurate estimates for project bids. In these applications computers greatly reduce tedious calculation time for materials and costs. To do this the computer typically contains large tables of data such as sizes and itemized costs of building materials. When the quantities are entered, the computer quickly makes the necessary extensions to estimate the project. The computer also saves many additional person-hours in recalculating costs after project updates.

Scheduling

For scheduling, the computer can decide when certain future events should take place. For example, the computer can easily handle the complexity of truck routing, air freight loading, or the multitude of activities in large construction projects. The system draws relationships among many pieces of information, such as equipment availability, machine capacities, labor, skill levels, etc. The computer then determines future activities by optimizing any number of variables that can be programmed into the machine.

Information Retrieval

Computers excel in disseminating up-to-the-minute information, such as stock quotations, credit card account status, or reservation availability for travel agents. Immediately after identification codes or account numbers are entered, the computer "looks up" the information in its large files and prints it or displays it on the video screen. No other interaction is required, and the user accepts the information passively the way one does from a TV or radio broadcast.

Data Collection

Only a few years ago punch cards were used to capture data from a manufacturer's production line for the large computer in the office. Preparing and handling the cards always involved extra, expensive steps, and errors usually were detected after the fact. Now, small computers cost so little that they can be placed in the production line and used to record the data, transferring it onto a machine-readable medium such as a floppy disk. In this situation the small computer only collects data to be fed into another computer, but with the advantage of on-the-spot data verification.

Word Processing

Word processing combines a computer with a typewriter. Its main purpose is to help prepare typed documents. The video screen component acts like an electronic blackboard, displaying the text during the entering and editing process. This feature allows typing the text into the computer memory and making corrections and changes before printing it on paper. Word processing does not deal with the meaning of the words, but lets you format and manipulate the text in other ways for printing letters, proposals, contracts, and other documents.

Graphics

Computer graphics means using the computer to draw pictures or to visually present stored data in other than a numerical format. In business, these may be bar graphs, line graphs, or pie charts, which may be shown on the video screen, printed on paper, or sometimes drawn on special devices called plotters. Graphics is a form of reporting that clarifies the relationships among numerical data. A special field of computer graphics called Computer Aided Design (CAD) is used by engineers, architects, and graphic artists in the design and development of new products. Here computer animation may be used. Computer graphics requires special hardware, such as high-resolution video displays or hard copy plotters, and graphics software packages.

Special Types of Applications

While the foregoing applications are those most commonly found in business, some special types of applications are listed here to show the computer's versatility. While some of these applications are found only on large computers, many are being developed for the micros.

Simulations. A simulation can be thought of as a laboratory experiment. It differs from modeling in that a simulation takes place in "real time" on the computer. Real time means the computer reacts or responds to additional data input while it processes the program. Coin-operated video games, for example, are simulations in real time. Simulation applications can be used with physical, organizational, or market forces in almost any environment. Management can thus study in advance the probable alternative effects of various decision choices. For example, the entire operation of the company can be simulated and the likely effects of future events can be known in a matter of hours. Various strategies can be quickly evaluated, the mistakes pinpointed, and response capabilities greatly enhanced. Computer simulations yield insights that would be virtually impossible to gain in the real world.

Communications. Sometimes computers are used solely for communications or high-speed data transmission. The best-known application for computerized line switching is the telephone system. In private enterprise the most common application is for small computers to facilitate communicating between large-scale computers. The computer quickly and automatically handles characteristics unique to this type of transmission, such as protocols, rate of transmission speeds, and other compatibility requirements.

Monitoring.   A computer can monitor events or processes. The computer is attached to a device in order to sense any discrepancy between actual and expected quantities or conditions. It can record or provide notice of these deviations. A program may also give it specific instructions in response to these changes in events. For instance, it can shut down a machine or speed it up, close or open a valve, and even provide warning of dangerous situations. For example, home and factory security systems use computers in monitoring applications.

Controlling Device.   The computer can also give instructions to other machines, such as heavy equipment used in manufacture or assembly. This is called numerical machine control. The computer orders the production machine to load, start, stop, or provide changes in production patterns, as well as test the accuracy or completion of the machine's output. Used in this way the computer is a great labor-saving device and helps increase the speed and accuracy of production processes. As in the monitoring type of application, the computer is attached to the machine for that purpose only and becomes a resident processor.

CHARACTERISTICS OF GOOD APPLICATIONS

The first part of this chapter outlines some common computer applications found in business and industry. As you have learned, the three ingredients essential to using a computer for any purpose are:

1. A computer with a CPU, main memory, video screen, and keyboard; a mass storage device, such as a floppy disk drive, and a printer

2. A computer program consisting of a predetermined set of instructions for doing what you want

3. Some data or information that the computer and the program will accept and process

You now know what an application is and what you need to put a computer to work for you. The next questions are: What makes a good application?, and, What makes some tasks better suited to computerization than others? This section provides insight into the characteristics of good applications, and will be helpful if you have in mind a new, as-yet-untried application.

Repetitive Process

The first characteristic of a good application is that it involves a highly repetitive process. Imagine the computer generating a series of invoices on the printer. As it proceeds, the program causes the computer to go to the customer file and pull out the ship-to and bill-to addresses. The program will then go to another file to list all of the line items on the invoice, and finally will add the appropriate freight charges and sales tax and total the invoice to prepare for sending out. Whether it is 100 invoices or 10,000, computers are good at a highly repetitive process such as in this example.

A good application may also involve handling large volumes of data. It doesn't matter if the computer is running 200 invoices or 2,000, it is designed to produce the results on the last invoice as accurately as it did on the first. Therefore, any task involving considerable volumes of data in similar transactions is a good candidate for a computer application.

To illustrate this point another way, suppose you want to paint the interior walls of your office and you want a computer to help calculate the required number of gallons of paint. First, you have to measure the height and width of the walls, subtracting the doors and windows as excluded surfaces. Then you write a program to accept the data and make the computations. Next you enter the information to get the results. No doubt this effort would require several hours of work before the computer could yield the correct answer. And if your project is a one-time effort, there's little question you could do it much faster and cheaper with a simple hand calculator. This problem does not have the characteristic of repetition.

Now suppose you own a paint store and each day fifty customers ask you how many gallons of paint are needed to paint an office. The repetitive nature of this problem justifies the time and effort to program a computer to quickly calculate the number of gallons.

Quantifiable Data

The second main characteristic of a good application is the ability to quantify the data you want processed. In other words, how well can you express your data in numbers or letters? Everything the computer does, everything it manipulates, must be reduced to symbols that it can understand. Accounting functions do well on computers for this reason, since most accounting data is in numbers, dollar amounts, dates, etc., which the computer readily handles.

Suppose you are doing market research and want to test consumer preferences for packaged goods. The test is to find out which one of the packages with various schemes of product identification are consumers most likely to pull off a store shelf. Let's say you have a total of four packages designed, with different colors, logos, lettering, and so forth, and you want the computer to tabulate the results of hundreds of consumer tests. It would be an easy matter to code the choices as Number 1, 2, 3, and 4. Assigning numeric codes is a simplified, accurate way to process this information through a computer in a way it understands.

Suppose you want to test further and learn how well consumers like the selected products. You might want to ask each consumer which product he or she likes best and why. The "why" part, however, is an open-ended question and poses a processing problem. The computer simply cannot handle non-numerical responses such as, "I like this color better than that one," or, "This one seems more reliable to me." The only way to process opinions or subjective responses is to have the researcher translate the responses into numerical data. The validity of this kind of research does not depend on the computer's ability to process coded information, but on the researcher's ability to accurately encode subjective information into quantifiable data.

Definable Problem

Third, a good application must be a definable problem. The catch about using the computer to solve a problem is that the program must contain a solution to the problem. The computer is a completely precise, logical machine. The development of the computer program must show some forethought to all the routines and possible exceptions it is expected to handle. A computer can add, multiply, divide, and subtract, but you must dictate the correct path for it to make these calculations. A computer can capture, store, process, and display data, but you must tell it precisely how to do so.

A computer program can also include instructions to test for certain conditions in the data and then branch off to a special routine if the test shows it to be a special case. These branches are called program sub-routines, and while they allow a departure from the main program routine they still represent part of the problem definition. For example, when you generate invoices at the month end, you want to avoid the extra cost of mailing to those customers who have no balance due. The computer can test for a zero balance and when it finds one skip to the next invoice.

Each of the applications listed at the beginning of this chapter is a definable problem the computer can solve. This definable problem aspect has been a barrier to answering questions such as, "Which way is the stock market headed?" or "What effect will new legislation have on my business?" These kinds of questions have too many variables of exceeding complexities to define and quantify.

Difficult Applications

It should be apparent by now why computers have not been able to solve all business problems. Computers are powerful management tools, but they have no knowledge beyond their program boundaries. Computers cannot create value judgments. Given the necessary conditions for a good match between the computer and the application, it's clear why computers have not penetrated well into the areas of forecasting, marketing, and advertising. Businesspeople can expect to continue facing a number of real life problems unaided by computers:

Will the unions go on strike this year? If so, for how long?

A competitor has taken certain steps that are hurting the business. What countermeasures should we use?

A recent IRS ruling will increase our income taxes. What steps should we take?

When will the economy improve and interest rates change?

What effect will new tariffs on international trade have on our business this year?

These characteristics of good applications should help you understand the fundamentals of business applications and why some are better than others. Also, since the new small computers are inexpensive and versatile, they will be used in "never-been-done-before" applications. Thus, the foregoing characteristics may help you explore new ways to use computers and guide you on new applications. The remainder of this chapter introduces three types of software you can expect to encounter in your search for a system.

TYPES OF SOFTWARE

The first part of this chapter discusses many kinds of computer applications. While thousands of commercially available programs have been written for these applications, four types of software have emerged so far as the most popular for the new small computers. They are general accounting, electronic spreadsheets, word processing, and data base management systems. Following an outline of these four is a discussion of two types of non-application software packages, called operating systems and programming languages.

Let's first look inside the computer for a moment and see how these software types function with each other. If you were to dissect the computer memory while it is operating, you would find the main memory divided into roughly three areas. (Recall that this memory typically has more than 64,000 positions, all of which can store programs or data.) The first part of the memory contains the computer's operating system, which is necessary software for running the computer. The next area contains the user's application program, such as word processing or general accounting. The third area contains the user's data, which are created by the application software and in turn are stored on the disk. While the computer is operating, these areas interact with each other. The computer runs, with this layered effect in its memory, as long as the application program continues to execute instructions. In a moment we will return to the definition and purpose of the operating system.

Application Software

Recall that an application is a task or job you want the computer to do. For this you need application software, or a set of computer programs. Many individuals and small companies in the computer industry have set out to produce packaged software to meet these application demands. While hundreds of thousands of programs have been written, the most popular packages fall into four types.

General Accounting. General accounting includes accounting routines used by almost all businesses; that is, a systematic production of information for general ledger, accounts receivable, accounts payable, sales order, inventory, and payroll. Software developers for accounting packages have attempted to reach the broadest market, since almost all businesses use one or more of these accounting functions. General accounting software packages, discussed thoroughly in Chapters 5 and 6, tend to be the most comprehensive and the most complex packages on the market. Among the best selling are: Easy Business Systems (Information Unlimited Software), General Accounting (BPI Systems, Inc.), Software Fitness Program (Open Systems, Inc.), Peachtree Accounting (Peachtree Software), and RealWorld Business Software (Micro Business Software, Inc.).

Electronic Spreadsheets. One of the most popular programs for small business computers is the electronic spreadsheet. While it is designed to make use of selected accounting information, as a program it stands apart from general accounting functions. With an electronic spreadsheet, the video screen displays rows and columns of figures and text, much the same as an accountant's columnar pad. The user can insert numerical data, formulas, or descriptive information, and manipulate and store data at the intersection of any row or column. The main advantage of this program is that it can quickly recalculate the entire set of figures when you need to make changes.

One simple application of the electronic spreadsheet is projecting net income. A column can be set up for each month of the year, with twelve columns across the screen. The rows going down the screen show gross sales, cost of goods sold, and expense information. When all the information is filled in and the command is given, the computer instantly shows net income at the end of the twelve-month period. This speed is why the electronic spreadsheet is so useful in financial planning. It allows

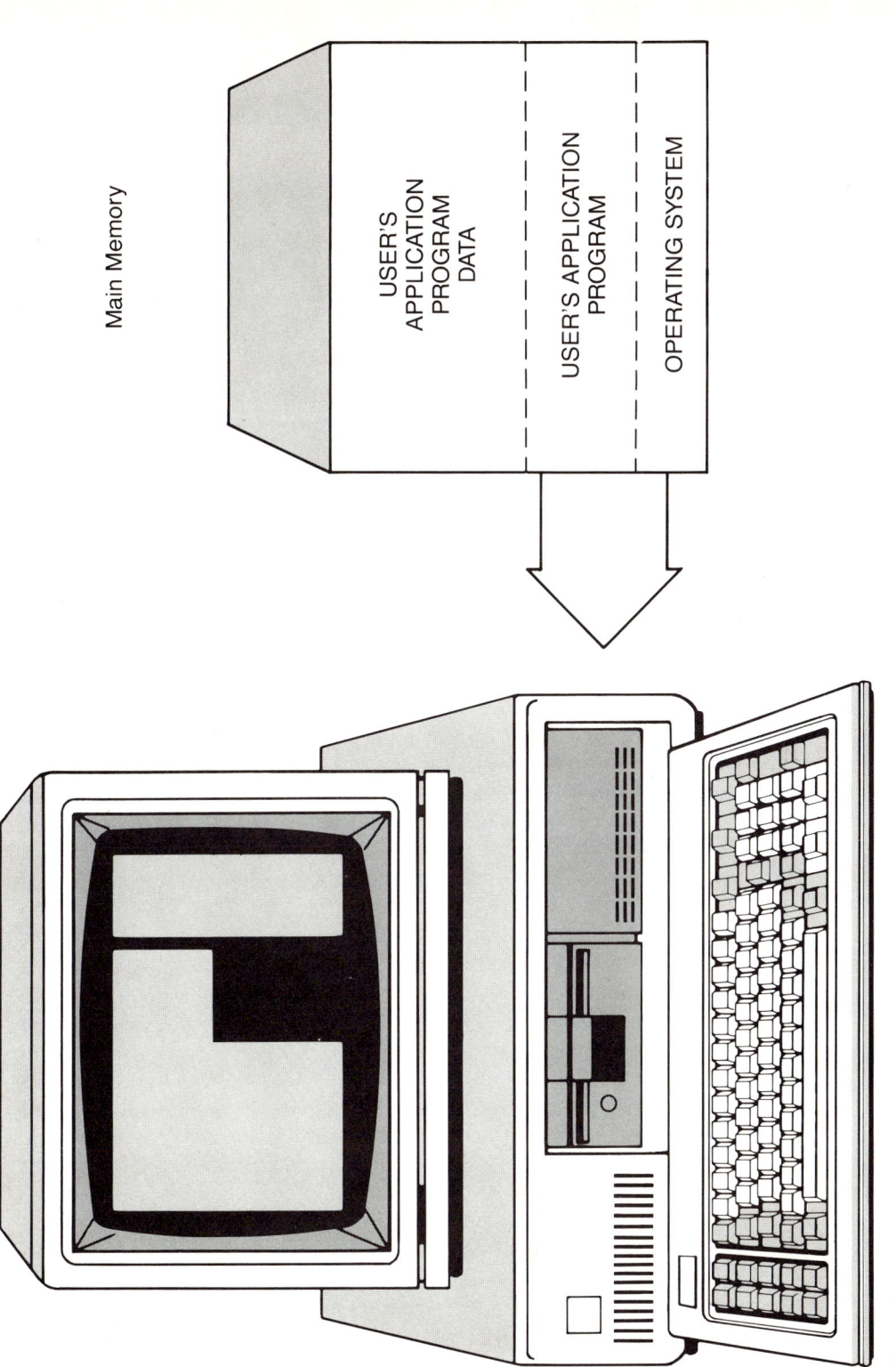

Main Memory

USER'S APPLICATION PROGRAM DATA

USER'S APPLICATION PROGRAM

OPERATING SYSTEM

Figure 3-2 Inside the Main Memory

frequent changing of the data, in effect asking "what if" questions about finances, and allows the user to explore many possible conditions and alternatives. This means you can change one or more numeric variables to see what effect they have on the total outcome.

This type of program has become popular with small computer users because it requires no particular programming knowledge. The concept and operation are simple and require only a few hours to master. Some of the popular brand names for these programs include: 1-2-3 (Lotus Software), Multiplan (Microsoft, Inc.), SuperCalc (Sorcim, Inc.), and Visicalc (VisiCorp, Inc.).

Word Processing. A small business computer with word processing capability greatly increases productivity in an office's ordinary typing chores. The demand for inexpensive word processing has been a major factor in the sales growth of small business computers in the last few years. As mentioned earlier, word processing combines the advantages of a computer's memory, speed, and accuracy with the printing of a quality office typewriter. The main benefit is that it saves many hours of the operator's time by avoiding the tedious editing and retyping of every document with even the slightest change in it. The new, lower prices of computers, combined with the convenience of having all the computer's resources at hand, have made word processing on a small computer more practical than doing the same job on a large computer.

Figure 3-3 Electronic Spreadsheet Program (Courtesy of Texas Instruments)

Briefly, here is how it works. As the operator keys in the text it appears on the screen and is also stored on the diskette for printing when complete. All changes, additions, or deletions are made electronically, at high speed and low noise. Once the information has been edited, the text is stored for printing future documents that are prepared repeatedly with only minor modifications. Large sections of text can be rearranged with a few simple commands, and finished documents can be reformatted for various printing effects. This kind of power and capability greatly assist the typist, who would otherwise have to continually retype until achieving a final, correct version.

In addition, many supplementary software programs are available to support the word processing function. For example, some software packages allow you to prepare form letters, each with separate addresses and other variable information, so that each letter looks individually typed. Word processing software packages also include programs for checking spelling. These programs contain computerized dictionaries that hold from 10,000 to 50,000 commonly used words. Each word in the user's document is compared with the dictionary to check correct spelling. The most widely used word processing software packages include: Easywriter II (Information Unlimited Software), Multimate (Softword Systems), PFS:Write (Software Publishing Corporation), Spellbinder (Lexisoft), and WordStar (MicroPro International).

Data Base Management Systems.   The remaining type of popular software packages is called data base management. What is a data base? Briefly, it's an organized collection of pieces of information that have some kind of relationship, such as names in a telephone book. Data base software is used to create application programs, but is not itself written for any particular application. In an accounting payroll program, for example, the user accepts the way the program is designed and the way the data is to be entered, stored, and reported. In a data base system, however, the user can specify the data to be keyed in, how the data is to be stored and used, and the reporting formats. In other words, a data base management system is a general purpose application program. While some liken it to a programming language, its chief advantage is that it allows one to produce an application in less time than it would take to do the same thing by writing a custom program.

In the wide spectrum of business software, a data base system falls somewhere between packaged software on one end and custom software on the other end. A canned package is fixed while a customized program is open ended. Data base systems offer some of the advantages of canned packages: They are low-cost and quick to implement. Like custom software, though, they can provide a precise fit for the problem you want to solve. A data base system can be set up to allow sharing or pooling of stored information among different users in an organization. Also, as the business's needs change over time, it offers an easier way to make changes in the application, compared to custom or packaged software.

Comprehensive data base management systems include these three primary functions:

1. **Data Entry.**   The user can determine the particular data items to be entered, like name, address, etc., as well as the length (number of digits or spaces in each item), and whether the data is alphabetical, numeric, or a combination of the two. The user can specify the format on the video screen and the sequence in which the data is to be entered. All of this is called data input, simply a structured method of entering the data, which are then stored on the diskette for later use.

2. **File Maintenance.**   The second primary function is file mainte-nance, the ability to change the data already entered. This includes an "inquiry" capability, which is calling to the screen at any time any piece of stored information and being able to delete or modify it.

3. **Reporting.**   The third primary function is reporting, or generating hard copy output for reference. The reporting capability should include selecting the data items to be printed and determining their sequence and format on the printed report.

The data base management packages found in a wide number of computer installations include: dBase II (Ashton Tate), Friday! (Ashton Tate), InfoStar (MicroPro International), PFS:File (Software Publishing Corporation), and VisiFile (VisiCorp, Inc.).

Operating Systems

If computers exist for the purpose of running application programs, then an operating system exists to run the computer. The operating system, sometimes called the "system software," is a set of computer programs that helps direct the internal functions of the computer for what the user wants to do. An operating system can be defined as the interface between the computer, its peripherals, and the user's programs. In other words, it resides in the computer's main memory and it "works" between the com-puter hardware and the application programs. Its main purpose is to pro-vide the user with a flexible means of control over the resources of the computer. It does this in three ways:

1. The operating system provides for the loading and execution of the application software (or user programs).

2. It provides a means for organizing files of data and for reporting the status of the disk drive units. It allows the user to find out what files are on a disk, how much disk space they have consumed, and how much unused space remains.

3. An operating system also takes care of the thousands of small tasks involved in transferring information from the main processor to the computer's peripherals, such as disk drives, printers, and terminals.

The operating system is essential. Every computer in the world, regardless of size, requires an operating system, as it is not possible to use a machine without it. Manufacturers of large-scale computers, such as CDC, IBM, Honeywell, and Univac, each create operating system software for their machines, none of which is transferable to any other brand of computer. Consequently, if a user changes from Univac to CDC he or she has to learn a different operating system.

In the world of micros, however, it's different. A microcomputer manufacturer can choose from a number of commercially available system software offerings produced by independent software companies. This means that many brands of micros use the same generic operating system. For instance, a Texas Instruments Professional Computer can run the same operating software as the IBM Personal Computer. With some computers, the operating system can be changed quickly just by changing a diskette. A user learns the fundamentals of a particular operating system, knowing it will work the same on one brand of computer as another. This adaptability in the marketplace is one of the major factors contributing to the popularity and widespread use of microcomputers, and it works to everyone's advantage.

Every microcomputer manufacturer supplies at least one (sometimes a choice) of the popular system software offerings that have been tailored to their hardware. This is how the manufacturers assure compatibility of the operating system with their equipment. However, just as the operating system has to work with the hardware, it also has to work with the application software. Thus the hardware, operating system, and application software are integrated with each other.

As an approach to your selection, start by looking for application packages that are compatible with the most widely used operating systems, like CP/M or MS-DOS (described below). This will give you a large selection of packages to choose from, since software developers tend to pick operating systems with the broadest possible market for their products. Thus the choice is not which operating system is best, but which operating system works with the software package you want to use. This need not be a major concern, however, since many computer manufacturers and software suppliers offer products that are compatible with more than one operating system.

The following is a brief description of some of the popular operating systems available for microcomputers. The names for them are usually abbreviations. An expanded description of these and more is included in Chapter 8.

CP/M.   CP/M is an abbreviation of Control Program for Microcomputers, which was created by Digital Research Corporation in 1976. It is a single user, hardware independent, general purpose operating system for microcomputers. CP/M's popularity is such that it is considered a standard for almost all small computers. The widespread use of CP/M means the user can choose from more than 3,000 application programs that can be adapted to almost any computer with this software.

MP/M.   Also developed by Digital Research, MP/M differs from CP/M primarily in that it is written for multi-user computers. Although more complex to install and use, MP/M's commands are largely the same as CP/M's. This similarity makes it easy for the user to switch from a CP/M single user computer to an MP/M multi-user computer.

MS-DOS.   MS-DOS was created by Microsoft, Inc. initially (and almost exclusively) for the IBM Personal Computer, which was announced in late 1981. MS-DOS (pronounced "M-S-DOSS") is called PC-DOS when associated with the IBM computer, and the DOS stands for Disk Operating System. It uses commands similar to CP/M, but the functional structure is more like the UNIX operating system mentioned below. A user must obtain application software written specifically for this operating system.

UNIX.   UNIX is an operating system developed by Bell Laboratories of New Jersey. It was originally written for the earlier minicomputers, such as the Digital Equipment Corporation (DEC) systems, and versions are now available for microcomputers. While it is designed for a multi-user environment, as is MP/M, UNIX is more sophisticated and is used primarily on the larger, or high-end, microcomputers. Another operating system, called XENIX (pronounced "ZEE-NIX"), is a UNIX look alike and was developed by Microsoft.

Programming Languages

Choosing a programming language matters only when you intend to develop or modify your own custom software. Since the advice of this book is to use packaged software, programming languages are mentioned here only to identify them and briefly describe their purpose.

Programming languages are software tools for programmers who want to develop applications software. All applications and programs have been written in a language of some kind. Many different languages are available, each for a different purpose in scientific, engineering, educational, and business use. No one language is best for every purpose—Programmers use a language that suits their needs for the software they want to develop.

When the programmer creates a program, he or she follows a set of rules that are logical and precise. The finished product, a set of detailed instructions, looks to most of us like a peculiar collection of symbols. Yet all languages yield the same general result: reducing the programmer's written instructions into a special set of symbols called machine code. This "translation" is necessary because in the end the computer understands only machine code. (See Chapter 5, Figure 5-8, for more on the process of converting the programmer's written code into machine code.)

Languages for Business. The most popular languages for business applications using microcomputers are C, BASIC, COBOL, PASCAL, and PL/1. Of these, BASIC comes in many different versions or dialects. Each of these languages is regarded as a high-level language, which means the computer generates a proportionally high number of machine instructions for each line the programmer writes.

Compilers and Interpreters. A compiler is a special computer program that translates the programmer's written code (called "source code") into machine language. Thus, what goes into a compiler is source code and what comes out is "object code." The object code, which becomes your application program, is the only type of instruction the machine can execute. Compiling consists of a special one-time computer step before the program can be used. It's similar to processing negative film before you can use the pictures. With an interpreter, however, each instruction in the program is translated and executed whenever the program is being run. No compiler step is required. This is similar to using instant camera film, and the results are immediate. BASIC is the language for microcomputers that is of the interpreter type. As with the different methods of developing pictures in photography, each type of programming code translation has its place in developing application software for computers.

Program Generators. Program generators are still another kind of software used mainly as a programmer's tool. Odd though it may sound, program generators are programs themselves that create other programs. While this may seem redundant, a program generator is useful in creating applications quickly by requiring a proportionally small amount of time for the actual writing of the program.

CHAPTER
4

Steps in Buying a Computer

One of the most important objectives in buying a computer is to find one that fits the organization. Select a system that matches your business requirements as closely as possible. A computer that is too small will invariably require a costly conversion to a larger computer later, but buying too much computer wastes money. Your goal is to find a system that is adequate for your present needs yet is expandable for your firm's future requirements.

You may already know that computer prices cover a wide range. Complete small business computers cost from $3,000 to $35,000. With all the choices in the market you can almost buy a different system for every additional dollar you have to spend. Furthermore, you can choose from a dozen or more different computers in every price bracket on the spectrum.

One Percent Rule. You need to know quickly if you can afford a computer for the purpose you have in mind. How do you determine what you can afford? One method is the 1 percent rule of thumb, a guideline established from a survey of various companies and their actual computer expenses. The rule is: The total annual system cost should not exceed 1 percent of your firm's gross income. The annual system cost includes hardware and software purchase prices amortized over a five-year period, plus annual maintenance costs. It also includes computer supplies and insurance, but does not include salary paid for the operator.

For example, a firm with $2 million a year in gross revenue should not spend more than $20,000 per year (for the first five years) for a computer and its operation. In other words, the one-time system purchase price spread over five years, plus maintenance, supplies, and insurance for each of those years, would come to $100,000. This means also that if you allowed $10,000 a year for hardware and software maintenance (which is more than sufficient) you could afford to look for a system with a price tag of up to $50,000. With the capabilities and prices of the small business computers available now, it is easy to stay within this 1 percent guideline.

NINE STEPS TO INSTALLATION

This chapter outlines the nine basic steps to your purchase and installation. The nine steps are divided into two groups. The first five steps are:

1. Decide what you want the computer to do

2. Determine single user or multi-user computer

3. Determine storage requirements

4. Evaluate the application software

5. Evaluate the computer hardware

If you've just started looking at computers, no doubt you have the proverbial "chicken or the egg" situation. You can't decide what to buy until you know what computers can do for your business (and at what price), and the computer people can't help much until you can tell them what you want to do. Thus, your search involves a repeating process of comparing what the marketplace has to offer with your business needs as they become clearer to you.

The first five steps are the iterative part of the process, and have several purposes. First, they represent a management summary of the most important criteria in the selection of a system. They are designed to help you quickly understand the fundamentals in choosing a computer. Second, these steps are the "qualifiers." They will save your time with vendors by providing a realistic approach to your decision process, and should also help to further qualify your own requirements. Third, the process will identify a number of qualified potential vendors from which to select a finalist. The remaining four steps contained in this chapter are:

6. Finalize system requirements

7. Select a vendor

8. Negotiate contracts

9. Install computer

Use these remaining steps after you have determined that computers are available for your purpose and are within your budget; that is, when you have found the concept worth pursuing and want to proceed with a purchase. These steps are better applied after you have narrowed the choice to three or four serious vendors.

STEP 1: DECIDE WHAT YOU WANT THE COMPUTER TO DO

The first step is to decide which business functions should be computerized. These usually include your most critical functional areas, the "heart" of your business. A simple "back-of-the-envelope" list of possible areas is sufficient for this step. Most businesspeople know what areas need improvement without a detailed study. For example, if you have a wholesale distributorship and your staff can't keep up with the paperwork, you should look for an order entry/inventory control system. A manufacturer requires a work-in-process and inventory control software package for the mainstream of his business. A service organization, such as a building maintenance firm, needs a job costing and client billing package. As you can see, the critical areas tend to be those that are capital intensive or that affect cash flow. Your list may look like this:

Computerize Now — Inventory Control
                                  Accounts Receivable
Computerize Later — General Ledger
                                  Accounts Payable
                                  Payroll

Your list should include all the things you would like the computer to do eventually, but for now, base your purchase on the top two or three items. The less critical functions are likely to fall within the same computer system requirements as the primary items. Once the initial applications are fully implemented and running smoothly, you can add the remaining items on your list to your system. Applications like general ledger or payroll, for example, can be installed later when your firm is ready for them. Accounting applications are commonly put on the computer first, but they don't have to be. If other applications are more important, such as word processing, information retrieval, or financial planning, focus on those first.

If you are uncertain whether your organization may benefit from a computer, look for answers to these questions:

Problems directly affecting costs and profits:

◪ Profits down due to excessive costs?
◪ Gross income lower than it should be?
◪ Collection of receivables consistently slow?
◪ Projects chronically over budget?
◪ Cost of outside services too high?
◪ Future labor costs create a profit squeeze?

Problems affecting organizational procedures:

◪ Personnel overworked or have poor morale?
◪ Areas with insufficient management controls?
◪ Present staff unable to handle expected growth?
◪ Lack of accurate and timely management information?
◪ Production consistently late in meeting schedules?
◪ Excessive paperwork restricting information flow?

In many ways, computers have resolved these kinds of problems. Answers to these questions should lead to clarification of critical areas and a list of potential computer applications. Remember, while you might at first feel intimidated by computer technology and its jargon, you are the best expert on your business and how it is run.

Although you need only make a brief list for this first step, studying your organization is helpful. Defining the ultimate tasks for the computer can only be done with an understanding of the present operation. The study might show not only where automating will do the most good but also where you can improve a manual system. Also consider your short- and long-range goals for the firm, and what benefits you might expect from a computer.

Have a clear idea of what's being done now, how it's being done, and the related problems. The study should show how the functional areas of your business relate to each other, and the critical points in the accounting procedures. This effort includes obtaining descriptions of documents and forms used, volume counts of the average and peak transactions, and the type of information to be included. The purpose and content of the preliminary study can be further served by a review of Chapter 12.

STEP 2: DETERMINE SINGLE USER OR MULTI-USER COMPUTER

Whether a computer can be used by one person or several persons at a time affects the extent of its use in a business environment. Some computers are designed for one user executing one particular task (computer program) at a time. With these systems different users have to "wait in line." Others can handle a number of users, each processing different tasks simultaneously. These two classes of computers generally are referred to as single user, single task systems and multi-user, multi-task systems. Deciding which you need can indicate a "fork in the road" in your search, since the two kinds of computers are designed differently and may have different choices of software packages.

Single-User Computer

A single user computer may be described as a small business "personal" or desk-top computer. It may have many of the same features as a multi-user computer—disk drives, printers, expandable main memory, a choice of similar application software—and it executes programs in the same manner. Nonetheless, a single user computer is designed to execute only one computer program at a time by one user. If software is to a computer what records are to a stereo, a single user computer is like playing only one record at a time. You can, however, have a collection of many different computer programs, just as you might have many different records in a stereo library. The main advantage of single user computers is their lower price, but the single user feature is generally a limitation for many small business environments.

Multi-User Computer

On the other hand, a multi-user computer can have several video screens (terminals) attached to it, each for a different user. This feature is necessary when more than one person at a time must use the system. For example, a multi-user computer allows one person to do invoicing while another updates the inventory. Or one person can process the general ledger while another adds names to the customer files. Each terminal is functionally interchangeable with the others, and all users have access to the same data files and computer programs, if desired. Because each user can run a different job, these systems are sometimes referred to as multi-tasking or "timesharing" computers. Multi-tasking computers can do more work per unit of time. This type of computer has the advantage of allowing many users to share a common set of data files, or data base, which contain the firm's operating information. It also has the advantage of providing computer power to a number of users for the cost of only one, albeit more expensive, central processing unit.

(A variation of the multi-user computer is the linking of two or more single user computers together, which is called "networking" and is explained in Chapter 8.)

Several criteria can help determine if you need a multi-user computer. First, if you have a half dozen or more employees in the accounting department, you probably need a timesharing system. When an employee specializes in one functional area on a full-time basis, he or she should have his own video screen and keyboard access to the computer. For instance, if one person does accounts receivable and another does inventory all day, they should each have their own computer work station. Otherwise, a conflict in work schedules results if they have to share a single terminal. Another criterion for a multi-user system is the demand, or the sheer volume, of data to be entered. If two people process orders all day, then they should each have a terminal. In this case, the function is the same for both (order entry), but the level of activity warrants two terminals for a normal day's workload.

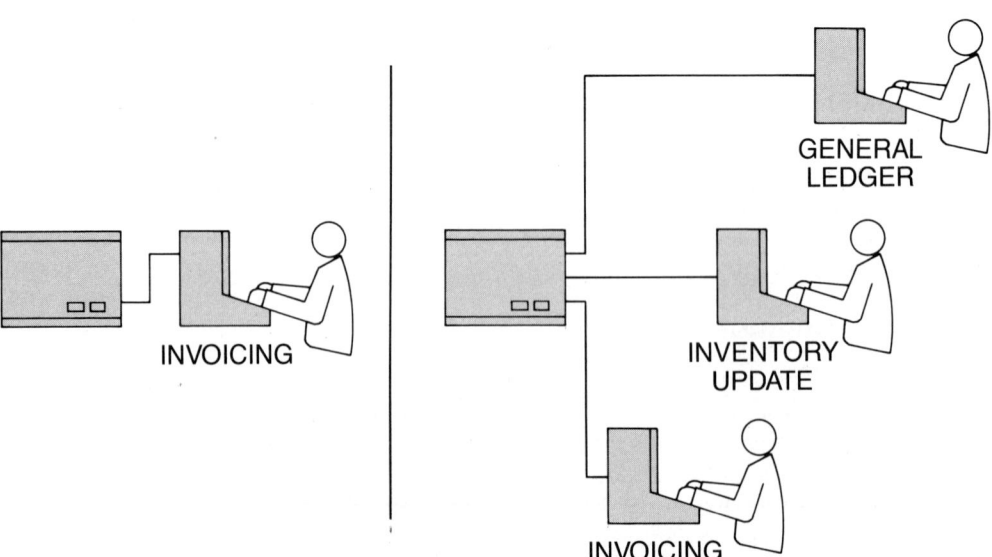

Figure 4-1 Single User and Multi-User Computers

Still another criterion may be the physical layout of your office or plant. The number and placement of the terminals may be decided as a matter of convenience. Some organizations have accounting functions spread throughout different floor levels, or even different buildings. Yet each user should have access to the computer through remote terminals. Many small business computers will support remote terminals by cables up to a hundred feet long without special equipment. For greater distances, the terminals can be connected by regular telephone lines using special communications adapters called modems.

One final note in making the decision between a single user and a multi-user computer. To begin, you can always use a multi-user computer as a single user system, just attach one terminal to it. The extra cost of a timesharing computer with a single work station may be only slightly more than a comparable single user system. If the system needs to be expanded later, the additional terminals, disk drives, and other peripherals can usually be installed on-site. This expansion feature will save you time and money by avoiding a conversion to a larger computer. Thus, in regard to the central processing unit, it's best to start with the "computer power" you think you will need over the next few years.

STEP 3: DETERMINE STORAGE REQUIREMENTS

Part of what determines the size of a computer is the amount of mass storage attachable to it. Aside from the multi-user feature, the disk capacity is the single most important factor in determining the size computer you need for accounting purposes. Disk drives are often purchased as peripheral attachments. Compared to magnetic tape used on large computers, disks are more efficient for storing data. The purpose of this section is to introduce the concept of information storage, and to show how to approximate storage requirements. A rough estimate is all you need for your window-shopping tour. Ultimately, your vendor should help calculate your final requirements, since the eventual file sizes will depend on the specifications in the software, which will vary from one package to another.

Small business computers can use the $5\frac{1}{4}$-inch floppy disks, the 8-inch floppys, or the "hard" disks. (See "Mass Storage Devices," Chapter 7.) These three types of disk offer a wide range of storage—from 100,000 characters to forty million characters (or bytes) per single disk. The larger your company the more information you will need to store, and the more you need a computer with large disk-storage capacity. As a point of reference, a business with $2 million a year in revenues will probably find five million characters of storage small, while more than forty million characters would be considered large. Make certain that the machine can add enough storage capacity for your future applications.

A computer's disk capacity is a function of its design specifications and the type of disk. Among the different brands of computer systems, the $5\frac{1}{4}$-inch floppy disk holds 90,000 to 750,000 characters of information. The next step up is the 8-inch floppy, which holds 250,000 to 1,200,000 characters. Many manufacturers state their capacities as a total of two floppy disk drive units, which doubles these figures. If you need more storage, hard disks have a range of capacities from five to forty million characters per drive unit. Normally, only one hard disk drive is specified in a system, although many computers can have up to four units attached. Therefore, you need only to approximate your storage requirements and base your purchase decision on the next higher disk storage level.

A brief clarification of the meaning of the term "memory" should be helpful. Even though all computers have a main memory in the central processing unit, all computer programs and data files are stored on disks. The disks are the only way to physically remove the stored data from the computer system, and the only way to retain the data after turning off the main power switch. The main memory goes totally blank when the power is off. Thus, while the main memory is an essential component for processing, it does not provide permanent storage the way disks do. Therefore, the following explanation of storage should not be confused with the main memory of the computer, which is discussed further in Chapter 7.

How Data is Stored

Starting at the most elementary level, the smallest unit of computer storage is one character of information. A character is a single letter of the alphabet, a single numeric digit, or a special symbol such as #, %, *, etc. A character can also be a blank space, such as a space between words. And, in computer jargon, a "byte" is one character of information. Characters make up the information you want the computer to store and manipulate. For example, "04321" is a five-digit customer code number (or account number) that consumes five bytes of storage. In computer talk, the customer number is called a "field" or "data item."

The number of characters shown for each of the data items in Figure 4-2 is the same number of characters reserved on the disk. For example, the data item called "City" takes fifteen bytes of storage, and the data item called "Last Yr. Sales" takes eight bytes. Quite simply, the numbers are the total amount of disk space allocated for each of the data items each time it needs to be stored. These space allocations usually have a fixed length even though some of them may not be used or fully consumed. For instance, the actual length of the "Customer Name" varies from one customer to another, up to the twenty-five positions allowed.

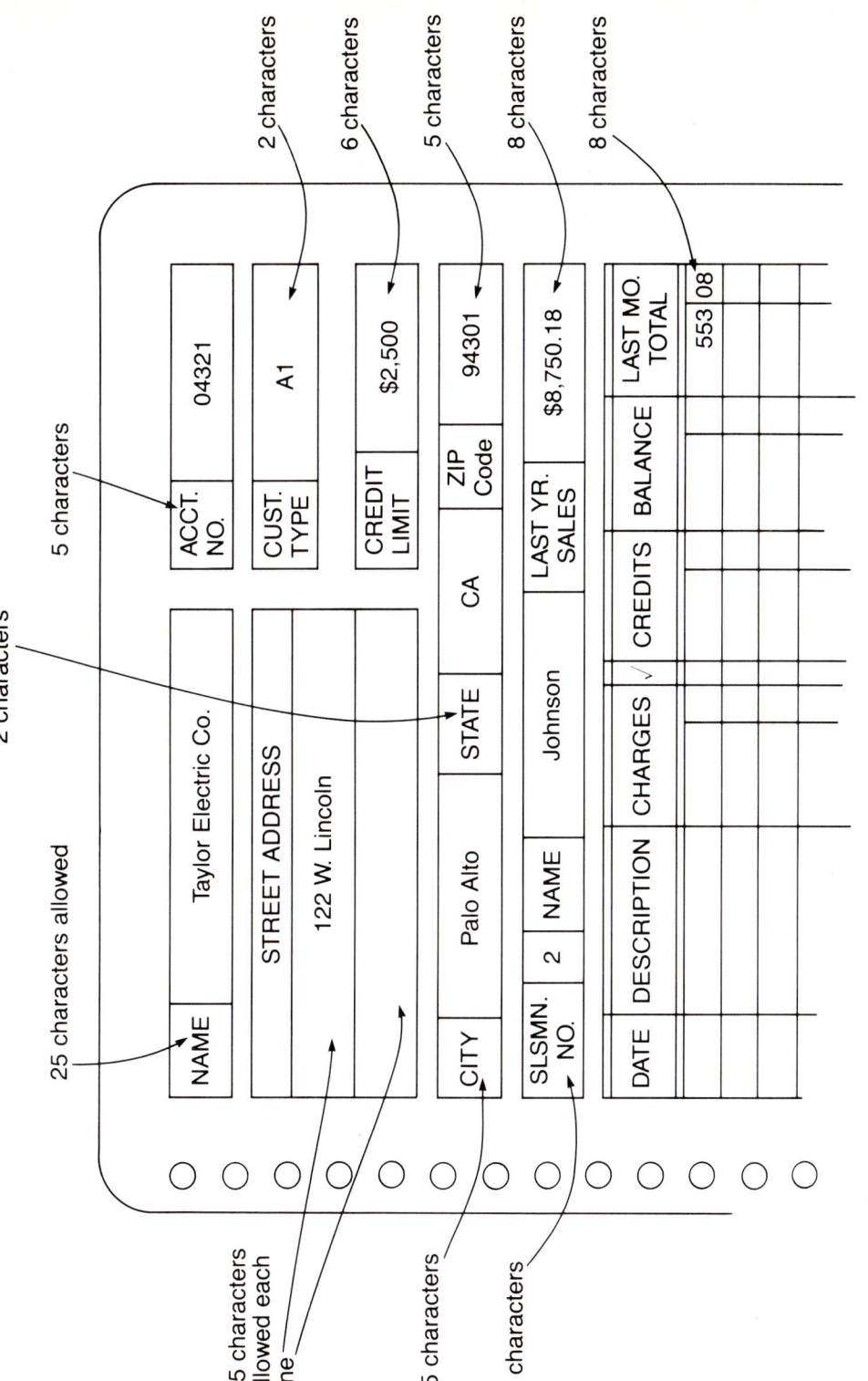

Figure 4-2 Customer Record Data Items

As we'll see in a moment, the fixed positions concept makes it easy to determine disk storage requirements. Other data items, like "Salesperson Number" and "Customer Type," each use two-position codes, which help conserve disk storage space.

So far we have defined data items as meaningful pieces of information. But what is it when we put these pieces together? A group of data items is called a "record." By industry definition, a record consists of one or more data items with a logical relationship. Journal entries, vendor masters, sales orders, cash receipts, and general ledger accounts, each made up of various data items, are typical of the types of records in computer accounting systems. Information such as name, address, city, state, etc., as shown in Figure 4-2, is the assembly of related data items that make up a typical customer record.

Data Files

Any number of records with the same set of data items makes a composite of information called a "data file." In the previous example, any number of customer records makes a customer data file. This file now contains background and accounting information about all the firm's customers. To determine the storage requirement for one data file you must first add all the characters for each of the data items in the record. This gives you the total record size. Then you multiply the record size by the number of records in the file. Thus, the disk storage space required for one file is the result of a simple arithmetic extension. In our example, 500 customer records with 128 bytes per record would consume 64,000 bytes of disk storage. A summary of the data hierarchy for one data file is as follows:

- ◪ Character—numbers, letters, symbols
- ◪ Data Item—characters grouped to specify a particular unit of information
- ◪ Record—one or more data items related in some meaningful way
- ◪ File—a collection or set of records

Each accounting module, such as accounts receivable, general ledger, or inventory control, usually contains a number of data files. By making computations for each data file in all the modules that you plan to use, you can calculate the grand total of disk storage required for your installation. The manuals that come with some software packages show storage capacities by the maximum number of transactions allowed per month and the maximum number of "accounts" allowed, such as general ledger, customers, vendors, and employees. This kind of information makes computing storage requirements somewhat easier. At the very least, your software supplier should provide you with a list of all data files, record sizes, and data items for your final calculations.

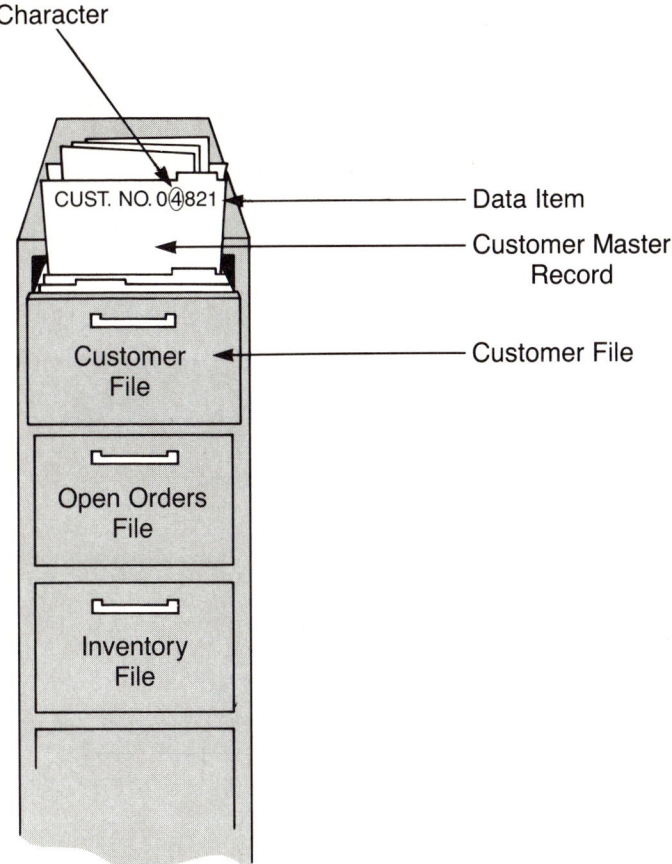

Character

CUST. NO. 0④821 ——————— Data Item

——————— Customer Master Record

Customer File ◀————— Customer File

Open Orders File

Inventory File

Figure 4-3 Data File Relationships

After you have determined the total disk storage requirements, add an extra 40–60 percent to the figure. This allows "headroom" for the files, as their size fluctuates from day-to-day processing activities. Also, all computer systems automatically create special file indexes, which are stored on the same disk as the data files. Finally, most systems need extra room or temporary space for the sorting and merging of data files. All of these extra space requirements are called "data file overhead." Have ample disk storage available and buy excess capacity beyond your immediate needs.

On-Line File Storage

The total disk storage requirements apply only to data files that need to be "on-line." On-line means having immediate access to information stored on disks that are already inserted in the disk drive unit. With data files

Accounting System Disk Storage Requirements

Module / File Name	Record Size	No. of Records	Total Characters
Accounts Receivable			
Customer Master	128	500	64,000
Open Items	50	250	12,500
Sales Orders	80	300	24,000
Cash Receipts	80	375	30,000
Sales Summary	40	150	6,000
Accounts Payable			
Vendor Master	120	250	30,000
Open Items	60	125	7,500
Transaction File	180	200	36,000
G/L Distribution	50	120	6,000
Partial Payments	60	100	6,000
Order Entry/Inventory Control			
Inventory Master	180	4,500	810,000
Receiving Transactions	110	150	16,500
Sales Orders	100	350	35,000
Back Orders	100	60	6,000
Customer Ship To	120	500	60,000
Customer Bill To	120	130	15,600
Salesperson Commission	40	25	1,000
General Ledger			
Account Master	120	140	16,800
Transaction File	60	350	21,000
Y-T-D Balances	80	140	11,200
Cross References	75	100	7,500
Posting File	60	25	1,500
			1,224,100
Headroom Factor 40%			489,640
Total Disk Storage			1,713,740

Figure 4-4 Accounting System Disk Storage Requirements

on-line you can call up any data item without loading another diskette. Information you use on an hour-to-hour basis should be available through the system without the operator having to reload the disk drives. Airline reservations and automated bank tellers are common examples of on-line systems with large computers. For most small businesses, however, only accounts receivable, order entry, and inventory control should be on-line. Payroll is processed only periodically and the data files are not normally needed during other routine processing. When you want to run payroll, just remove the on-line disk and replace it with the payroll disk. Therefore, the disk storage device need only be large enough for the on-line data files, not for all the files in your diskette library.

Be sure to figure that your largest data file will fit on a single diskette, even though your computer has two or more disk drive units. A single data file may be spread across multiple diskettes, but this arrangement often requires breaking the file into logical entities. This method is awkward and file maintenance can result in headaches. Single disk files are easier to handle and most software systems are designed that way. Also, it's best if the data files for all *active* accounting modules are stored together on one disk. This method is essential for multi-user computer systems and requires a hard disk. The "all-files-on-one-disk" concept saves changing disks when moving from one accounting module to another and thus makes the system easier to use.

Before the final purchase decision, make projections for future disk storage requirements. Since the life expectancy of a business computer is at least five years, consider what your needs might be at that distant date. Disk drive units can be added to the computer after the initial purchase, and most computers will accept up to four drives of equal size. However, you should avoid buying a computer whose total design capability is something less than your projected future requirements. The system you buy today should be expandable to meet all your future needs, especially if your business is rapidly growing.

STEP 4: EVALUATE THE APPLICATION SOFTWARE

In the beginning of their search for a business system, most people focus only on the computer hardware. The hardware is the most tangible part of the system and, as with buying television sets or cars, the hardware features are easier to compare with other computers than are the software features. While the application software plays a much larger role in the day-to-day operation of your business, the merits of a software package are more difficult to judge. Thus, you can expect that most of your effort in qualifying a system will be spent on software. Choosing the right software is the key to a successful installation, and it is so important that the next two chapters are devoted to this topic. Some preliminaries here, however, should be helpful.

Your computer works for you through application software, a set of related computer programs that addresses a functional area of business. Accounting areas such as general ledger, accounts receivable, accounts payable, inventory, and payroll are examples of application software. Each of these five areas is often referred to as an accounting software module. In most cases, a module is self-contained and may be purchased and installed separately from the others. One or more of these modules is called a software package, and a vendor may offer all five modules as a complete accounting package. Application software also applies to many non-accounting functions, such as word processing, mailing lists, production scheduling, and statistical analysis.

Many software suppliers offer the above modules, since these five accounting functions are common to most businesses. The software package comes preprogrammed and ready to use. You need only load the programs into the computer and create the data files (after some set up and training, of course!). Accounting software is generally available through independent software firms, computer dealers, original equipment manufacturers (OEMs), and hardware manufacturers. Some suppliers offer different versions of their package, each for a different name-brand computer, which gives some flexibility in the choice of hardware. You should, in fact, avoid a package that will run on only one particular computer.

The application software generates the information by which you run your business on a daily basis. Many computers execute programs in much the same way, but wide differences can be found in the way software handles your data. You must recognize these differences in selecting a system. With a specific application in mind, locating the software first makes hardware selection much easier.

Software tends to mystify a beginner, since it's intangible and difficult to "see" in the machine. Computers operate at near the speed of light, making it impossible to observe program execution. For example, a computer can add a quarter of a million pairs of numbers in one second. Consequently, we only see the resulting effects of software in any computer operation.

Video Screen Display

In reviewing application software, however, two of these effects can be easily observed. The first is the information on the video screen (or CRT terminal). Terminals with keyboards are used for three basic functions: first, to control and monitor the execution of the computer program (system control); second, to enter information into the data files (data input); and third, to make inquiries about stored information (data output). Each software package will have different methods of displaying this information, but in each case the screen format should be clear and easy to read. The test here is that you should be able to understand the screen display without feeling like you need to be a programmer.

A well-designed package should seem friendly to the user. It should be designed for individuals with no special training in computers. For example, when you first use the system it will present you with a list of choices, called a "menu," and wait patiently for your keyboard response. After you've entered your selection, the system will continue with a series of choices, prompting you through each step of the process. Messages on the screen will tell you if you've made a mistake and how to correct it. These and many other features that make the system easy to use are explained further in the next chapter.

Printed Computer Reports

The software also produces reports that come as a standard feature with the package. Reviewing these does not require a live computer demonstration, since you only need copies of the reports. Your vendor can provide a set of sample reports for this purpose. Listed below are some of the reports normally found as standard items in the accounts receivable module:

Cash Receipts Journal	Sales Analysis
Aged Accounts Receivable	Customer Listing
Statements/Invoices	Sales Summary

Computer generated reports often look very impressive—and very neat compared to manual reports. You should, however, remain objective about the report information you're about to pay for—all the reports you want must be included in the package. If you need sales analysis by type of customer, or an unemployment tax report, make sure it's provided. A good generalized accounting package will have more reports than you will probably use.

Check the report headings across the top of each sample and make certain they contain the type of information you need. The headings normally include items like reference numbers, descriptions, quantities, transaction dates, and dollar amounts. Check the sequence of the information detailed in the body of the report. Reports are normally generated in a strict ascending sequence on items such as customer numbers, dates, part numbers, account numbers, etc., which usually appear on the left side of the report. This sequence is called the sorting sequence. Finally, check the body of the report for the data detail and readability. Compare the information in the report samples with your current method of reporting.

Although no software package will perfectly suit your requirements, what you choose should be an improvement over a manual system. As a rule, if the package comes within 80 percent of meeting your needs, then it is a good compromise for the money. This does not mean you must live with a totally rigid package. Nor does it mean overhauling the way you operate your business. If the package can be modified, it's possible the remaining 20 percent can be changed for less money than buying fully-customized software. In this way the package becomes the basis for building software uniquely suited to your business.

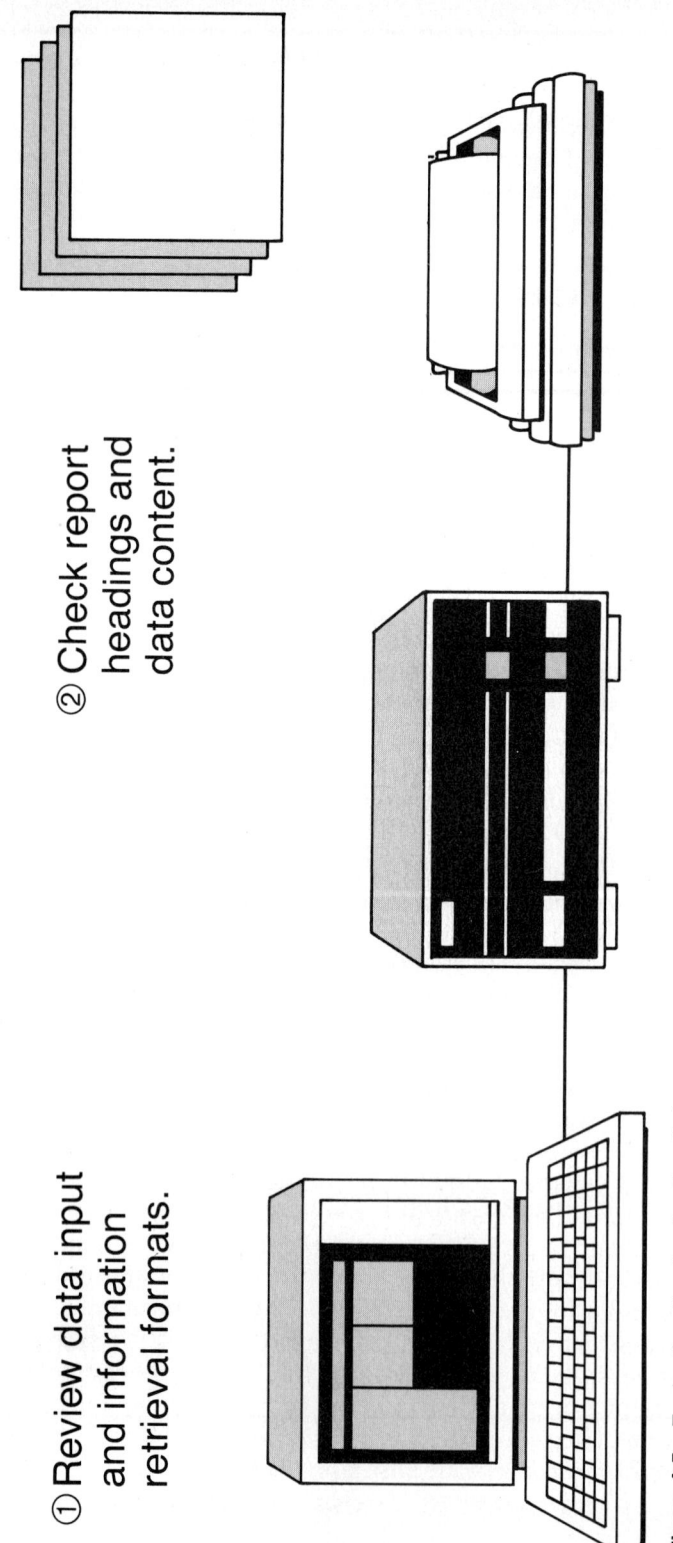

① Review data input and information retrieval formats.

② Check report headings and data content.

Figure 4-5 Evaluating the Application Software

STEP 5: EVALUATE THE COMPUTER HARDWARE

After finding the software, deciding on the hardware is relatively easy. The previous step should narrow the hardware choice to just a few systems, and in most cases the software package will dictate which computer system to buy. This step should also lead to an accurate estimate of the hardware and software costs for your purchase considerations.

As discussed in Chapter 1, even the smallest business computer has four basic components: a central processor unit (CPU), which is connected to all the peripherals and houses the main memory; a video screen console with a keyboard for data input; floppy or hard disks for storing programs and data files; and a printer for producing the hard copy reports. Each of these components is described in greater detail in Chapter 7.

Expandable Systems

One of the most common mistakes in buying a computer for business is getting one that cannot be expanded. Make sure the unit you purchase can be expanded by adding hardware modules. The painful alternative is converting to another system. For this reason, it's best to buy first at the low end or mid-range of a particular brand, providing it meets your initial requirements, and add to it as your needs grow.

Most single user and multi-user computers are designed to increase the disk storage capacity by adding more disk drive units, either floppy or hard, to the central processor. These extra drives can be added later as they are needed. This flexibility allows keeping the initial system cost in line with current requirements while assuring future storage capacity.

Multi-user computers can also be expanded with additional terminals. These become necessary as more people need access to the computer, either as more accounting modules are adopted or, for example, to add a word processing station. Make sure your future requirements are within the maximum number of terminals the computer can accommodate. Some computers will handle up to sixty-four terminals, while others are limited to four or fewer. Generally, adding more terminals to the system requires increasing the amount of disk storage, usually with a hard disk unit.

Many small business computers are designed to expand the main memory as an option, although this is more easily done on a "bus"-type computer, as explained in Chapter 8. Most systems start with 64,000 memory positions (bytes) as a standard feature, but some computers can be increased to more than one million positions of main memory. This is done by inserting additional printed circuit boards in the central processor

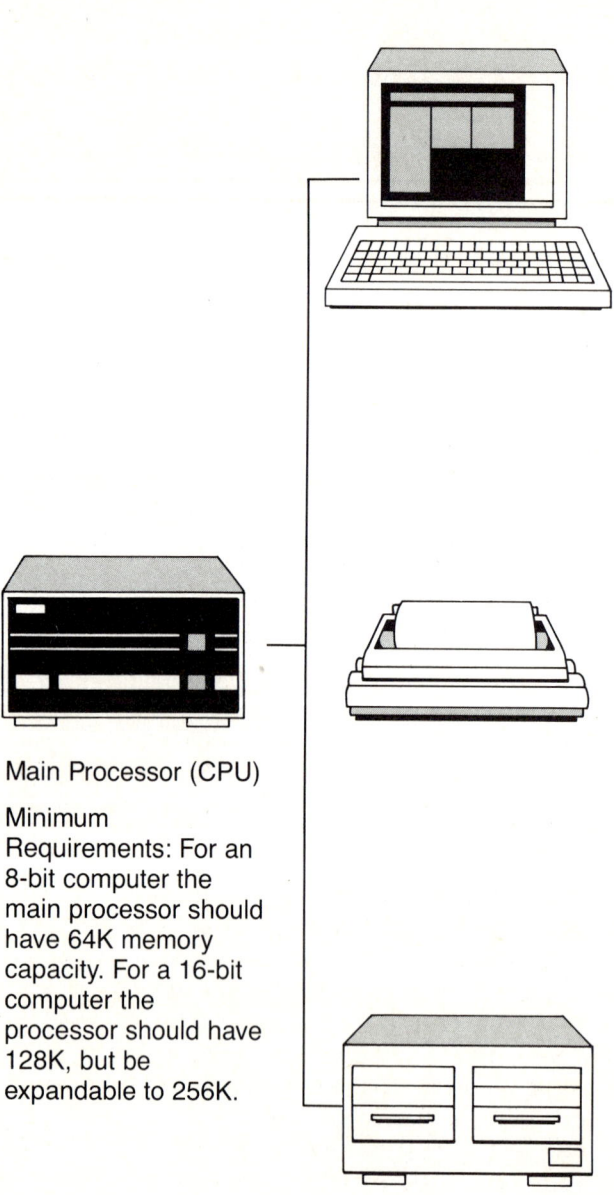

Video Display

Minimum Requirements: The video display should be one designed for computer use, not a television set. The display should measure 12 inches diagonally and show 24 lines down and 80 columns across. Also, it must display both upper and lower case letters. The keyboard should be separate and attached by a cable, with full typewriter-style layout and a 10-key numeric pad.

Printer

Minimum Requirements: The printer, either dot matrix or letter quality, must be able to print across 132 columns, which is required by most accounting packages. The print speed for a dot matrix printer should be 120 to 200 characters per second (cps). A letter quality machine should print in the 30 to 55 cps range. The printer should also have a tractor feed mechanism for the paper.

Disk Storage

Minimum Requirements: A single-user system for non-accounting applications should have two floppy disk drives, each with a minimum of 360K storage capacity. Accounting requires at least 500K per drive. For multi-user systems, the main storage unit should be a hard disk with a minimum of 5 megabytes (5,000K).

Main Processor (CPU)

Minimum Requirements: For an 8-bit computer the main processor should have 64K memory capacity. For a 16-bit computer the processor should have 128K, but be expandable to 256K.

Figure 4-6 Basic System Components: Minimum Configuration

cabinet. Memory boards typically come in capacities of 64,000, 128,000, and 256,000 memory positions. The upper limits of main memory are determined by the type of CPU computer chip and the number of available slots in the computer mainframe cabinet. An eight-bit processor chip, for example, is limited to addressing 64,000 memory positions. Generally, more memory is necessary when the number of terminals is increased or when running very large computer programs. (See Figure 8-1 for information on eight-bit computers with more than 64K memory.).

Remaining Steps in Buying a Computer

Ideally, with the first five steps you have found that: computer systems are available that meet your requirements; they are within your budget; and you have decided to continue searching for a system. In other words, by now you should be able to state confidently that a computer is, or is not, a justifiable acquisition. You have also identified several potential vendors. But which one should you choose? The remaining steps outlined here are the final ones in selecting a system and a vendor. The underlying premise is that you want the system to support the mainstream of your business activity. However, if you intend for your system to operate on the periphery of your business, like a word processor or a personal computer, then you may want to skip Step 6 and proceed with the others.

STEP 6: FINALIZE SYSTEM REQUIREMENTS

Steps 4 and 5 were your window-shopping adventures. Now you need to arrange what you've learned into a meaningful statement of your requirements. A written statement is best, since it prods objective thinking and helps clarify possible solutions. The statement will also help you define a system that is consistent with what's available in the marketplace. Buying the right system will save time and money in the long run. Put the statement in the form of a Request for Proposal (RFP), a document that is sent to potential vendors so they may bid for your business. While this formalizing may seem like a lot of tedious work, the extra effort in the beginning prevents later problems.

The RFP is detailed and specific. It's the blueprint of the computer system that will do what you need. It identifies the software modules you want, with all the critical features needed, such as the open-item method of processing accounts receivable and separate order-entry and invoicing functions. The section on hardware states the amount of disk storage you need, the number of terminals, type of printer, the amount of main memory, and so on. And, equally important, it includes the general terms and conditions of purchase you want from a vendor.

The RFP method enables vendors to respond to a set of specifications made equally available to all participants. It becomes a fair and objective process for them and allows the buyer an easier "apples-to-apples"-type comparison and evaluation. You will have better control of the buying process because you tell the vendors what you want, rather than dealing with their various proposed solutions. It keeps you in the driver's seat. Also, developing the RFP is particularly worth the effort because it can become the specifications part of your final contract with the vendor. Chapter 12 shows how to construct a formal RFP.

STEP 7: SELECT A VENDOR

The process of selecting a vendor is much like selecting your accounting or law firm. You do it with some forethought. Careful preparation of the RFP, however, makes selecting a vendor an easier task. Since you have specified a particular response format in the RFP, you need only prepare a simple vendor evaluation chart. This is a form that allows easy side-by-side comparison of the facts and figures you have requested from the vendors.

Many things about the vendor are important to know beyond the hardware and software considerations. Your RFP should contain questions like:

How long has the vendor been in business?

How many systems have they installed?

How many are similar to your proposed installation?

How well qualified are the technical people?

What kind of service and support record do they have?

Answers to these questions are important, since the success of your installation will depend on the experience of your vendor and his ability to provide continuing quality service.

You must, of course, pay attention to the price of the system. The evaluation chart should include detailed line items for hardware components, system and application software, and installation and training costs. However, choose the lowest-priced only when all other things are equal in proposed systems. Only rarely does this happen. By providing various features and capabilities, a system with a higher purchase price may cost less in the long run than the seemingly low-cost system. In the final decision, give equal consideration to the vendor's performance record along with the quality of the computer system. Chapter 14 explains all the necessary considerations in selecting a vendor.

STEP 8: NEGOTIATE CONTRACTS

It is not uncommon to have two or three separate contracts for the computer installation and on-going support, even when there is only one vendor. A contract to purchase and install the system, a software license agreement, and a field maintenance contract are the most common written agreements. Understanding the terms and conditions in the contracts is an important part of the buying process.

Many vendors prepare a "boiler plate" contract for their services and ask you to sign without any changes. Most preprinted agreements are written to protect their interest more than yours. Thus, you should aim to negotiate the terms and conditions to ensure they serve your interest equally well.

A good contract contains definitions of the hardware and software to be delivered. Since the vendor proposals often contain these definitions, it's an easy matter to append the proposal to the final written agreement. The contract should also outline who does what, where, and when. This minimizes communication problems and lessens the chance of expensive legal battles. Chapter 15 covers the basics of vendor contracts.

STEP 9: INSTALLATION

The installation of your computer system involves more than just uncrating the hardware, plugging it in, and flipping the On switch. Installation means a thorough checking of all system components, including peripherals, software, and documentation. Numerous checkout procedures and test steps are necessary, and it isn't done overnight. Next comes the implementation of the application software with your firm's live data entered by your own people. The installation is actually a combined effort, a specific set of activities shared between you and the vendor. You are better off taking command in managing these steps.

A complete system installation can take a few weeks to ensure that the actual performance meets the contracted specifications. Phase in the application modules over a period of time. This allows your staff to become familiar with each new accounting function and its effect on the way you operate your business. Several months are usually required for full adaptation, with the first or second months running concurrently with the previous methods. This "running in parallel" is a common method used to test the accuracy of the new computer. Chapters 16 and 17 outline the installation and implementation procedures in detail.

SUMMARY

A summary of the nine basic steps to your purchase and installation outlined in this chapter is as follows:

Step 1. Decide What You Want the Computer to Do

You must first decide which business functions should be computerized. Your list should include all the things you want the computer to do, now and in the future, but base your purchase on the most important two or three functions. Making a study of your organization to determine your needs is not only helpful but essential. (Chapters 4 and 12)

Step 2. Determine Single User or Multi-User Computer

Decide whether you need a single user or a multi-user computer system. The single user computers are fine for jobs like word processing, while multi-user systems are better for full accounting applications. The initial extra cost to purchase a multi-user computer with only one terminal may save money in the long run if you're certain you will eventually need more than one work station. (Chapters 4 and 11)

Step 3. Determine Storage Requirements

In an accounting application, the disk capacity is the single most important factor in determining the size of the computer you need. You only have to approximate your data storage requirements, but you will need to add 40–60 percent more for file storage overhead. Also make certain that you can expand the disk storage capacity for all your future applications without having to buy a larger computer. (Chapter 4)

Step 4. Evaluate the Application Software

Choosing the right software is imperative for a successful installation—it's more important than the hardware decision. The best way to observe what the software package does is to view the information on the video screen and check the reports the programs generate. To find out if the package does what you want, check the features. The best way to learn if the programs work properly is to ask other companies who have already used them. (Chapters 5 and 6)

Step 5. Evaluate the Computer Hardware

Finding the right application software will help narrow the choice of hardware. Make certain you will be satisfied with basic features like the disk capacity, size of main memory, video display, keyboard layout, operating system compatibility, and a choice of printers. It's best to buy at the low end of a manufacturer's line to assure future expandability. This step should also conclude accurate cost estimates for the total system. (Chapters 7 and 8)

Step 6. Finalize System Requirements

Now you need to prepare from your findings a definition or statement of your overall requirements, and write a Request for Proposal. This is essential since it is the master plan for your system. It details things like the hardware and software, vendor services, and the terms and conditions of the purchase. (Chapter 12)

Step 7. Select a Vendor

Your vendor should be able to demonstrate the hardware and software products, configure a system , install it, and assist you without depending on outside expertise. They should know enough about business procedures to apply computers effectively and offer practical solutions to problems when they occur. The success of your installation depends on the abilities of your vendor since they're your standby data processing department. (Chapter 14)

Step 8. Negotiate Contracts

A contract to purchase and install the system, a software license agreement, and a field maintenance contract are the three common legal documents you will have to contend with. You should be prepared to negotiate the terms and conditions to make sure they serve your best interest. (Chapter 15)

Step 9. Installation

The installation of the computer system involves many steps that are shared between you and the vendor. It includes training the staff, preparing the computer site, testing the software, converting the accounting information, and running the old and new system side by side. It can take anywhere from a few hours to a few weeks to complete the process. (Chapters 16 and 17)

CHAPTER
5

Accounting Software Selection

Choosing software can be perplexing because of the many software packages on the market and their diverse functions, features, and prices. Yet the accounting software is the most critical component in your computer system. Finding the right software for your business computer will take the most time. This chapter explains five basic software selection criteria and helps you narrow the wide number of choices. These preliminary criteria are:

1. The software package meets your present needs.

2. The package is easy to learn and easy to use.

3. The programs can be modified if necessary.

4. The vendor provides technical assistance.

5. The software meets your planned future requirements.

These five criteria are not *all* you need to choose a package, but with a basic understanding of them you can formulate easy questions for your first talks with vendors. They are offered as a "first pass" set of judgments to help you save time. Disqualify any software package that fails on any of the five. On the other hand, if a package passes on all criteria, review it more thoroughly.

Although accounting examples are used in this chapter, the five criteria are general enough to apply to non-accounting packages. Chapter 6 provides more detailed selection criteria for general accounting software, including general ledger, accounts receivable, accounts payable, inventory control, and payroll. Chapter 11 discusses the cost considerations for packaged software, including purchase license fees, program modification costs, and on-going maintenance. To appreciate some of the advantages of packaged software, let's first compare it with custom software as an alternative.

CUSTOM VS. PACKAGED SOFTWARE

Buying custom software is like having a suit tailor-made—you get a precise fit. Custom application programs are developed by programmers whom you hire independently or contract with through a local programming service. Packaged software is like buying a suit "off the rack." It may not fit perfectly, but it can be a very good compromise for the price. Application packages are generally available from independent software suppliers, computer dealers, and (sometimes) hardware manufacturers.

Custom Software

The main advantage of custom software is that it precisely meets your requirements because you tell the programmer exactly what you need. Custom software is best when you have a special project for which packaged software is not available. Also, if you've contracted with a programmer on an exclusive basis, you own all the rights to the programs.

Compared to the packages, however, custom programming is an expensive alternative. You can expect to pay from five to twenty-five times the cost of a packaged system. Also, custom programming requires

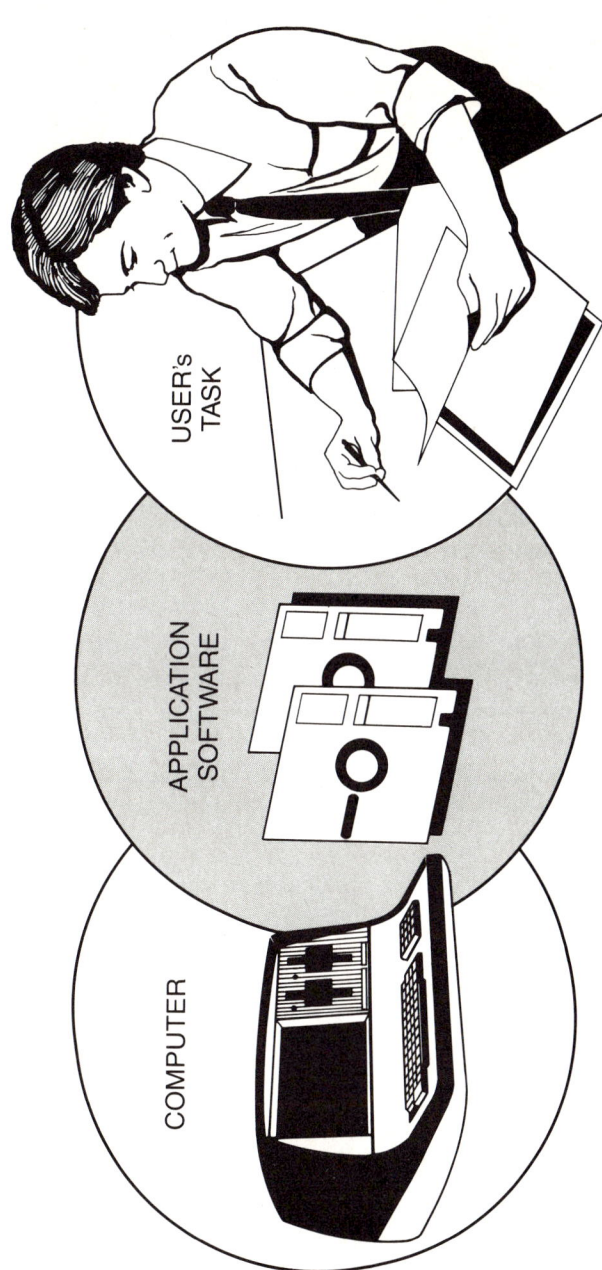

USER's TASK

APPLICATION SOFTWARE

COMPUTER

Figure 5-1 Application Software: The Primary User Interface

Custom Programming	**Application Packages**
Advantages	
Meets Exact Requirements	Fixed Cost Purchase
Customer Ownership	Market/Field Tested
	Ready to Use
	Superior Documentation
Disadvantages	
Very Expensive	Requires Changes in
Development Lead Time	Organizational Procedures
Resolve Program "Bugs"	or Program Modifications
Programmer-Dependent	Extra Costs to Modify

Figure 5-2 Custom Programming vs. Application Packages

development time because the programmer must start from scratch. While he works, you will have to wait weeks or months before you can use your new program. Also, unless the programmer can use his own computer for development, he will need yours, which means you're paying for the hardware before gaining any benefits. Even after the programs are completed you will need a test period to find and resolve all deficiencies, called program "bugs." All newly created programs need de-bugging.

The custom route is also programmer dependent. If for any reason he/she is not able to complete the job (and the progress has not been documented), you may need to find someone else and start again. Programming is a highly personal skill, and often does not lend itself well to a team effort. Packaged software suppliers and dealers, however, usually have more than one person who knows their system intimately.

Packaged Software

If you want one of the common business applications, like general accounting, the packages resolve almost all the disadvantages of custom software. Packages are designed to appeal to a wide market of a large number of users. While they are generalized, the more comprehensive packages have many features, some of which are incorporated as user options. This means you can tailor the package somewhat without using a programmer. Thus a package may come close to meeting all your present needs while having some of your future requirements already built in.

Because packaged software is generalized, it actually costs more to develop than custom software. But the purchase price to the consumer is low because the development costs are shared by many users. Producing a software package is similar to publishing a book—the profits are made when a large number of buyers purchase a copy. Also as with books, you buy a package at a fixed, known price, and you can inspect the merchandise before you buy.

Application packages are field-tested and ready to use, so you need no development lead time. Field-tested means the supplier has installed the software in several test sites to determine the program's integrity before release to the general market. In fact, the better packages have established a customer base, which is some assurance that the programs work well. In addition, many suppliers offer a software warranty to help protect you against defects. (See Chapter 15.)

Commercial software packages usually have superior documentation, manuals that tell how to install, operate, and maintain your system. Most software suppliers who are committed to their product take great pains to offer complete and easy-to-understand manuals. Good documentation is essential.

One disadvantage of application software is that it may require program changes to meet your specific requirements. (See the discussion of "Modifiable Programs" later in this chapter.) Briefly, program modifications involve determining what changes need to be made and what they will cost. This means using a programmer, and the costs of even small changes can easily approach the original cost of the package. Cost estimates and modification services are usually available through your vendor, but you may elect to hire a programmer to do it independently. If you do not change the software, you may need to bend your organization's procedures to accommodate the package.

In summary, give priority consideration to packaged application software. Use custom software only when no package is available, or when the cost of a software package plus the cost of tailoring approaches the expense of customized development.

APPLICATION SOFTWARE CRITERIA

CRITERION 1: MEETS PRESENT REQUIREMENTS

The first step in your search for a computer in Chapter 4 was "Decide What You Want the Computer to Do" by listing all the functional areas of your business that you want to automate. The example used showed accounts receivable and inventory control as the priority computer applications. By the steps in Chapter 4 you have identified a few software packages whose capabilities seem to match the needs on your list. Now you will need to further qualify the software for your present business requirements. Let's look closer at the packages containing the modules and features you've selected.

To begin matching software to your requirements, see if it suits your particular industry. Some packages say they are used "in a wide variety of businesses." No package works equally well for all types of industries, or for even a few industries. Inventory reporting for a manufacturer is different than for a retailer. A book publisher will use a different procedure for accounts receivable than a wholesale distributor. Even companies in the same industry use different accounting methods.

Also, ask if the package is appropriate for the size of your business within your industry. Find out the size of other businesses that bought the same package. Are you in the same league? An accounting package designed for a company with annual sales of ten million dollars will probably be wrong for a "mom-and-pop"-type operation. For example, larger firms often require multiple capabilities, like multi-division reporting, multiple warehouse locations, multiple branch offices, and so on. Larger businesses also need extended reporting features, such as two sets of general ledger budget figures for alternative planning.

Step 4 in Chapter 4 shows how to evaluate accounting reports by checking the headings, report-sorting sequences, and the information detailed in the body of the report. Do this kind of evaluation again but with closer scrutiny. In any business operation, computer generated reports serve a number of purposes. They show the status of such items as inventory levels and the outstanding amounts in accounts receivable. They should provide accurate and timely information for managing the business, such as daily cash receipts and inventory re-order points. They should also provide information to support major decisions, such as setting new policies or changing the course of the business to meet new objectives. And the computer should generate government-required reports without extensive manual preparation.

Any of these reports can be developed with a manual system. One of the main benefits of a computer, however, is that it provides information for analysis with little manual effort. For instance, the data captured from the invoicing operation can be used to produce sales analysis reports by customer, product, salesperson, or geographic area. A computer does this kind of analysis without extra or redundant manual effort. The computer program simply reorganizes, or re-sorts, the invoicing data files and prints the reports using the same information in a different sequence. And it does this in a matter of minutes.

Therefore, the reporting capabilities of the package should exceed any manual reporting system. The software package should improve management decision and operating information. But be certain the reports contain the kind of information you need on a daily basis. Figure 5-3 is a model list of reports found in each of the five accounting modules. Use it as a checklist for your requirements.

General Accounting Software Reports

General Ledger

General Ledger Transaction Register
General Ledger Trial Balance
General Ledger Source Cross Reference
General Ledger Account Master File

Balance Sheet
Profit and Loss Statement
Supporting Schedules

Accounts Receivable

Sales Journal
Cash Receipts Journal
Accounts Receivable Aged Trial Balance
Statements
Monthly Sales Summary
Customer Mailing Labels
Credit Memo Edit List

Sales Analysis by Customer
Sales Analysis by Salesman
Sales Analysis by State
Sales Analysis by Customer Type
Alphabetical Customer List
Order Edit List
Billing Memo Edit List

Accounts Payable

Accounts Payable Voucher Register
Cash Requirements Report
Accounts Payable Checks
A/P, G/L Distribution Cross Reference
Alphabetical Vendor List

Accounts Payable Aged Trial Balance
Pre–Check Writing Report
Accounts Payable Check Register
Vendor Analysis Report
Expense Account List

Order Entry/Inventory Control

Inventory Receivings Report
Back Order Report by Item
Price List
Sales Analysis by Product Category
Invoices
Inventory Master File

Picking Tickets
Purchasing Advice Report
Inventory Stock Status Report
Commissions Due Report
Back Order Report by Customer
Salesman File

Payroll

Payroll Attendance Register
Payroll Register
Payroll Checks and Stubs
Payroll Check Register
Payroll Deductions Register
Payroll Manual Transaction Register
Attendance Distribution Report

Overtime and Sick Pay Report
941A and W-2 Forms
Alphabetical Employee List
Payroll History Report
Payroll Savings Bond Register
Unemployment Tax Report
Employee Master File

Figure 5-3 General Accounting Software Reports

Other application requirements are based on the particular methods used in your present accounting system. The compatibility of a package with your business procedures may depend on features like the following:

◪ Balance forward or open item accounts receivable
◪ Automatic calculation of finance charges

◪ Partial payments of accounts payable items
◪ User-defined general ledger chart of accounts
◪ Separate order entry and invoicing functions
◪ Manual override of inventory prices
◪ Partial billing with adjustments to quantity shipped and quantity back-ordered
◪ Payroll processing with labor distribution reports
◪ Out-of-state payroll tax tables

Features like these and many others vary greatly from one software package to another. No single package will have all the features you need, so carefully check the must-have items. Chapter 6 discusses these and other features to help with your selection.

CRITERION 2: EASY TO LEARN/EASY TO USE

The real test of packaged software is how well you can understand and use it. Both are important factors, particularly in a small business where a computer expert is generally not available. Most package ads say "easy to use," but you may have difficulty cutting through the advertising hype to establish what this means.

First of all, software should be designed to ease the initial learning period. This is especially important when clerical-level people are expected to use the system. A short learning curve means your staff will make effective use of the system soon after the installation. Genuine easy-to-learn software means you can easily train others in the firm when the key operators are absent. Also, it helps cut down the cost of training a new key operator. Easy-to-understand software helps reduce the "people" cost throughout the life of the system.

Secondly, software should be designed to help prevent serious mishaps during operation. These features focus on preventing mistakes, as well as correcting them once they occur. The real effort in the package's design and construction should be to make it as foolproof as possible. (There may be limits, however. Shaw's Principle says, "Build a system that even a fool can use, and only a fool will want to use it".)

The following items, which are discussed in this section, are criteria to help you assess how easy or difficult it is to use a particular software package. The list is not inclusive of all the things you may want to consider, and some elements are subjective depending on the user's experience.

◪ The features that determine how well the user interfaces with the software
◪ User-conducted software tests
◪ The package's ability to handle routine exceptions
◪ Software error recovery procedures
◪ Readability and completeness of user manuals

Application Software Features

Menu Selection of Function. You command what you want the computer to do under "menu" control. A menu is simply a list of operator choices that appears on the video screen. This feature makes it easy to tell the system to do inventory updates at one moment, run general ledger reports the next moment, or to do anything else the computer is programmed for. Figure 5-4 is an example of the first menu (the main menu) to appear when you begin your session with the computer.

This is how it works. For each function the system will display on the video screen choices such as: "General Ledger," "Accounts Receivable," "Accounts Payable," "Inventory," or "Payroll," each with its own selection letter or number. When you enter the appropriate code via the keyboard, you advance to a sub-menu, the next step in the program. If you choose "Accounts Receivable," then the sub-menu choices might be "Enter Daily Transactions," "Customer Master File Update," "Run A/R Reports," or "End of Month Processing." Figure 5-5 is an example of a general ledger sub-menu. Thus, menu control allows the operator to proceed from one accounting module to another, or from one function to another within a module. This feature makes it easy to operate the computer system without having to memorize procedures. Most of the popular software packages use the menu feature for control.

Prompting for Data. Computer terminals (keyboards with video screens) are used for three basic functions: to execute programs and control the system; to enter data; and to make inquiries about previously stored information. During each of these functions the computer needs specific data or instructions. For example, after you turn on the computer in the morning, the system will "prompt" you for the current date, a numeric variable. (The date automatically appears on all transactions, computer reports, and other computer activities during the day without you having to re-enter it each time.) Any logical date is accepted. In other cases, the prompt is for a predetermined set of choices like, "Do you wish to continue transactions? Yes/No." Here the computer accepts only a "Yes" or "No" answer. In Figure 5-4, the selection number "3" was entered to select "General Ledger" as one of eight possible choices.

When the computer prompts for data, it will ask for a particular response and stop all processing until it is entered. Thus, prompting helps guide the operator and keeps the data input in correct sequence with the steps in the program. Prompting is part of the "conversational" nature of using computers, and helps the operator avoid confusion and errors.

Validation of Information Entered. One of the advantages of using a computer over a manual system is that it can automatically verify the accuracy of entered data. This is called "on-line editing" and is done at the time of data entry, but before the computer passes the information to

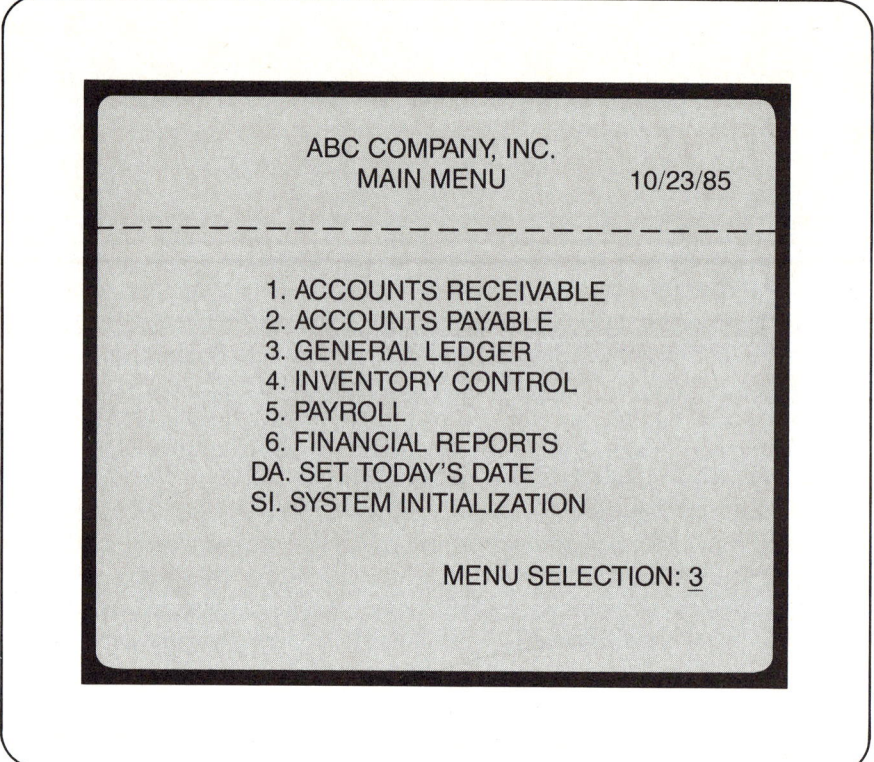

Figure 5-4   Screen: Menu Selection

its disk files. Aside from maintaining accuracy, the main benefit of catching errors at the point of entry is to save the staff time needed to trace entries that would happen in a manual system. The programs can instantly check the validity of numbers and other data in several ways:

1. Data Item Size.   The size or the length of the data item can be verified. Many items, like zip codes, telephone numbers, customer codes, general ledger account numbers, vendor numbers, and salesperson codes, contain a predetermined number of characters or digits. Once these data items are installed in your system they each will have a fixed number of digits. The computer can tell the operator if the keyed entry deviates from the prescribed field length.

ABC COMPANY, INC.
GENERAL LEDGER—SUB-MENU

— —

1. MASTER FILE MAINTENANCE
2. ENTER DAILY TRANSACTIONS
3. ACCOUNTING TRANSFER
4. DELETE AN ENTRY
5. QUERY ACCOUNT STATUS
6. FINANCIAL REPORTS
7. MASTER FILE LIST
8. TRANSACTIONS FILE LIST
9. MONTH END PROCESSING
E. RETURN TO MAIN MENU

MENU SELECTION:_____

Figure 5-5 Screen: Sub-Menu Selection

2. Alphanumeric Data. Some data items, such as inventory quantities, will always be numeric, and others, such as city and state, will always be alphabetic. The computer can test for each of these two conditions without regard to the values entered. Thus, the system can help eliminate "garbage" from creeping into the data files. Still other items, like company names, street addresses, and inventory part descriptions, may contain both alphabetic and numeric data, and no such test is made. Figure 5-6 shows examples of alphabetic, numeric, and alphanumeric data items entered in an employee master file.

3. Account Codes. The computer can check for previously assigned codes and account numbers when entering transactions. Any unassigned numbers are rejected and the operator is asked to correct and re-enter, set

```
┌─────────────────────────────────────────────────┐
│                                                   │
│   EMPLOYEE MASTER FILE—ADD NEW EMP                │
│   ─ ─ ─ ─ ─ ─ ─ ─ ─ ─ ─ ─ ─ ─ ─ ─ ─ ─ ─ ─ ─ ─   │
│                                                   │
│    1. EMPLOYEE NO.: 1234      12. OVT. RATE:       │
│    2. NAME: TOM SMITH         13. SPC. RATE:       │
│    3. STREET: 123 ANY STREET  14. EXM FWT:         │
│    4. CITY: YOURTOWN          15. ADD FWT:         │
│    5. STATE: CA               16. FICA FLG:        │
│    6. ZIP: 96510              17. PROJECT:         │
│    7. SOC. SEC.: 487-56-8970  18. TITLE:           │
│    8. EMP. TYPE: 2            19. FUNCTION:         │
│    9. DEPT. NO:               20. LOCATION:        │
│   10. BASE PAY:               21. MARITAL:          │
│   11. REG. RATE:              22. PENSION:          │
│                                                   │
│   INVALID ENTRY—PUSH "RETURN" TO RECOVER          │
│                                                   │
└─────────────────────────────────────────────────┘
```

Figure 5-6 Screen: Data Entry Validation

up a new code, or proceed to the next step. For instance, when making journal entries, the operator enters a general ledger account number. The computer program then searches and verifies the number from its general ledger master file. If the number was not previously assigned, the system informs the operator with a message on the video screen: "Invalid account number." If the account number is correct the computer verifies it by accepting the transaction or showing the appropriate detail.

4. Numeric Range. The computer can also check for a range of numeric values. For example, the system will present a "flag" message when a new customer order exceeds the approved credit limit. Depending on the program, the credit limit can be tested for a single order or for an accumulation of all outstanding orders. In this example, the range is for any dollar amount up to the specified credit limit, but almost any type of range can be set for other critical data items.

5. Control Totals. Batch totals are useful in making sure the computer has properly received all entries for a group of transactions and that the total amounts are correct. Here the operator compares the computer total with a total previously run on an adding machine. With this method, any problems are associated with a particular group of transactions, which helps save staff time in finding them.

System Defaults for User Options.   Good software helps the operator avoid tedious repetition. Consider the situation in which an operator has to enter the current date for every transaction processed in a day's time. This amounts to a lot of repetitive keystrokes to post the date with the transactions. With a system default, however, the user strikes only a single key when asked for the date (usually the "Return" or "Enter" key), and the current date is automatically entered. (The current date is normally entered only once at the beginning of the day.) If the operator wants to process a transaction held over from the previous week, the default is manually overridden and the proper date is entered. This example shows only one type of system default.

Defaults are designed to minimize operator effort by assuming that most of the routine processing is done in a prescribed manner. Yet they will allow other choices when necessary, or handle the exceptions without making changes in the computer programs. For example, another kind of default causes all reports to be printed on the main printer unless the operator choses to print at a remote work station. Still another kind sorts a file for a report in ascending order, unless descending order is requested as an exception. Thus, system defaults help save time and maintain program flexibility by allowing changes in the operation when necessary.

Self-Explanatory Error Messages.   Processing errors are likely to occur from time to time and error messages will then appear on the video screen. Basically, an error occurs when something happens for which the computer was not programmed. This can happen either through operator error, machine failure, or an internal condition, such as filling all the available disk space. A good software package notifies the user by displaying a short message on the video screen. (In some systems the error message is accompanied by an audio "beep".) Figure 5-6 shows an example of a self-explanatory error message on the bottom line of the screen.

Messages like "Disk storage not available," "Invalid entry—please re-enter," "Account number not found in file," or "Customer number previously assigned" need no further explanation. These kinds of messages help the operator by identifying the problem so he or she does not have to look up an error code number in a reference manual.

On-Line File Inquiry.   Every software package should allow the user to display or print any stored items of data, or selected portions of the data files, at any time. This is the equivalent of reviewing a ledger card or files in an office file cabinet. Immediate inquiry is an essential feature, since the magnetically coated disks are not manually readable. One main reason for on-line inquiries is to give users access to the company data base to obtain current information without running a lengthy computer printed report. Some common questions the inquiry feature can assist with are:

◪ How much does a particular customer owe?
◪ How much of an inventory item is on hand?
◪ When was the last shipment made to a given customer?
◪ Who is the assigned salesperson for this account?
◪ How much is owed a particular vendor?
◪ What are all the recent transactions for a particular general ledger account?

On-line file inquiry is a neat and consistent way to give all users current information about the accounting data. The information appears on the video screen quietly and efficiently and helps eliminate excessive paperwork. In Figure 5-7, the employee number "0010" is entered and the system immediately displays the master file information for Kevin Driscoll.

Testing the Package

Every software package will have its own operating style, since each is a uniquely created product. While many packages act similarly in processing information, they can have many differences as well. For someone trying to decide on a package, these differences can make it difficult to compare one software product with another. It often seems like an "apples-to-oranges" kind of comparison. One way to ease the evaluation process is to step through a logical sequence of events as they might occur in your own business. If you perform the same test sequence for each package, the differences and shortcomings become apparent.

Most of your operator's activity will involve entering and changing data, since the information in an active business never stands still. New customers are added to the customer master file, inventory balances change as orders are shipped, and paid invoices are deleted from the open-order file. These examples constitute the three basic ways of affecting the data base by additions, changes, and deletions. Any software package should make changing information in its data base easy, accurate, and straightforward. To test the ease of use in making data file changes, ask for a live demonstration from your prospective vendor.

Pick two or three of your frequent kinds of transactions and ask to operate the system yourself, with the salesperson's assistance. For exam-

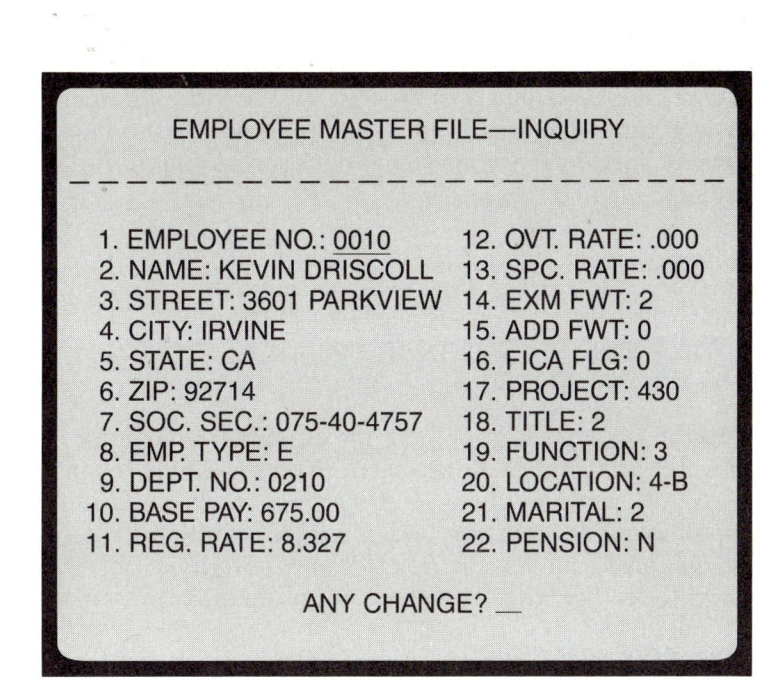

EMPLOYEE MASTER FILE—INQUIRY

1. EMPLOYEE NO.: 0010   12. OVT. RATE: .000
2. NAME: KEVIN DRISCOLL   13. SPC. RATE: .000
3. STREET: 3601 PARKVIEW   14. EXM FWT: 2
4. CITY: IRVINE   15. ADD FWT: 0
5. STATE: CA   16. FICA FLG: 0
6. ZIP: 92714   17. PROJECT: 430
7. SOC. SEC.: 075-40-4757   18. TITLE: 2
8. EMP. TYPE: E   19. FUNCTION: 3
9. DEPT. NO.: 0210   20. LOCATION: 4-B
10. BASE PAY: 675.00   21. MARITAL: 2
11. REG. RATE: 8.327   22. PENSION: N

ANY CHANGE? __

Figure 5-7   Screen: Data File Inquiry

ple, try adding a new item to the inventory file. Learn what kind of information you must have before you can command the system to record it in the inventory file on the disk. Almost all systems require a part number, but data items like description, re-order level, and product category can sometimes be added at a later time if necessary. See how easy it is to enter the information through the keyboard, and see if you can understand the screen format. Also check to see how easily you can change the data appearing on the screen if you make an entry error. Then after completing the step, recall the item from the system disk file and make some changes, such as entering a new description or updating the unit cost. You might also create an invoice to see if the quantity on hand is affected properly and if the other pertinent information went through the system as it should.

Taking the testing a step further, you should deliberately make wild and crazy mistakes (chances are that's what will happen anyway) to see how well the system holds up. Well-designed software should help avoid critical problems even when you've done something wrong. Here are some examples:

◪ Type in a menu choice that isn't displayed
◪ Ask for a file on a disk that's not in the drive
◪ Enter alphabetic data where numeric should go
◪ Inquire about a record that doesn't exist
◪ Exceed the number of digits in an account code

With this approach you take the computer system for a "test drive." You walk through making transactions as you would in your own operation. You'll see how the system responds, how much information the operator needs at each step, and how easy or difficult a transaction is to do. This approach makes it easy to compare various packages and should give you a feel for what's involved in operating the system daily.

Handling Exceptions

Most day-to-day business transactions are handled as a matter of routine. Invoices are created with the customer name and address, items ordered with quantities extended, freight and sales tax added, and the invoices totaled. The majority of invoices are created by this procedure without exception, but what if management wants to give one customer special treatment? A good software package should be flexible enough to handle the kind of exceptions that occur in any business.

One kind of exception is allowing special discounts for selected customers. This discount is separate from the regular discounts that might apply to all other customers. It could be a reduction in price for orders based on total dollar amount, seasonal sales, goodwill, or any other reason. Two ways of solving this situation are to process the exceptions manually outside the computer system, or to add a special program routine for just those few customers. While neither of these methods is totally satisfactory, management should be able to apply a special discount to any customer in its computer files.

When using computers, one common method in handling exceptions is to provide a "manual override." In our example, this is done at the time the invoice is created, and the computer is programmed to allow the override as an operator option for every invoice and every customer. The computer prompts the operator for special discounts, and when an amount is entered it's automatically included in the system accounting. Thus, the manual override feature permits flexibility for management in handling exceptions while maintaining accounting integrity.

Other common exceptions are split commissions between two or more salespersons on one sale, and manually writing payables and payroll checks in advance of the computer processing. If the package does not allow processing the exceptions you need, you may find it acceptable to handle them manually outside the system rather than pay for expensive program modifications.

Error Recovery Procedures

Murphy's Fourth Law says: "If there is a possibility of several things going wrong, the one that will cause the most damage will be the one to go wrong." How well a software package recovers from an operator error is part of its ease of use. With few exceptions, such as outright hardware malfunctions, the program should show what kind of error has been made, and allow recovery either by making a correction or disallowing the error so as to maintain data accuracy. Good error procedures provide recovery without having to push the panic button or pull the power cord from the wall outlet.

Since loss of data files represents the highest risk in using computers, the system should force the user through a two-step procedure before erasing any data. Suppose you have absentmindedly given the computer a command to delete an active customer from the master customer file. The system should respond with a "fail-safe" step asking "OK to delete this record?" Once you have realized your mistake, you can reply "No" without losing any data. Or suppose you have inserted the wrong diskette in the disk drive unit. The system should show the error by identifying the incorrect diskette on the video screen and halting further processing until it is corrected.

To cancel an error is to correct it before the information on the disk is affected. To reverse an error is to correct it when it's discovered after it's been stored on the disk. The better software packages have both cancel- and reverse-error procedures. The reversals, however, should automatically be posted to the system audit trails. Good error recovery procedures mean your operation runs with less trouble and you become self-sufficient in dealing with such problems.

System User Manuals

The manuals supplied with the software package are often called "documentation." Good documentation is usually a sign of a quality software package. It should be written for a clerical-level operator and not for a programmer or system engineer. If the manuals are well prepared, and good training has been provided, they should also minimize the need for an in-house expert. Documentation is the one part of the package that you can thoroughly preview before committing to a purchase, and often the manuals can be borrowed or purchased separately. (The best-selling software packages are often the subject of commercial paperbacks, which is an inexpensive way to review them.)

The reference manuals serve a number of purposes. First, they explain how to install the system, including computer site preparation, hardware switch settings, software implementation, and loading the initial data files. Second, they show general procedures, the logical progression of steps in using the system on a day-to-day basis. These may include flow charts to help explain the sequence of activities. And third, the manuals are used as a reference for troubleshooting, including a detailed explanation of error messages and what to do when they occur. Look for these features when you review the documentation:

1. Introduction. An overview that identifies the basic components of the software package and the inter-relationships among them. This section shows how the manual is organized. It also shows the software specifications, and the minimum hardware requirements.

2. Installation. Shows how to properly install the software on your particular computer configuration. Each package has to allow for different brands of terminals, printers, and other devices. This also includes initializing the software for your particular operation.

3. Tutorial. Provides an approach to learning how to use the package. This is often done in the form of lesson plans that can be followed while using the machine. This section includes basic operation of data entry, file updating, and report generation.

4. Sample Reports. Shows a sample page for each kind of report the system is designed to produce, including preprinted forms. Sample reports help in qualifying the software package for your requirements before the purchase. They are also useful after the installation in matching the reports you run off the printer with the report specifications stated in the manual.

5. Data File or Record Formats. Shows all the data items in the files (or records) and the number of positions allowed for each; whether they contain numeric or alphabetic information; number of decimal places in the amount fields; and the data items or "keys" used in sorting the files for reports. This is useful in determining whether the software includes the detail information you need to process.

6. System Commands. Includes a brief explanation or summary of all the program commands used in operating the software package. This is a handy reference once you have become proficient in using the programs, and it minimizes the need for referring to the full documentation. A summary of all possible error messages should also be provided.

7. Backup Procedures. Backing up programs and data files means making exact duplicates of all programs and files on separate, removable diskettes to "back you up" in case the primary disks are lost or destroyed. Various software packages have different procedures for this step. (Backup is explained further in Chapter 9.)

8. Owner Maintenance. What the user can do, or should not do, to take care of the system. Maintenance includes proper handling of the diskettes, running system diagnostics, and environmental considerations.

CRITERION 3: MODIFIABLE PROGRAMS

Since few accounting packages will fit a business perfectly, it is important that the programs can be changed or modified. (Generally, you should get to know the system thoroughly over ninety days before making changes.) Modification means reprogramming sections of the package, or writing new programs to supplement the package. These changes close the gap between the unique way you run your business and the software package as it comes off the shelf. You may want to add a new sales analysis report, include a new data item in the inventory master file, or change a report sort sequence. Even if no modifications seem to be needed at installation, you may need to make modifications later as your business changes. Some of the most frequently requested types of changes are:

◪ Adding a new report not included with the standard package
◪ Adding new data items to files or records
◪ Changing printing formats to conform with preprinted forms
◪ Changing sort sequence for existing reports
◪ Adding capabilities to conform with new government requirements
◪ Adapting the data files from one software package to operate under another software package

For the money, a modifiable package is a good compromise between a fixed software package and the expense of all-new custom software. This recommendation assumes that less than 20 percent of the software's program instructions need to be reprogrammed. If you must change more than 20 percent of the software to meet your requirements, look for another package or consider custom software. Program changes are expensive. Treat them like making changes in the floor plans of a house after the foundation has been poured.

To make program changes usually requires having the program "source code." The source code is the set of computer instructions created by the programmer. With a subsequent computer step this code produces the final machine instructions that the computer actually follows. These machine instructions are called "object code," and are separate and distinct from the source code. Object code is, normally, the programs you receive when you buy a software package. Most computer programs cannot be changed or modified without the source code, since it is like the key used in decoding secret messages. Many software suppliers make the source code available only to the dealer or user under a special license agreement (and price).

Even if you can afford the source code, it's often more practical to have your vendor make the modifications. One reason is that programming is a tedious and time consuming effort. Most managers do not have any more time for programming than they do for their own building maintenance. Also, when you make changes to the basic structure of the software package you may void the warranty. If the supplier or dealer is authorized to make the modifications, the warranty remains in effect, which offers additional protection for your investment.

CRITERION 4: TECHNICAL SUPPORT

The small business computer is designed to be operated in a firm without any programmers or computer experts on the staff. Occasionally, however, you will need someone with extensive knowledge of the entire computer system, called a technical support person. This person is someone available from outside the firm, from either the dealer or the software supplier, who can help with problems during system ownership. This person essentially becomes your data processing department. Good technical support, particularly in the early stages, can help ensure a successful installation.

A full-service dealer will have available someone with a working knowledge of both the hardware and software, who also knows general business procedures. Ideally this person is involved from the beginning and helps determine the initial computer configuration, installs the system, and provides training and on-going maintenance. When problems arise, support from a local vendor is the best choice, but the dealer may in turn depend on assistance from the software suppliers.

At the very least, technical support should be available by telephone. Some vendors establish a "hot line," which is a special phone number used to reach a technical person whose sole responsibility is to answer questions from users. While a hot line is ideal for specific questions or a preliminary diagnosis, it's best if the vendor has the staff available to make follow-up calls to your office. These personal visits are necessary when the support person needs to review your office procedures, troubleshoot the system on-site, or discuss new application requirements. On-site follow-up is one of the main reasons for doing business with a local vendor.

Another method of vendor support is called "remote dial-up." It requires communications equipment, at an extra cost of only a few hundred dol-

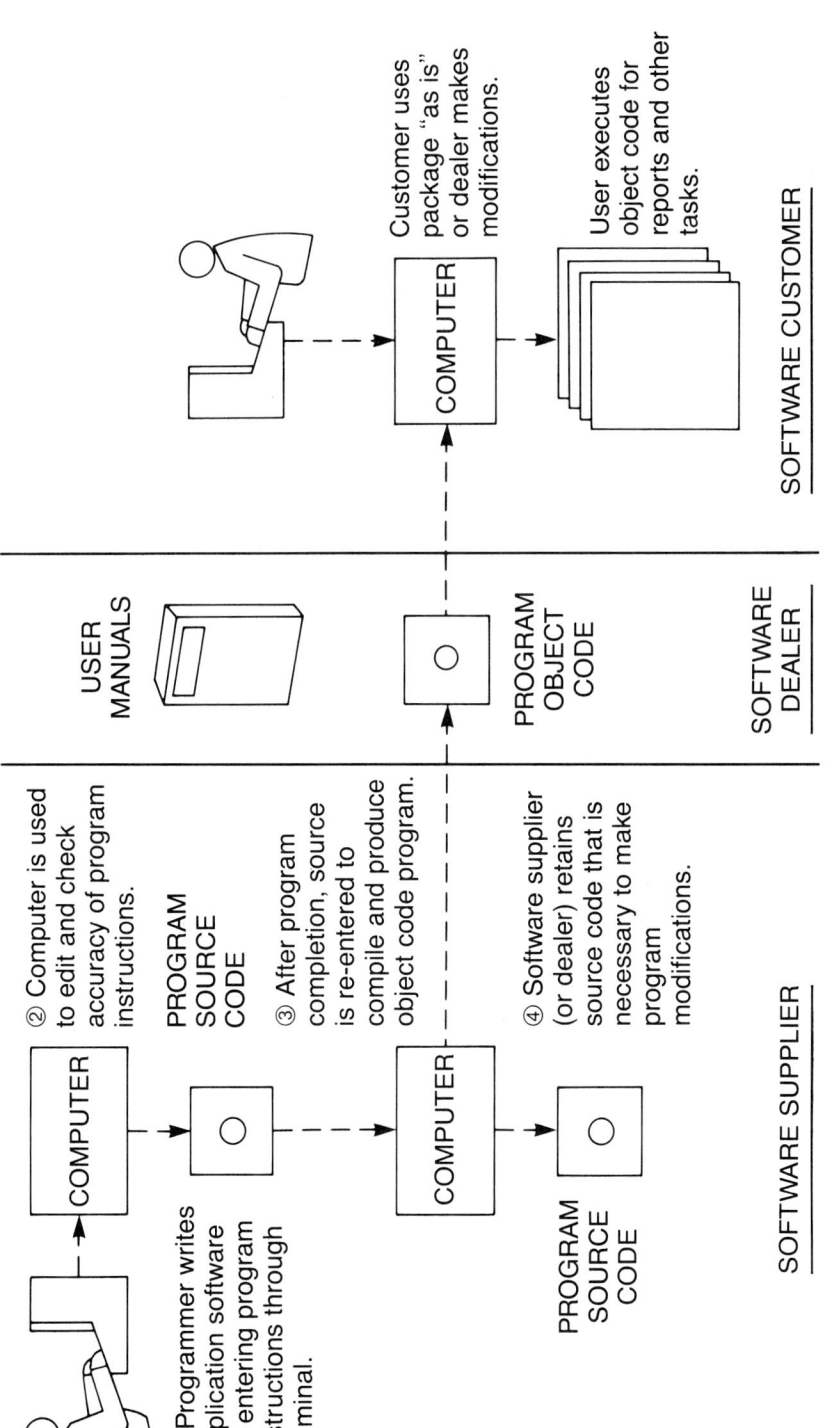

Figure 5-8 Application Program Development and Distribution

① Programmer writes application software by entering program instructions through terminal.

② Computer is used to edit and check accuracy of program instructions.

PROGRAM SOURCE CODE

③ After program completion, source is re-entered to compile and produce object code program.

④ Software supplier (or dealer) retains source code that is necessary to make program modifications.

PROGRAM SOURCE CODE

COMPUTER

COMPUTER

SOFTWARE SUPPLIER

USER MANUALS

PROGRAM OBJECT CODE

SOFTWARE DEALER

Customer uses package "as is" or dealer makes modifications.

COMPUTER

User executes object code for reports and other tasks.

SOFTWARE CUSTOMER

lars. The data communications equipment is installed with your computer and allows the vendor to connect to it directly, via a telephone line, from a terminal in his office. Remote dial-up uses a regular voice-grade telephone line. This connection provides the technical support person with access to your computer as though he or she were operating one of your on-site work stations. This arrangement often allows diagnosis and correction without a personal visit to your office.

Software suppliers should provide users a number of services as support. The supplier should notify all users when program deficiencies (bugs) are discovered and correct them, even if the errors are found by only one customer. Periodically the software "fixes" are sent to all users so they may install them in their systems. This is one of the reasons suppliers ask for owner registration of their products.

A supplier committed to supporting his customers through his products offers updates or "enhancements" for his software package. Enhancements are planned improvements that do not materially change the basic functions of the software. For instance, including income tax tables for all fifty states in the payroll module, instead of just one or two, is an enhancement. Extended capabilities, which the supplier may also choose to offer, do materially affect the system. Adding sales analysis reporting to the accounts receivable module is an example of extended capability. These enhancements and extensions consist of all new programs, or program sub-routines, and are made available on diskettes along with new or revised documentation. An annual subscription fee is usually charged for this service as an option, or the upgrades can be made available on a per copy basis.

CRITERION 5: FUTURE APPLICATION NEEDS

Your immediate needs may call for only one or two accounting modules. Recalling our list from Step 1 in Chapter 4, inventory control and accounts receivable had top priority, while general ledger, accounts payable, and payroll were planned to be added at a later time. Thus, your initial system purchase will focus on the top priority items.

Nonetheless, in order to take full advantage of the computer you should, over a period of time, plan on implementing all five modules. These often can be installed and operated independently of each other. Most accounting packages allow separate module purchase, and each additional module is only a small portion of the total cost of the computer system. Since the computer is primarily a fixed cost item, the more work your system can do for you, the greater the return on your investment.

The five modules should be integrated as a total system, which means they work together. For example, some data files may be shared by two or more modules, such as the customer master file, which is used between the order entry/inventory and accounts receivable modules. Integrated also means that single data entries set in motion a chain of events necessary for full accounting purposes. For instance, a single accounts payable transaction automatically generates entries to general ledger cash, expense, and payable accounts.

Therefore, for your future considerations, look for a software supplier that currently has all five accounting modules. If the package is incomplete, keep on looking; It is not wise to depend on a developer's promise for future modules. Also, mixing one supplier's receivables with another's inventory usually does not work. Buy all the modules from the same supplier to assure compatibility.

In conclusion, evaluate the software as carefully as any other investment, since the quality and capabilities of the package play a major part in the return on your investment.

SUMMARY

The five basic criteria for selecting application software as suggested in this chapter are as follows:

1. Software Meets Present Requirements

After the first five steps in Chapter 4, you will need to further qualify the package for your current business needs. Check if the software is suited for your industry, and if it's appropriate for the size of your company. Check the printed reports for the operating information you need. The reporting capabilities should be an improvement over your present methods.

2. Easy to Learn/Easy to Use

The real test of the software package is how easily you and your staff can learn it, and how well it does what you want. The way the software interacts with the user; how gracefully it allows recovery from operator errors and other mishaps; and how good it is at handling exceptions in the accounting routines are among the important considerations. The user manuals play a significant part in this evaluation as well.

3. Modifiable Program

Don't expect a software package to fit the way you run your business perfectly. Nor should you have to change your business to fit the package. These differences can be resolved by making programming changes called modifications. The caution here is it's expensive. Make sure the changes are absolutely necessary, and get an estimate and specifications in writing before you begin.

4. Technical Support

You will need to call on your vendor from time to time for help. Make certain he has a staff that knows the hardware and software on a technical level, has a telephone "hot line" service, and, more importantly, can make house calls. This vendor support should be available for the life of your computer system.

5. Software Meets Future Requirements

Don't buy an accounting package that doesn't offer all the basic modules. Even if you don't plan on using them all, there's no other way to assure compatiblity in the event that you decide to do so later. If a package you like is incomplete, keep on looking—too many times a software supplier's promise of future modules never materializes.

CHAPTER
6

Accounting Software Features

Chapter Five explained the basic criteria for selecting an accounting package and the general considerations for meeting your requirements. This chapter discusses the specific features of accounting packages. These features will help you distinguish one package from another in ways that are not readily apparent when searching for the ideal package.

This chapter covers the following accounting modules: general ledger, accounts receivable, accounts payable, inventory control, and payroll. These accounting functions are sometimes called "the big five," because they are the most common in all types of businesses. Accounting packages vary, however, in the number and types of modules they provide. You can find modules for such functions as sales analysis, job costing, purchase order, order entry, fixed assets, bill of materials, and materials requirements planning (MRP).

Any of these may be as important to you as those in the big five. While this chapter covers only the five basic modules, the same considerations apply to the others. The first section below discusses general features, while the last part covers specific features.

While each of the five modules serves a particular accounting function, they all have the common, underlying capabilities to accomplish the following basic tasks:

1. Create master files, stored on the disk,containing information such as customer name,inventory balances, and general ledger chart of accounts. The modules allow for both creating the files and maintaining them.

2. Enter, edit, and store daily transactions as they occur.

3. Correlate daily transactions with both the correct master files and files of other accounting modules.

4. Complete required computations by crediting or debiting accounts.

5. Provide a means to verify, correct or change any data on the disks at any time.

6. Produce reports with detailed listings of accounting activity and management summaries.

While many accounting packages are good products, offering all the essential features at a fair price, choosing accounting software is difficult because it involves so many variables. The packages are complex, and each product brings trade-offs that you must consider. No perfect system exists; nor is there a "best" program for all situations. Selecting an accounting package, then, is a matter of making intelligent compromises.

For example, in addition to the features, you must consider style. Each software firm designs a package from its own point of view on accounting and the world of business. You may like the way accounting is handled in one package, and be frustrated by the programmer's approach in another, even though both accomplish the same thing.

If you are not fully confident of your accounting knowledge, get the help of your CPA or an accountant. Seek the advice of someone who knows both accounting and microcomputers *before* you buy any software. Compared to other application software, accounting packages are not quickly evaluated. Expert advice is usually valuable and may help you avoid expensive mistakes.

GENERAL FEATURES TO LOOK FOR

The general features apply to all modules of the accounting package. These concern basic operational capabilities such as:

Package Integration
Adequate Security
File Lockout
Adequate Audit Trails
Batch or Interactive Mode
Single User or Multi-User
Supplemental Capability

Beyond the general features, all accounting packages have small differences for you to consider. These lesser features usually do not swing the decision to buy a particular package. Some are desirable, while others simply add to the distinction of one package from another. Some examples:

◢ Rounding off cents to the nearest dollar amount. In most cases, this feature yields more readable financial statements.
◢ The user can determine the divisor for calculating percentages shown on the financial reports. Some managers like to have the divisor equal total revenues, while others use total expenses or net income. This kind of flexibility can improve the meaning of the information in these statements.
◢ Some programs show the placement of dollar signs only at the top of the column and at the total. Programs that print the dollar sign beside each figure in the columns clutter up the statement with redundant information.

The seven general features to look for in an accounting package are as follows:

1. Integrated Packages

In Chapter Five the term "integrated" meant an accounting package with all modules working together as a unit. Although this meaning is the general use of the term, "integrated" appears frequently in advertising and has several different meanings. While these differences may not be obvious in sales brochures or even the documentation, so-called integrated packages work differently in daily use. Thus, a further definition is essential, and you should be aware of the two basic approaches used in accounting packages.

To some software firms, integrated simply means offering all of the big-five accounting functions as one package. Each module, however, is installed and operated almost separately from the others. This limited level of integration means only that the data file formats in each module are compatible with the others. Each module allows you to transfer data *only* to the general ledger by creating a summary transaction file which is then updated once a month. Thus, a sales transaction requires the operator to make a separate entry into both the accounts receivable and inventory control modules, since the accounts receivable does not automatically deduct product sold from the inventory. This type of package places more work on the operator, is redundant, and is therefore less than ideal for most users.

In the other approach, integrated means that all of the modules are bound into one comprehensive accounting system. For example, a single transaction entry sets in motion a chain of events in the computer necessary for full accounting purposes. When the operator records a sales transaction, the program simultaneously updates the accounts receivable and the inventory. Complete integration means the payroll data is communicated to the general ledger; product shipments update the inventory; and purchases in the payables system also update the inventory. Therefore, each module is interactive with the others without extra operator intervention. This approach is preferred for a truly efficient accounting package.

In addition to automatic posting to the respective modules, an integrated package should disburse transaction information according to established procedures. For example, the receivables module should allow the user to spread sales entries into several sales accounts. The payables module should allow splitting vouchers among several accounts. An integrated package should also properly handle partial payments, partial shipments, and partial cash disbursements as they might be handled in a manual system. The list below shows some typical transactions and the accounting modules they affect.

Received Goods   ⎫   Accounts Payable, Inventory,
Returned Goods ⎭   General Ledger

Product Sales   ⎫   Accounts Receivable, Inventory,
Product Returned ⎭   General Ledger

When closing the accounting period, each module should automatically submit its accumulated totals to the general ledger. Also, the general ledger module should verify these totals before posting them to its accounts.

2. Data Security

The mark of a good accounting package is how well it protects your stored data from abuse and misuse. Any computer installation must have the controls to prevent unauthorized use of the system. One method to restrict access uses passwords, which act like keys to a lock. A password is a secret code known only to the user and the manager of the system.

An accounting package with good data security also provides various *levels* of passwords, since a single password may not be sufficient. For example, one password should first limit access to the system itself; then another to particular functions such as accounts receivable; and still another to particularly sensitive files such as payroll. Look for a package that offers multiple password protection, especially in a multi-user system. (See "Unauthorized Use of Computer," Chapter 9.)

Another security matter is how the system protects the disk files in the event of a major mishap. In computerese this is called a "system crash." Although the term sounds like a total loss of the system, physical damage is rare. More often the magnetic recordings on the data files become distorted so as to make them unreadable by the computer. Such a mishap could be caused by excessive "glitches" in the power line, hardware equipment failure, or static electricity. (See "Physical Environment," Chapter 9.)

The better packages have a way to recover from a system crash. For example, many accounting programs use complex file structures that are controlled by sub-files called indexes. These indexes are separate files that simply point to the location of a particular data record originally entered randomly. Index files are an important key to using the main data files, and the system can be rendered inoperable if they are damaged or destroyed. Therefore, you should look for an accounting package that has a special index rebuilding program. This is a "utility" program, and you should question any package that does not have this file-saving software.

3. File Lockout

File lockout is an essential feature on multi-user computers for maintaining data integrity. (It is not necessary for single user computers.) The inherent characteristics of a multi-user system require measures to prevent users from inadvertently destroying each other's files. (See "Multi-User Computers, Chapter 8.)

For example, consider two users, each unaware of the other's activities, trying to access the same accounts receivable file at the same time. One is using the customer master file to generate invoices, while the other wants to update a customer name and address. Without file lockout, the computer may be confused as to which command to follow. To avoid this problem, some systems have a "File busy" message, which simply forces the second user to wait until the first user finishes. This file lockout feature must be present in both the operating system and the accounting package.

4. Audit Trails

The accounting package's internal controls should include audit trails, which are a sound practice whether the accounting is computerized or not. An audit trail is the automatic recording of every transaction entered, including the time, date, and source of the activity. When an entry must be checked, audit trails make it easy to trace errors through the transactions. Also, audit trails should be incorporated into all the modules of a computerized system, not just the general ledger.

Audit trails can either be displayed on the video screen or produced as hard copy by the printer. Hard copy is especially important for a company that must provide a certified audit.

The accounting package should also provide an easy, identifiable way to use the audit trails. Using batch numbers is one method. When an apparently erroneous entry needs to be checked, batch numbers enable you to narrow the problem down to a particular group by a previously assigned number. For example, while there may be a large number of checks to petty cash for $15, it's likely that no more than one or two are in batch number 325.

Instead of batch numbers, the system may assign a transaction number, which is almost as good. The system automatically assigns a line number to a keyed-in transaction, thereby making each entry unique. The package should not, however, begin renumbering each session with number 001 unless the date and time are also posted as part of the transaction number. (Many computers have built-in clocks for date and time posting.) Beware of accounting packages that do not have such audit trail controls.

Also, every accounting package, no matter how elementary, should be based on the double-entry method of bookkeeping. For every debit there must be an equal credit (or credits) in the system. Amazingly, some programmers create accounting software with only a single entry provision, which omits the verification that most accounting systems demand. A single entry system can actually become a liability. Make sure the package you are looking at uses the double-entry method.

5. Batch or Interactive

Although most accounting packages are designed to run in what is called "interactive mode," some run in "batch" mode. The batch method is a carryover from the kind of processing originally found on large mainframe computers. With the big computers, you put some data in one end, stand by while things shuffle around for a while, then receive your output from the other end, like taking your suit to the dry cleaner. The differences between batch and interactive are important, though, in the day-to-day operation of an accounting system.

With batch mode the microcomputer takes entered data and stores it in a temporary, or "suspense," file for further processing. Some time later, at the operator's command, the temporary file is processed and the account activity updated. In the old days, batching was the only way to do anything on the giant computers. Now microcomputers can be dedicated to accounting tasks, and batch is no longer the only choice. Batch processing offers the advantage of finding errors before the data is transferred to the disk active files. The main disadvantage of batching is that the files are not "up-to-the-minute" current.

The other type of processing is called interactive or on-line. In this mode the accounting files are affected immediately after the information is entered. (The computer still helps to edit and verify some of the data before it goes to the disk files.) Since the update occurs instantaneously, the interactive method assures that all data files are current. The batch method is slow by comparison, since it involves a series of steps, both on and off the computer, to edit and correct the information before it is finally posted to the accounts.

The interactive method also helps the operator save time by not having to trace through transaction edit lists (hard copy) to correct the data. The disadvantage of interactive processing is that correcting an error requires a system designed to reverse everything and provide audit trails showing the change. For most installations, however, interactive processing has the advantage over batch. Some accounting packages provide both methods as an option.

6. Multi-User Software

Given the large number of eight-bit, single user computers sold by the industry, most accounting packages were written for these machines. Nonetheless, some accounting packages now come in both single user and multi-user versions. This book recommends a multi-user computer for the more demanding business environment. Make certain that your multi-user computer has a multi-user accounting package.

While single user packages work fine, their programs are not designed for the complexities of a multi-user computer. Also, a local programmer can rarely modify or convert a single user package to a multi-user system. Generally, only the original software developer is best equipped for such a conversion. Keep in mind also that a multi-user accounting package requires a multi-user operating system.

7. Supplemental Packages

In general, look for an accounting package whose data files can be accessed or read by other popular application software, such as word processing, electronic spreadsheets, graphics, and data base management. This "data crossover" greatly extends the usefulness of your financial information. Using these packages with your accounting data, however, depends on the ability to transfer files from one package to another. Fortunately, software suppliers make this kind of interface commonplace in the industry. Some examples of using non-accounting packages with your system are:

◪ A word processing program that reads the data files of the accounting package can format the data for special one-time reports.

◪ An electronic spreadsheet can be used for analysis beyond the standard reporting by creating "what if" scenarios with the accounting data.

◪ A graphics package that accesses the accounting files can present data in simple graphic form, such as line graphs, bar charts, and pie charts.

◪ A compatible data base management program can create special reports that may not be available as standard items in the accounting package.

A data base management system gives you a flexible way to access and rearrange accounting information. These reporting capabilities are highly desirable, since they often provide a versatile way to extract and manipulate data without involving a programmer. Some accounting pack-

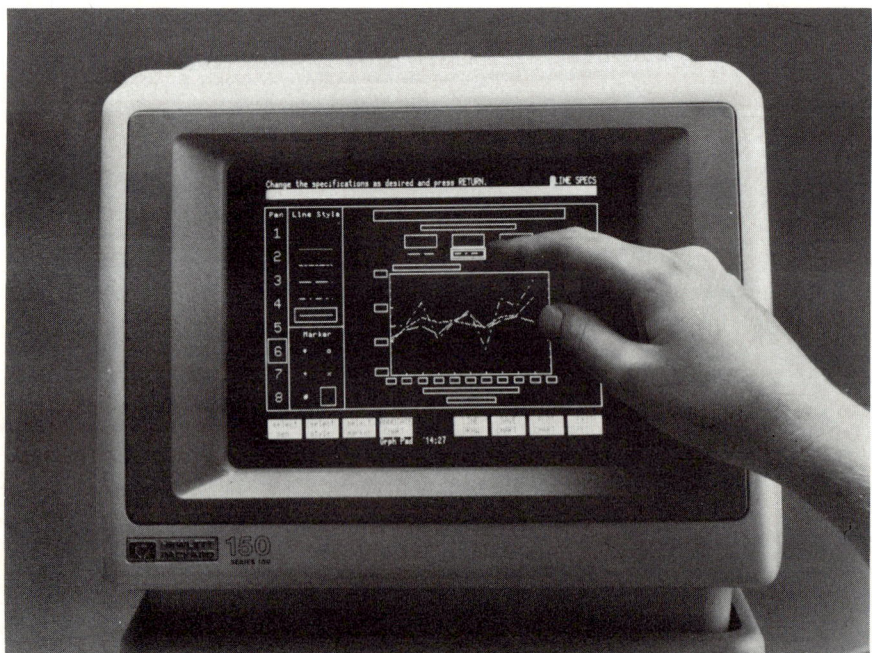

Figure 6-1 Graphics Program: Line Graph (Courtesy of Hewlett-Packard Company)

ages are originally created with a data base management program, so this flexibility is already built into the system.

For instance, accounting packages invariably report sales activity in customer number sequence. A data base management program can generate the same information sorted by total sales for each customer, so that the largest customers appear at the top of the report. Or you might want to have your customers presented in the order of largest percentage increase in sales. A data base management program can also extract information with a different perspective on your financial data if, for example, you are considering a merger or an acquisition.

ACCOUNTING MODULE FEATURES

This section offers a module-by-module look at detailed accounting package features. This is not intended to be complete since there are many items to consider. Rather, it is a summary of features that may be critical enough to affect your overall decision.

You can decide on and indicate the importance of each feature by marking the "Must Have," "Would Like," or "Don't Need" columns beside each feature in the checklist. "Must Have," of course, are the features that are absolutely essential in your operation, and their absence is reason to reject the package. The "Would Like" features will enhance your accounting procedures but are not cause to reject the package if they are missing. The "Don't Need" features would never be required in the forseeable future. This last category helps since fewer explicit demands widens your choice of accounting packages. Include the results of your feature requirements in the application software section of your Request for Proposal. (See "Section V., Application Software," Chapter 12.)

First, consider two items that apply to all modules: the number of digits allowed for account numbers and dollar amounts, and the maximum number of accounts and transaction volumes.

Data Item Size

You need to check the number of digits allowed for the various account numbers before you buy. This is the number of spaces the system permits for the numbers (or codes) used to control the processing. For example, the computer matches employee numbers on time cards against employee numbers in the master file. These user assigned numbers are also used for the chart of accounts, customers, vendors, and inventory parts. Look for a system that has enough positions for each of the codes that you want to use. (This is sometimes called the "field size" of the data items, as explained in Chapter 4.)

Accounting packages vary in the number of digits allowed for each controlling number. For example, the typical allowance for customer and vendor numbers is five digits, although these range from three to six digits among the packages. The chart of accounts in the general ledger varies even more, with a range from three to sixteen digits.

The field size for inventory items can be a problem, especially if you do business under government contract and are required to report their inventory part numbers. Most packages allow ten- or twelve-digit part numbers. However, federal government part numbers are among the longest in the industry, with some requiring up to twenty-two digits.

Field size also applies to the space allowed for text such as journal entries and inventory item descriptions. You should have at least twenty characters in order to write intelligible descriptions.

Field size as applied to dollar amounts (such as single transaction amounts) is especially important in accumulating sub-totals and grand totals in reports. For example, some packages provide up to nine digits ($9,999,999.99), while others allow up to eleven digits ($999,999,999.99) as the largest possible totals.

A package that allows more digits than you need is less of a problem than one whose field sizes are too small. The package *must* meet or exceed the number of digits necessary for your account numbers and total amounts, since they usually cannot be modified. Look for a system that has a sufficient number of positions for your critical data items.

Capacities

An equally important feature includes the limit on transaction volumes and the number of accounts, which are sometimes restricted by the file sizes or disk capacities. Be certain the accounting package does not place any undue constraints on the transaction volumes or on the number of accounts to be stored on the disk.

Accounting software brochures typically state, for example, "up to 99,999 customers," or, "up to 9,999 chart of accounts." The number of accounts, however, is limited by the disk space available or the field size of the account numbers, whichever is lower. Thus, if the customer account number is limited to four digits, the package cannot handle more than 9,999 different customers, even when the disk storage can accommodate more. (See "How Data is Stored," Chapter 4, for a discussion on data items, and Figure 12-2, which is a Transaction Volume Checklist).

Finally, consider the types of reports the package generates and determine if the information shown and the report formats are suitable. A complete list of types of reports appears in Figure 5-3.

General Ledger

The general ledger is the primary ledger, containing the balance sheet and income statement accounts. It is the core of recordkeeping for all secondary ledgers, such as accounts receivable or accounts payable. The general ledger is organized by a chart of accounts and provides financial reports including balance sheets, profit and loss statements, and statements of changes in financial position.

The general ledger may function by itself, or operate in conjunction with other accounting modules. When used with other modules, the journal entries originate from activities of sales, purchases, cash receipts, or payroll transactions.

Feature	Must Have	Would Like	Don't Need
1. User-defined chart of account numbers and descriptions			
2. Designates sub-account numbers			
3. Ability to include job or project numbers			
4. User-defined financial reporting formats			
5. Month-to-date, year-to-date totals of accounts			
6. Monthly budget/historical comparative figures			
7. Multiple division/branch reporting			
8. Multiple division/branch with different chart of accounts			
9. Consolidates division/branch reporting			
10. Designates period beginning and ending calendar dates			
11. Opens new month before closing previous month			
12. User-definable percent denominator on statements			
13. Reporting for selected profit centers			

Accounts Receivable

The accounts receivable is a supporting ledger that records all customer sales of goods and services. This accounting module helps manage customer billing and receipt of cash. Control of the processing is normally by the assignment of numbers to the customer accounts. Customer information can usually be recalled at any time.

In most accounting packages, this module will produce invoices or statements, generate an aged-accounts report, and provide sales analysis reporting. The statements can be by the open-item or the balance-forward method. In a fully integrated system, the accounts receivable will automatically interact with the inventory control module by deducting product balances.

Feature	Must Have	Would Like	Don't Need
1. Permits combination of open-item and balance-forward methods			
2. Allows multiple billing cycles			
3. Ability to do fixed or recurring billing monthly			
4. Automatic pricing with manual override			
5. Finance charges are user-set and automatically computed but can be manually overriden			
6. Performs credit limit check			
7. Late charges computed and added to statements or invoices			
8. Allows special messages to show on customer statements			
9. Handles customer partial payments and shipments			
10. Processes a single-check payment for multiple invoices			
11. Charges single-invoice amount to several general ledger accounts			
12. Adds new customers at time of order			
13. Invoice shows sales order number and/or product serial number			
14. Automatic update of inventory on-hand balances when invoice is entered			
15. Manual or automatic invoice numbering			
16. Allows processing by customer types or class codes			
17. Permits sales transactions without printing an invoice			

Feature	Must Have	Would Like	Don't Need
18. User-defined "terms of sale" codes			
19. Ability to apply payments to specific invoices/line items			
20. Ability to report sales tax on taxable and non-taxable sales by city, county, and state			
21. Allows taxable or non-taxable miscellaneous charges			
22. Handles multiple ship-to names and addresses			
23. Prints name and address labels			

Accounts Payable

The accounts payable is a supporting ledger used to record the activity of creditors for the purchase of materials and services by the business. The main purpose of this module is the tracking of bills to be paid, but accounts payable is also important in the monitoring and control of cash flow in the business.

The creditors, called "vendors," are controlled by assigning account numbers. This module should maintain a complete record for each vendor, and help determine who and when to pay by due date, discount date, and by specified cash requirements. The system should also have an override feature that allows the option to hold or defer payments.

Feature	Must Have	Would Like	Don't Need
1. Applies credit to specific invoice in vendor file			
2. Automatic posting of fixed or recurring monthly payments			
3. Allows partial payments			
4. Permits adjustments, prepaids, and cancellations			
5. User option to pay by due date or discount date			
6. Deferred payments by vendor account or selected vouchers			
7. Places an indefinite hold on invoices for payment			

Feature	Must Have	Would Like	Don't Need
8. Manual approval of invoices/line items for payment by vendor			
9. Maintains month-to-date and year-to-date totals by vendors			
10. Charges single payments to multiple general ledger accounts			
11. Permits manual writing of checks			
12. Uses prenumbered checks with controls by computer			
13. Tracks sales taxes paid			
14. Full cash requirements reporting			

Inventory Control

The inventory control is a supporting ledger that is used to account for products held for sale and/or for materials held for manufacturing. Inventory items are continuously being purchased and sold, and this process generates the major portion of the firm's revenues (except in the services industry where inventories are small). In addition, a large amount of capital is usually invested in inventory, and it is normally the largest of current assets.

The inventory control may interact with the accounts receivable, accounts payable, and general ledger modules. This module should allow special adjustments of inventory quantities for items that have become damaged, lost or obsolete.

Feature	Must Have	Would Like	Don't Need
1. Supports work-in-process and raw materials inventory			
2. Allows option of inventory costing by average cost, FIFO, or LIFO methods			
3. Flagging of low-point reorder amounts			
4. Provides for inventory item multiple cost/price figures with manual override			
5. Allows for multiple vendor pricing and recommended vendor			
6. Provides for inventory of bulk items with units of measure			
7. Can track quantity on-hand, allocated, and on-order by inventory item			
8. Allows for processing and adjustments to items back-ordered			
9. Allows multiple warehouse/bin locations and transfer between locations			
10. Permits designating inventory items by product group or category			
11. Provides for cycle count method of inventory accounting			
12. Automatically allocates inventory for customer orders			
13. Allows posting and tracking of product serial numbers			

Payroll

The payroll is a supporting ledger for the recording of employee compensation, including payroll deductions and the reporting of taxes to state and federal governments. This module is designed to perform many repetitive calculations with variables of hourly and monthly rates, overtime, part-time, commissions, payroll deductions, and different but concurrent pay periods. A payroll application also keeps track of all employee earnings and deductions for quarterly and annual reporting to authorities.

The payroll module differs from the others by the need to contain different tax withholding tables for federal, state, and possibly county or city taxes, if the business has employees in more than one state.

Feature	Must Have	Would Like	Don't Need
1. Handles hourly, salaried, bonus, and commission pay types			
2. Handles overtime, piecemeal, contract, and special pay rates			
3. Includes non-taxable items such as meal allowance, credit-union savings, and employee purchase			
4. Handles retroactive changes			
5. Computes vacation pay for terminated employees, and/or severance pay			
6. Permits multiple but concurrent pay periods			
7. Subscription to annually updated tax tables			
8. Provides for labor distributions and/or department reporting			
9. Ability to write paychecks manually			
10. Provides for union deductions and reporting			
11. Computes federal and state unemployment taxes			
12. Accrues and tracks sick/vacation days for each employee			

CHAPTER
7

Computer Hardware: What To Look For

If you like irony and odd facts, the insides of a business computer will fascinate you. This precise, highly complex, technical machine is created by rare design and engineering talents, and manufactured to microscopic tolerances under antiseptic, dust-free conditions. Yet for all its complexities, the most important part of the computer begins as one of the earth's most common and ordinary materials: sand. From sand comes silica, the same hard material used in making glass. Silica is processed into silicon wafers for making computer chips. The rest of the computer is made of aluminum, copper, plastic, and other common materials.

For all its apparent sophistication and mystery, a computer is only an information processor. Recent vast improvements in the speed, size, and cost of the processors have enabled the computer to alter forever the way we handle information. Yet the computer does only what business managers have always done with information: collect it, rearrange it, store it, and recall it in a useful form for making decisions.

Recall from Chapter 1 that this book defines a small business computer by how it is used, not by its size or price. The purpose of a computer is to give a manager the information he needs to plan for, operate, and control a business. In particular, it handles the primary accounting functions. Although this chapter discusses business computers from the accounting perspective, the criteria apply well to other business uses.

The main sections here describe the four basic hardware components: main processing unit, work stations, mass storage devices, and printers. Each section concludes with a "Features To Look For" sub-section. This chapter also focuses on single user computers, although many of the features apply to multi-user systems as well. Multi-user systems are described in Chapter 8, which also includes a description of the operating system (system software), considered part of the hardware purchase.

MINIMUM SYSTEM REQUIREMENTS

The following is a brief description of the four basic hardware units, including the recommended minimum requirements for a small business computer as described in this book.

Main Processing Unit

The heart of any computer system is a group of small electronic circuit boards inside a "box" called the central processing unit (CPU). Depending on its design, the CPU can reside in its own separate enclosure, or be in the same cabinet with the visual display and disk drives. The CPU contains the computer's main memory, which is expressed in kilobytes, or units of "K" such as 128K. It also contains the back panel connectors for other components, such as a printer, and the main On/Off switch and reset button, usually on the front side.

> *MINIMUM REQUIREMENTS: For an eight-bit computer the main processor should have 64K memory capacity. For a sixteen-bit computer the processor should have 128K, but be expandable to 256K.*

Mass Storage Device

The computer must store the information it processes in a durable form. The most common device for business use is a disk drive that holds a

FIG 7-1 SMALL BUSINESS COMPUTER

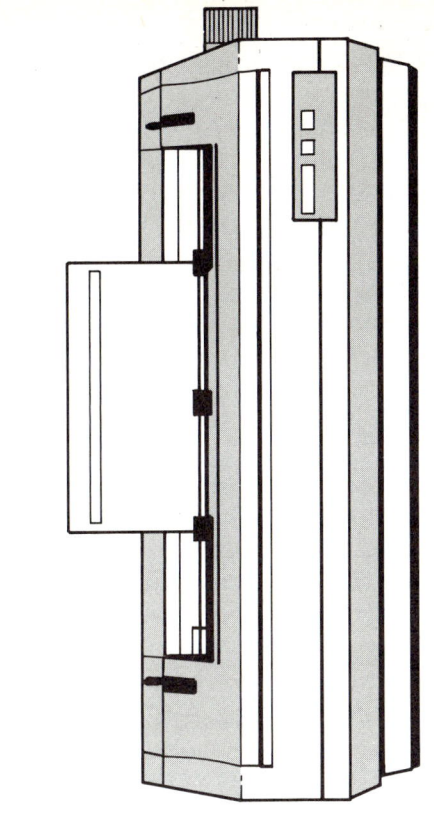

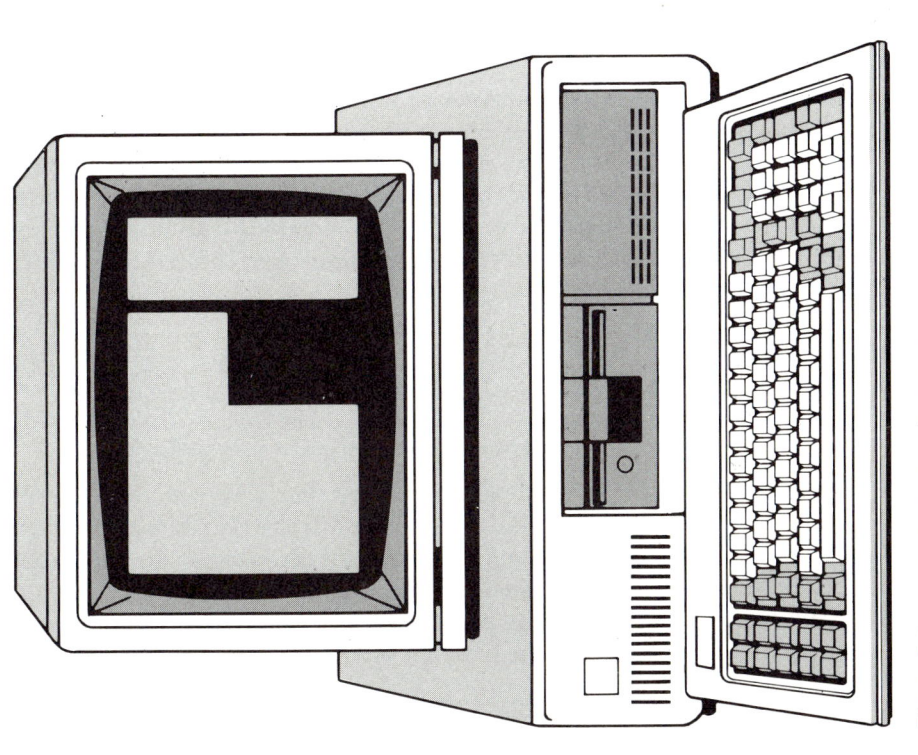

Figure 7-1 Small Business Computer

round magnetic disk (called a floppy disk) in a square protective sleeve. The two most common floppy disk sizes are $5\frac{1}{4}$-inch and 8-inch. Most business installations have two drives side by side, called dual drives. For even more storage capacity you may use a sealed unit called a hard disk.

MINIMUM REQUIREMENTS: A single user system for non-accounting applications should have two floppy disk drives, each with a minimum of 360K storage capacity. Accounting requires at least 500K per drive. For multi-user systems, the main storage unit should be a hard disk with a minimum of five megabytes (5,000K).

Work Stations

The work station (or terminal) is the main device for entering and retrieving data, as well as controlling the computer. It consists of two parts: a video display and a keyboard. The video display is also known as a CRT (for cathode ray tube) and is similar to a television set. The keyboard and video screen may be separate physical units or housed together as one unit.

MINIMUM REQUIREMENTS: The video display should be designed for computer use, not a television set. The display should measure twelve inches diagonally, and show twenty-four lines down and eighty columns across. Also, it must display both upper and lower case letters. The keyboard should be separate and attached by a cable, with full typewriter style layout and a ten-key numeric pad.

Printer

The printer is a super-fast first cousin to the electric typewriter and serves the same purpose. While printers come with a variety of features, they use two basic technologies to print characters on paper: dots in patterns (called dot matrix), or fully-formed, molded characters like a typewriter (called letter quality). Dot matrix printers are suitable for accounting reports and mailing labels, while letter quality printers are required for the highest quality printed documents.

MINIMUM REQUIREMENTS: The printer, either dot matrix or letter quality, must be able to print across 132 columns, which is required by most accounting packages. The print speed for a dot matrix printer should be 120 to 200 characters per second (cps). A letter quality machine should print in the 30 to 55 cps range. The printer should also have a tractor feed mechanism for the paper.

Computer *systems* are available almost any way you want, from a complete "system in a box" sold as a single unit, to individual components that you choose separately. A complete unit is often called an "all-in-one" or packaged computer and usually comes with everything you need to get started except the printer. The pros, cons, and unknowns of each type are similar to those facing the hi-fi stereo buyer. Buying a packaged system requires you to accept each part regardless of its individual merits, but removes the "little" decisions. On the other hand, buying components lets you assemble a system closer to your specific needs, but it may cost more.

A packaged system has certain advantages for the first-time buyer. These systems have no hardware compatibility problems, since everything has been designed to work together. Matching separate computer components can be difficult and requires the hand of an experienced dealer. Also, a package may be simpler and cheaper to buy, since it comes from one manufacturer who can pass on greater economies of scale. Whether you buy your computer "a la carte" or "on the dinner," it's most important to find a system that solves your business problems. Let's look at the main characteristics of the four basic components.

MAIN PROCESSING UNIT (CPU)

With current technology, most small business computers use one of two types of microprocessor: eight-bit or sixteen-bit. These "bits" (an abbreviation for binary digit) are the computer's word length, or the amount of information the processor handles in a single operation. While the sixteen-bit word length is only twice the eight-bit, doubling the word length yields a geometric increase in computing power. For example, the memory addressing of an eight-bit computer is limited to 64,000-plus positions (64K), while a sixteen-bit system can address memory up to a million positions (1,000K)—more than fifteen times as much! The longer the word length, the more powerful the computer. This discussion, incidentally, parallels the difference between sixteen- and thirty-two-bit computers. (See Figure 8-1 for details on special memories larger than 64K for eight-bit computers. See also "Should You Buy an Eight-Bit or Sixteen-Bit Computer?" and "Dual Processor Machines" in Chapter 8.)

The microprocessor, of whatever kind, does its calculations within the main memory, also known as "random access memory" (RAM). The size of the computer's RAM determines the amount of information it can work with at any moment. RAM size also limits the amount of data flowing to and from the disk. Most single user computers are commonly supplied with a 64K RAM memory, while some multi-user systems can be expanded to 2,000K

RAM is also called "user-programmable memory" because it can be changed, or "programmed," as you work. But RAM stores information only temporarily. When the computer is turned off, its contents are instantly erased. This volatile nature of RAM is why you need floppy diskettes or other means of permanent storage.

Briefly, this is how disk storage works: Programs and data from your computer session are stored on diskettes outside of RAM before you turn the power off. When the switch is pulled the main memory goes blank. In your next session, after you turn the power on, you must reload the programs and data back into RAM—that is, "copy" them into RAM after it is reactivated.

As the computer responds to your instructions it retrieves information from the disk, processes it in the CPU, and returns it to storage by "writing" it back to the disk. Storage outside of RAM is called mass storage because the quantity of information stored is far greater than the RAM's capacity. For instance, a floppy disk with a capacity of 400K can hold ten to fifteen times the main memory's storage capacity for user data.

Main Processor—What To Look For

Growth Capacity.   In choosing your computer you must find a system that suits your business, both as it is now and as it is likely to become. Both your present needs and future growth are important in choosing the core of the system, the central processing unit. Look for a system that can expand as your requirements change. It is false economy to buy a limited, inexpensive "OK for now" system that will be all wrong in three to five years. Better to spend extra on a flexible system that can grow with your company. When you shop, the questions to ask are:

Can I add more RAM memory?

Can I add more work stations?

Can I attach more disk storage?

Can I change to a different kind of printer?

In searching for a computer with expansion capability, look for a machine that can accept additional circuit boards in the central processor cabinet. The IBM Personal Computer, for instance, has four internal "expansion slots." More RAM memory, communications, networking, and graphics are some of the add-on capabilities. Printed circuit boards for these functions can be bought separately and installed by the dealer at any time. Expansion memory boards come in capacities of 64K, 128K, 256K, and 512K. Total RAM memory is limited by the type of processor chip (eight-bit or sixteen-bit) or the number of expansion slots in the computer chassis. Usually you need more memory to add more terminals in a multi-user system or to run very large programs, such as color graphics or multi-tasking software. (See "Expandable Computers," Chapter 8.)

Processing Speeds.   Another important aspect of your computer's operation in the business environment is speed. How quickly does it perform its various operations? While computers may seem magical because they operate at nearly the speed of light, some are noticeably slower than others due to differences in electronic design. For example, the Compupro runs twice as fast as the IBM PC, even though it has the same processor chip, the Intel 8088. Look for a specification called megahertz (or MHz), which refers to the number of cycles per second. The higher the number the faster the processor. Many single user computers run at four MHz, which is acceptable, but a multi-user computer should be rated between eight MHz and twelve MHz or higher to better accommodate many users. (The disk drives also vary in their operating speeds and can affect overall performance. The programming language used is also a factor.)

Peripheral Connectors. All the system's peripherals are attached by cables to the central processing unit. The back panel of the CPU has a number of connectors or openings called "ports." Almost every type of peripheral (i.e., disk drives, terminals, printers) has a different type of cable connector. The number of actual wires in each cable ranges from two to fifty depending on the device. Despite this range, most manufacturers use connectors of two general types: serial and parallel. The terminology is confusing since both types are used for printers, while terminals always have a serial interface. Neither is clearly superior, however, for overall system performance.

The serial interface is often called "RS-232." The parallel is sometimes called the Centronics, or "IEEE-488." These designations refer mainly to the physical shape of the connector. However, because of the lack of standardization within the electronics industry, a serial connection on Brand X computer will not automatically work with a serial connection on Brand Y printer. Such compatibility has three aspects. First, the physical connector and the designated use of each wire inside the cable, which are called the "pin assignments," must match exactly. That is, Pin 1 out of the computer must be "assigned" to the same task as Pin 1 into the printer, and so forth with the rest of the connector pins. Second, the electrical specifications, which are the voltages and current directions at each pin, must match. Third, the software specifications, called "protocols," must also match. Protocols are the rules for formatting and exchanging data between devices as they "talk" to each other.

As a buyer you must beware. Because the industry has no widely accepted standards for connecting peripherals, you must be certain your dealer, or a knowledgeable consultant, can do all the interfacing for you.

Also important is the number of ports available for adding external devices. The more the better, and a mix of both kinds, serial and parallel, is best. (Notice that connector ports are different from the expansion slots mentioned above.) With an all-in-one computer, you should look for a way to hook up a printer, a modem for data communications, and a hard disk drive. For a component system, in addition to the above you should look for connections for floppy disk drives and a terminal. Some designers of less expensive computers cut corners by eliminating connections for modems and hard disks.

Computer Enclosure.   Besides what is inside your computer, you should consider what surrounds it, namely the cabinet. An all-metal cabinet is more durable than plastic and helps to minimize radio frequency interference (see "Radio Frequencies," Chapter 9). You should also look for a rugged chassis that provides easy access to components that may need service. Other features to check for are a cooling fan to draw off excess heat without adding much noise, and front panel controls that are clearly marked, easy to reach, and protected from accidental movements. In short, if you plan to run your computer more than just a few hours a day, make sure it's built for heavy use.

MASS STORAGE DEVICES

Many people remember punched cards, which became widespread in the 1960s and early 1970s as a way to store information. The most popular card format was developed by IBM, and came with the infamous message, "Do not fold, spindle, or mutilate." The cards were perforated with tiny rectangular holes, which made up codes that represented letters of the alphabet, numbers, and other characters. The cards contained eighty columns, which, by no coincidence, is the same number of columns across the standard video display. These cards, used primarily on very large computers, worked well, but were expensive to prepare and maintain.

In the mid-1970s, with the appearance of the first small home computers, magnetic tape cassettes of the kind used in audio recorders became a common method of storing data and programs. While cassettes were inexpensive, they were too slow and cumbersome for business use. For these and other reasons these two storage methods are now obsolete.

Types of Storage

Three new storage methods have emerged that offer greater convenience and economy: floppy disk (diskettes); magnetic tape (which is different from audio cassettes); and the newest technology, video disk, which shows promise but is not yet widely available. Magnetic tape is used primarily with hard disks to back up files and is discussed later in this section. By far the most popular of these storage forms is the magnetic disk or diskette, better known as the floppy disk. The two prevailing sizes of diskettes (measured across) are $5\frac{1}{4}$-inch and 8-inch. Smaller diskettes, such as the $3\frac{1}{2}$-inch found in the Apple Macintosh, and Hewlett-Packard 150, may become more common with portable hand-held computers. Also popular is the hard disk, which is sometimes called the Winchester-type disk drive.

The sole function of any of these devices is storing information for the computer to process, whether it be office memoranda, customer names and addresses, or accounting information. At your command, the computer records (or "writes") information onto the diskette similar to the way music is recorded onto an audio cassette. Conversely, once information is on the disk, you can command the computer to play it back (or "read" it) into the computer's main memory for processing.

In addition to its low cost, disk storage is popular because of a characteristic called "random access." Because the disk head can seek out and pinpoint a particular piece of information anywhere on the diskette, random access allows the computer to read programs and store data very quickly. Magnetic tape, by comparison, is relatively slow because it searches sequentially. Here the computer must first wind the tape all the way to the point where the information is stored before retrieving it. A secretary using a random access disk can retrieve a typed letter in two or three seconds, while the same search on tape storage might take one to three minutes. This difference in retrieval speed is not only a convenience but a significant time saver.

Floppy disks differ from hard disks in that you can quickly and easily change them in the disk drive the way you change records on a stereo system. This flexibility allows your computer to store programs and data on an unlimited number of floppy diskettes. By comparison, hard disks remain fixed in the system, but their much larger capacity makes for more convenient data storage. The main features and buyer considerations of these two drives are covered in the following sections.

Floppy Disk Drives

Floppy disk drives appear almost uninteresting. All you see is a black rectangular panel with a slot or door. Their mechanical operation is simple and straightforward. A button or a latch allows you to open the drive and insert the diskette—as easy as putting bread in a toaster. When the door is closed the computer is ready to engage the disk-drive head to read or write data. Most drives have a small red "activity" light to show when the disk head is engaged, which is similar to a phonograph arm touching the surface of a record. The purpose of the light is to warn you not to disengage the diskette when the delicate head is active on the disk's surface.

Floppy disks are so called because they are flexible or non-rigid to the touch. These circles of plastic mylar are coated with iron oxide, the same material found on audio and video cassette tapes. Floppy disks are permanently sealed in a black cardboard envelope to protect them from dust, dirt, and gooey things that melt in your hand. The disk is inserted in the drive unit complete with its protective cover. Once inside, the cover remains stationary, while the mylar disk rotates at several hundred rpm.

Figure 7-2 Eight-Inch Dual Floppy Disk Drives (Courtesy of Compupro)

Disk drives that read/write on one side only have one read/write head, while a drive that uses both sides of the diskette has two heads. These are referred to as "single-sided" and "double-sided" disk drives. Both kinds of disks are inserted in the drive only one way. In other words, you cannot flip them over for additional recording the way you can an audio cassette.

Any computer used in business or a profession should have two floppy disk drives to ease making backup files, which is the copying of data from one disk to another. (See Chapter 9.) Dual drives also make it easy to separate program disks from data disks, which offers advantages when operating the computer.

Due to the way the microcomputer industry has evolved and its changing technologies, floppy diskettes now have a wide range of storage capacities. To no one's surprise, what once could be stored on an 8-inch diskette, now fits on a $5\frac{1}{4}$-inch diskette. But even with the same size diskette, the range of storage varies widely. Because of varieties in design by manufacturers, a $5\frac{1}{4}$-inch diskette can now hold up to about 750K bytes, and an 8-inch disk can hold up to 1,200K bytes. Recall from Chapter 4 that the smallest unit of storage on a disk is one character and the total number of characters is expressed in the number of bytes, or K bytes for every thousand. Specifically, a one-page letter takes about 2K of storage, and the entire contents of this book consumes about 750K of mass storage.

Recording Formats. What factors determine the actual disk capacity for a particular computer? The first is whether the disk drive records on one or both sides of the disk. The double-sided drive gives almost (but not always) twice the storage of a single-sided drive. Second is the "density" of the storage. Some drives record in double density, while others record only in single density. You can find the double density feature in both single- and double-sided disk drives. (Drives that are both double-sided and double density are sometimes called "quad density.")

The third factor determining the storage capacity is the manufacturer's design specifications, known as the recording format. For instance, two different brand name computers, each with $5\frac{1}{4}$-inch double-sided, double density disk drives, can have different capacities. One computer may have a total capacity of 400K per drive, while another has only 320K storage. Almost every computer manufacturer has its own format for storing information on the disks. Except for the single-sided, single density 8-inch drive, no formatting standards have yet been established. These format differences create a disk compatibility problem that prevents the easy exchange of diskettes from one make computer to another. For example, a disk formatted on a DEC Rainbow microcomputer will not run on an IBM PC even though both machines use $5\frac{1}{4}$-inch drives and the same operating system. (See "The Compatibility Problem," Chapter 8, for more on transferring files between computers.)

Figure 7-3 shows the general range of storage capacities for both disk sizes in each of the three formats. Generally, $5\frac{1}{4}$-inch drive units are relatively inexpensive and work well for personal computer applications such as word processing and electronic spreadsheets. The 8-inch units can be more than twice as expensive, but their extra capacity makes them suitable for data-intensive applications such as accounting. Another advantage of 8-inch diskettes is that IBM's single-sided, single density format has become a standard throughout the micro industry. Only data stored in this format can be easily transferred from one brand of computer to another by simply inserting a diskette.

Floppy Disk Storage

	Single Side- Single Density	Single Side- Double Density	Double Side- Double Density
Single 5¼-Inch Floppy Drive	90K to 250K	250K to 400K	350K to 750K
Single 8-Inch Floppy Drive	250K to 300K	250K to 600K	1,000 to 1,200K
Winchester Hard Disk	5 Megabytes to 40 Megabytes		

Figure 7-3 Floppy Disk Storage

Floppy Drives—What To Look For

A recap of the advantages of floppy disk drives shows why they have become so popular for microcomputers. Their low cost ($350–$600 per $5\frac{1}{4}$-inch drive unit; $3–$8 per diskette, depending on size and quality), convenience, and portability make them a practical choice over hard disks or magnetic tape. Floppy disks also offer good storage capacity for many small computer tasks. And they have the convenience of identifying stored information with hand-written labels attached to the disk. Here's what to look for.

Storage Capacity. The main disadvantage of floppys is the limited storage capacity for accounting applications, which require storing many files on the same disk. Be certain that the largest file of any application will fit on a single floppy disk. While you can sometimes store part of a file on one disk and the rest on another, it is always awkward and inconvenient.

Also make certain that all the *programs* for one function will fit on one disk. Usually in an accounting package the accounts receivable program is on one disk and the inventory control program is on another, requiring that you change diskettes. This is an inconvenience, and it sometimes confuses the operator. (See Chapter 4, Step 3, "Determine Storage Requirements" for accounting.)

The best way to guarantee future storage expansion is to buy a computer that can accommodate additional disk drives. Most computers are designed to increase the disk storage by adding more drive units, either floppy or hard, to the central processor enclosure. These extra drives can be added as accessories. If you have a choice, however, it is better to expand by adding a hard disk rather than a third or fourth floppy disk. A hard disk not only adds considerably more storage, but greatly improves the performance of your computer with faster processing speeds. This arrangement gives you a system with the advantages of both a hard and a floppy disk.

One item worth noting here is the difference between formatted and unformatted disk capacities. Computer manufacturers typically advertise the unformatted capacity of their drives, which is a larger amount. The formatted capacity is a lesser amount actually available to the user. In one case, a disk drive rated at 400K storage "unformatted" actually has only 368K available for use, which is 8 percent less. This notation applies to hard disk drives as well as floppys.

Format Compatibility. If you need to exchange information with another computer by shuffling diskettes back and forth, make sure the other computer can read your data without going through a disk conversion. The best way to ensure this exchange is to use computers of the same make and model. Some business computers, however, such as the Morrow

Micro Decision, can read and write in the same disk format as several other computers, including the Xerox and IBM. (See "The Compatibility Problem," Chapter 8.)

Other Features. Some disk drives tend to be noisy, whether or not they are built into the same enclosure as the computer. Disk drive noise tends to go unnoticed in the dealer's showroom, but it can be annoying to the user and distracting to others in a relatively quiet office. If this is of concern to you, look for a computer with quiet drives.

An important consideration in choosing a computer is speed, which includes how long it takes to access the disk. When you instruct the computer to find a file on the disk, how long must you wait for it to appear on the video screen? Even a few seconds makes a difference when repeated many times while working continuously at the computer. This access speed is not normally shown in the brochure information, but you can get a feel for it as you try different computer systems. (A fair comparison, for example, would have each machine do roughly the same task, such as save a one-page letter.)

A number of factors determine access speed. Double-density drives give faster access than single-density. An 8-inch drive continuously rotates the disk, which increases its access speed. Many $5\frac{1}{4}$-inch drives use a start-and-stop method, however, in which the disk doesn't rotate until the user instructs the computer to retrieve information from it. This disk access factor is even more important in a multi-user computer, which is one reason it should have a hard disk.

Hard Disk Drives

A hard disk is a fixed or rigid platter with a magnetically coated surface much like a floppy disk. The relative firmness of the hard disk, compared to a floppy, allows much closer tolerance in recording data, thereby creating greater storage capacity. Recording and playing back data are the same as on a floppy disk, with a read/write head moving rapidly back and forth across the radius of the disk.

The hard disk may be contained in its own enclosure, with a cable connecting it to the central processing unit, or the smaller ones can be built into the computer's enclosure. Either way, the hard disk unit looks simple. The front may have only an activity light showing when the drive head is engaged. When housed in a separate cabinet the hard disk may have nothing more than a power On/Off switch and one or two indicator lights.

Unlike the floppy, the hard disk platter remains inside its enclosure. There are no doors on the front through which to remove the disk. With a rotational speed of 3,600 rpm (about ten times faster than the floppy disk), it has much faster access time and better overall performance. One

Figure 7-4 Corvus Hard Disk Drive (Courtesy of Corvus Systems, Inc.)

particular type of hard disk, called the Winchester, is contained in a permanently sealed enclosure, making it highly tolerant of environmental hazards that create problems for non-sealed hard disks. Because of this design, Winchesters have proven to be very reliable.

Like floppy disks, hard disks come in different physical sizes, with diameters such as $5\frac{1}{4}$, 8, 10, and 12 inches. However, the physical size of a hard disk is less important than with a floppy disk. The storage capacity of the hard disk is the main buying consideration. Hard disks come in storage sizes such as five, ten, twelve, twenty, and forty megabytes. (A megabyte is one million characters.) The initial cost of a hard disk is much more than a floppy, but with the greatly increased capacity the cost of storage per byte is actually lower. This larger storage capacity also makes it easier to put all of the user's application programs and data on a single disk. A hard disk is mandatory for a multi-user installation, especially with accounting applications.

Since the hard disk remains in the computer, a special means of file backup must be used. (Recall that proper backup requires being able to physically remove the data from the machine and put it in a secure storage location.) One way to provide backup is to use floppy disks, but their limited capacity can make this cumbersome.

Another solution is to use removable cartridges. One type of cartridge contains magnetic tape, similar to a standard audio cassette. Another type contains the hard disk itself, and using it for backup is similar to using a floppy disk. Both of these kinds of cartridges are removed from the machine after copying the data. (An ideal variation of this concept is to have half the hard disk storage contained on a fixed disk, with the other half in a removable cartridge.) At this writing the cartridge-type hard disk is not readily available because of production problems. Here again, no standards exist for removable hard-disk cartridges to make them readily interchangeable with other computers.

Hard Disk Drives—What To Look For

Storage Capacity.   Compared to floppys, hard disks have the two advantages of storing more data and processing it faster. In deciding how much capacity to buy, consider both your current needs and future prospects. You must also estimate how you will allocate the hard disk storage, since this type of drive has a finite capacity. In other words, you cannot buy more diskettes for it when you start running out of space the way you can with floppy drives. If space becomes tight, you can take files off the hard disk and store them on removable media—but this detracts from the convenience. Thus, when buying a hard disk, lean toward more capacity than you think you will need.

Disk File Backup.   Providing data file backup for a hard disk is different from providing backup for a floppy disk, because the hard disk

Figure 7-5 Magnetic Tape Cartridge (Courtesy of 3M)

media are not removable from the drive unit like a floppy. For business applications, especially accounting, you should make certain that you have some means of backing up the hard disk. As mentioned, floppy diskettes are generally limited for this purpose. For example, to copy all the files stored on a five-megabyte hard disk requires ten to thirteen diskettes, each capable of holding 400K. You can get by in some cases by copying only selected files rather than the entire hard disk. For optimal backup, though, you should consider magnetic tape or removable hard-disk cartridges.

Additional Drives. Most computers provide only one physical connector for a hard disk. Most hard disks, fortunately, are designed to be connected in series of up to four units, with one unit attached to another. This is called "daisy chaining," and allows you to add three more units, each the same size as the first. Even though most computers are used with only one hard disk, you should check to see if your computer will accept additional units.

WORK STATIONS

The work station, better known as the computer terminal, is made up of two parts: a glassed-in, TV-like screen and a keyboard. The video screen is an output device, since it displays portions of the computer's main memory. The keyboard has buttons that you push and resembles the keyboard on a typewriter. Together the keyboard and video screen (or terminal) make up one of the four basic units of the computer system.

When you type on the keyboard, the characters appear immediately on the video screen, much like producing letters and numbers on paper when using a typewriter. This immediacy gives the illusion that you are typing on the screen. However, when you press the letter "A" on the keyboard, for example, the electronic code for that character is transmitted to the computer's main memory, which simultaneously flashes the letter "A" on the screen. Thus, what you see on the screen is an echo of a character that has been entered into the central processing unit. The screen display, then, merely verifies what you have just keyed in through the keyboard.

The video display can be either in full color (multi-color) or monochrome, only one color. Monochrome colors for business computers are green, or amber, or white. The characters usually appear in one of these three colors against a dark background. For example, the characters on a white monochrome display appear light against a dark background, which is the opposite of the normal hard copy produced by a typewriter.

The terminal is actually the main device used to tell the computer what you want to do. It is the part of the system that your operator spends the most time with, either looking at the screen or working the keyboard.

Therefore, take some care to buy a terminal that is comfortable for your operators. Let's look at the main features of the video display, followed by a section on keyboards.

Types of Display

The three most common types of video display are televisions, CRTs, and monitors. A television display is just that, an ordinary television hooked up to display the contents of the computer. While color televisions are

Figure 7-6   Qume Computer Terminal (Courtesy of Qume Corporation)

fine for home computers, they are unsatisfactory for business use. Why? A television cannot display all the information on the screen the way a CRT or monitor does. Also, a television image is not sharp enough for letters and numbers, and the fuzzy display causes operator eyestrain.

The CRT, sometimes called a monitor, is the display part of a computer terminal. (CRT stands for Cathode Ray Tube, which is confusing since all three display types have this type of tube.) It is the most common device used for business computers. The standard information display on a CRT is eighty columns across by twenty-four lines down. Thus, a CRT is superior to a television because it has a fuller, sharper character display.

A computer monitor is the third type of display. It is much like the CRT in physical size, display characteristics, and function. Both CRTs and monitors are available in multi-color or monochrome. Yet, a subtle difference separates a monitor and a CRT: The monitor is simply a display device with no input capability, while a CRT generally includes a keyboard. You can tell if a computer requires a CRT or a monitor by noticing where the cable from the keyboard is attached. If it connects to the enclosure of the central processing unit, the system uses a monitor. If the cable from the keyboard is connected to the video display, then it uses a CRT (or computer terminal).

For example, both the IBM Personal Computer and the Texas Instruments Professional Computer require monitors. Component systems like the Compupro and TeleVideo use CRTs. Being aware of this difference provides more options when assembling a computer system, even though each manufacturer may offer its own monitor or CRT.

Monitors are either single color or multi-color. Multi-color monitors are more expensive than single color and come in two types: composite and RGB. A composite monitor operates like a television, with one internal electron gun creating all the different colors to be shown. An RGB monitor has three electron guns creating the colors for the display. (RGB stands for Red, Green, and Blue.) This technical difference makes the RGB superior in creating a sharp, clear image on the screen. With this type of monitor, the three primary colors are controlled separately, and each can be more precisely addressed to a particular dot on the screen. However, the computer itself must be designed to produce the proper electronic signal for an RGB monitor.

Screen resolution is a key variable for displays. Resolution on a computer terminal is stated in characters, such as an eighty-column-by-twenty-four-line display; on a monitor, resolution is measured in a unit called a pixel. The more pixels per square inch on the screen, the better the quality of the picture. A typical RGB monitor resolution is 720 by 300 pixels.

With the exception of a television set, all video displays are suitable for day-to-day operations such as word processing, accounting, and so on. The RGB monitor is best suited for high-resolution graphic applications.

If this is your interest, be certain the computer you are considering can provide the proper signals for an RGB monitor. Generally, the sharper and clearer the image display, the more expensive the computer terminal or monitor.

Visual Displays—What To Look For

Size and Color.   Since you spend most of your time at the terminal, look for one that is comfortable and minimizes fatigue and eyestrain. Don't pick a porthole-sized screen: For most people a screen of twelve to fourteen inches (measured diagonally) is best. A smaller display is fine for computer hobbyists and in portable units, but a poor choice for a true small business computer.

Figure 7-7   TeleVideo Computer Terminal (Courtesy of TeleVideo Systems, Inc.)

Except for multi-color graphics, a monochrome screen works well for business processing. Again, the three most common colors are white, green, and amber. Although studies have attempted to determine the relationship between color and eyestrain, no conclusions have been drawn as to which color is best. Currently, green and amber outsell white, but the choice is strictly a matter of personal preference.

Two other factors *are* important in reducing user fatigue. One is the resolution of the characters, which consist of a series of tiny dots. The more dots in the character matrix, the higher the resolution. Sharp, crisp images of letters and numbers on the screen go a long way toward making the terminal pleasant to use over long periods.

The screen's readability is also affected by the amount of light generated by the CRT. Generally, this is not a problem, since each terminal or monitor has a brightness control much like that on a television set. You should adjust this control when evaluating video displays.

The remaining factor determining the screen's readability is an optional feature called reverse video. Computer terminals usually show light characters on a dark background, but on most displays this can be "reversed." That is, most can be changed to show dark characters on a light background, as we are accustomed to seeing the printed word on white paper. Reverse video is usually controlled by a switch on the back panel or some other built-in control. Ask the dealer to show you the reverse video feature.

A non-glare screen may also improve visibility. Some manufacturers specially treat the glass surface of the display to reduce the mirror-like effect. Reducing glare is highly desirable when the computer is placed in a strong-light area, such as near south-facing windows.

Upper/Lower Case   Most computers display both upper and lower case letters and other symbols shown on the keyboard. While this capability is desirable for displaying business information (unless you like the all-caps style of telegrams), it is mandatory for word processing. The upper/lower case feature is actually a function of the main processing unit and not the terminal. The video display only "echoes" what the computer sends to it. Only a few home-type computers are limited to showing upper case only.

Screen Resolution.   For business applications you should insist on a screen display with no less than 80 columns by 24 lines. With it you can display about one-half page of text, single spaced, which is sufficient for word processing and other applications. Most packaged software is written to use these screen dimensions. (Some displays, like the DECMATE II, by Digital Equipment Corp., can show up to 132 columns across.)

You can judge the clearness of the display by seeing how easily you can distinguish letters, like "w" from "u" and "m" from "n." You should be able to do this at a comfortable sitting distance from the display. You should also check for descenders. These are the lower case letters with tails: "g," "p," "q," and "y." In normal print these tails extend below the print line, and they should do the same on the display. Remember that the system's ability to display lower case letters is a function of the computer, while the clarity of the display is a function of the terminal or monitor. Therefore, you may get different display results on the same computer by changing terminals.

One last item to check on the video display is overscan, a condition in which the body of the display comes close to, or touches, the edges of the screen. In extreme cases this can cause the loss of text or data lines at the sides of the screen. A quality computer eliminates the overscan problem by putting a dark border around the display area. These blank areas are called guard bands, and make the display easier to read by creating borders like those around a printed page. Look for a display that's centered and has evenly spaced borders around the edges.

User Controls. Look for brightness and contrast controls like those found on a regular television receiver. The brightness control sets the amount of light coming from the display. You will probably need to adjust it depending on the amount of ambient light in the room. The contrast control adjusts the difference in brightness between the on-screen characters and the background. Both of these controls are likely to need occasional adjusting, especially if the computer has different users. Check to see if the controls are within easy reach while sitting at the terminal.

Many users enjoy being able to tilt and swivel the video display by moving its enclosure. This feature is especially desirable if the display must be adjusted for users of varying heights.

Terminal Emulation. One feature often overlooked when purchasing a computer is called terminal emulation. It is of particular concern when buying a component system, in which you choose the terminal you like best. It is of less concern when buying a packaged computer like DEC, IBM, or Hewlett-Packard, because with these you accept the terminal or monitor that comes with the computer.

Terminal emulation is the ability of a computer terminal to act electronically like other name-brand terminals. For example, by setting switches on a back panel, a TeleVideo 925 can perform with the internal design characteristics of a Hazeltine 1500 or a Lear Siegler ADM3A.

Why is this technical feature important to the buyer? If your computer terminal can emulate others, it gives you more flexibility in adapting different kinds of software packages to your computer. When you buy application software you must first configure it to your system. A special Install program (supplied with each package) contains a list of different brands of terminals and printers from which you indicate the one you have. (This is a quick, one-time operation normally done by the dealer.) Once this is done, the software is tailored to your system and ready to use.

The most popular printers and terminals are likely to appear on the

Install program list, which makes this step easy. However, if your chosen peripherals do not appear on the list, then the dealer has to perform the time-consuming and sometimes expensive step of customizing the software to your computer. Therefore, a terminal that can emulate other terminals can save time and money on installation.

Computer Keyboards

The keyboard is purchased either as a standard item with the computer, or with the terminal as a separate component. The keyboard, combined with the display, has three main purposes: enter data, display data (retrieval), and control the computer. Therefore, the computer terminal becomes your "command center" for communicating with the computer.

A full keyboard has an impressive array of keys, far beyond those on a standard typewriter. Each key shows a letter of the alphabet, a single digit, or symbols like #, %, and &. Computer keyboards also have special function keys not found on typewriters. Each key is attached to an electrical switch. Whenever a key is depressed, a contact is made and a specific signal is sent to the computer.

Keyboards vary from one brand to another, and each has a unique feel and layout. For instance, the spacing between the keys varies, some give an audible click with each keystroke, and the special control keys are positioned differently.

For the first-time buyer, keyboards are easier to understand if the keys are divided into three basic groups. First are the alphabetic keys, positioned the same as on a standard typewriter. The letter "Q" always appears on the left of the second row down, and the letter "M" is always on the right of the bottom row. The second group is the numeric ten-key pad, usually in a cluster on the right-hand side. This sub-group contains the numbers zero through nine in the standard calculator layout: the numbers "7," "8," and "9" across the top row, and "1," "2," and "3" across the bottom.

The third group is the special function keys. They are generally placed in a separate row across the top of the keyboard, with some on either side of the alphabetic keys. The special function keys have labels such as "ESC" for the escape key, and "CTRL" for the control key. The four cursor control keys each have an arrow for moving the cursor in a compass direction. Some keyboards also have programmable special function keys with generic labels such as "F1," "F2," and so forth. On some keyboards these keys are color-coded to identify their function. No standard exists, however, for placement of the special function keys on the keyboards.

Keyboards—What To Look For

Detachable Units. Many computers have a detachable keyboard connected by a flexible cable. The keyboard can be moved around while the

Figure 7-8 Keyboard Layout (Courtesy of Hewlett-Packard Company)

video display remains stationary. This flexibility is a desirable feature that adds comfort for those who spend long hours at the computer. Someone who has to enter a long list of figures, for example, can sit back and place the keyboard in his lap instead of remaining hunched over a fixed keyboard. Most manufacturers offer this feature now as a standard item.

Subjective Qualities. The feel of the keyboard to the user is important, but it is almost entirely a personal or subjective quality. Individual tastes are formed in part by prior experience with typewriters or other keyboards. When you look at different keyboards, notice that some have keycaps that are concave, while others have flat. Some keycaps are glossy plastic, while others are made with a dull finish to minimize overhead glare. Some keyboards require a heavy touch, while others are feather-light. Be aware that because computer keyboards are electronic rather than mechanical (unlike typewriters), they do not have an adjustment for touch sensitivity.

Layout. The layout of the alphabetic keys on standard U.S. machines is known as the "QWERTY" system, so-called for the first six letters on the left in the second row. This layout comes from the standard typewriter configuration and is found on all computers except inexpensive home-type computers designed for children. An experienced typist will not have to relearn key placement in order to use the computer. A terminal with a separate calculator keyboard or ten-key numeric pad can greatly improve the speed of entering numeric-only information.

All video displays have a position indicator, called a cursor, which the operator moves around the screen. The keys to do this are on the keyboard and are called cursor controls or cursor arrows. Look for an easy-to-find, logical placement for these keys, since they are used frequently.

Also important is the reset key. It restores the main memory to a blank condition without having to turn the computer power off. Obviously, it should be used with caution and should be designed to prevent absent-minded or accidental usage. On some computers it is located on the CPU enclosure, while on others it requires two or three simultaneous entries on the keyboard.

Auto Repeat. A common feature now is automatic repeating keys, which allow you to repeat a letter or number as many times as you want simply by holding down the key. This feature is handy in word processing, for example, when you need to print a series of hyphens or underscores to create lines across the page. Most computers are designed to begin repeating after a delay of a few tenths of a second so as not to interfere with normal, single keystrokes.

Given the personal, lengthy nature of the operator's interaction with the terminal, it is wise to involve those persons who will be spending most of the time at the computer in the decision on the terminal and the keyboard.

PRINTERS

If you plan on using a computer in your business, you should count on using a printer with it. Printers, which are "output" devices, transfer the information from the computer to paper, called "hard copy." Think of the printer as a typewriter-with-no-keyboard connected to the computer. This device produces reports of accounting information such as customer listings, invoices, and monthly statements. It also produces correspondence and other documents developed in word processing. The printer is a sizable investment and can sometimes cost more than the computer itself.

Generally, the qualities you want in a printer are attractive print and high speed. Print speed is a consideration, especially for a small business. If you expect your computer to crank out fifty letters and office memos each day, a printer that does the letter in thirty seconds will save about an hour a day over a printer that takes ninety seconds for the same document. But good quality print and higher speeds come at a correspondingly higher price.

Types of Printers

At least six different types of printers on the market are designed to work with small business computers. Thermal printers and electrostatic printers, for example, are inexpensive, but require special paper which costs more than plain paper. Both printers are quiet and very reliable because they have no impact mechanism to wear out. But they do not allow the use of multi-part forms for making copies, and this makes them unsuitable for office use.

Ink-jet and laser printers are among the latest in printer technology. Ink-jet printers form characters on regular paper by forcing a small, neat blob of ink from the printhead. These printers have the strong advantage of producing multi-color printouts, but higher manufacturing costs have kept them non-competitive with other forms of printing. Laser printers actually use a tiny laser beam to burn characters onto the surface of the paper. Your monthly telephone bill is probably produced by a laser printer. Like ink-jet printers, laser technology remains too expensive for the small business market.

The two most popular types of printers are dot matrix and letter quality. They are called impact printers because, like a typewriter, they work by means of a character striking an inked ribbon against paper. (They are also called character printers, as opposed to line printers, because they print one character after another across the page.) The dot matrix printer forms each character with a series of tiny dots; the letter quality prints each character with an individually molded hammer-key. Dot matrix printers are good for accounting reports, memos, and other internal doc-

those with no previous experience .... and makes it easy to learn WordStar as each student will have access to the classroom computers. Word processing concepts are explained in a clear, easy to understand manner. This seminar allows you to quickly become proficient with you own system.

those with no previous experience .... and makes it easy to learn WordStar as each student will have access to the classroom computers. Word processing concepts are explained in a clear, easy to understand manner. This seminar allows you to quickly become proficient with your own system.

Figure 7-9 Dot Matrix/Letter Quality Print Comparison

uments, while letter quality printers are better for word processing and finished documents.

Briefly comparing the two, the dot matrix has the advantages of low cost, faster printing speeds, and the ability to print graphics. Letter quality printers are sometimes called "daisywheel" or "thimble" printers. Letter quality printers give clear, highly readable print, with some producing print quality good enough to be used as camera-ready copy. Letter quality printers also offer a wide selection of print fonts by using quickly-changed print wheels. Dot matrix printers outsell letter quality by three to one because of their versatility and lower cost.

Both printers come in two basic carriage widths. The smaller width is about nine inches, and is capable of printing up to 80 columns across the page. The larger width is about fifteen inches and prints 132 columns across the page. Both width dimensions are at the standard ten characters to the inch, but some printers can handle up to sixteen characters per inch. The remainder of this section details the main features of these two popular types of printers.

Dot Matrix Printers

The enclosure for a dot matrix printer is typically smaller and lighter than for the letter quality printer. A dot matrix printer has several front panel display lights, with at least two or three operator control switches, and a knob for manually feeding the paper through. It also has a mechanism for automatically feeding the "fanfold" paper, called a tractor feed. Also placed inside is a hard rubber platen, like that on a typewriter, which feeds through single sheets of paper, such as letterhead stock.

In front of the platen is a printhead that moves horizontally as it prints

Figure 7-10   Epson Dot Matrix Printer (Courtesy of Epson America, Inc.)

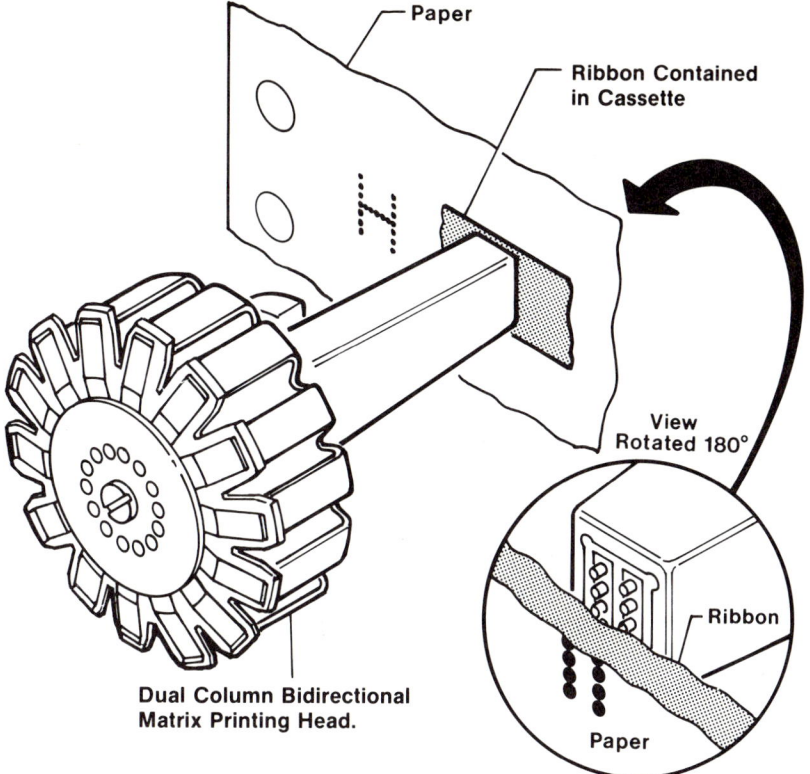

Figure 7-11 Dot Matrix Printing Technique (Courtesy of Dataproducts Corporation)

one character at a time. The printhead contains a series of vertically stacked wires, each about ten thousandths of an inch in diameter. These are individually activated by an array of small electromagnetic plungers, which in turn are energized to print a character on the paper. Firing alternate pins at different times allows printing of many different characters. This technology makes a dot matrix printer less expensive to produce and faster than a letter quality printer.

The print quality of a dot matrix depends on the number of dots (or wires) used to form the character. More dots produce more precisely shaped characters. An Epson printer, for example, uses a 9×9 array (81 dots total) to print 96 different characters. Some dot matrix printers use arrays on the order of 9×18 or 17×17 dots, called "correspondence mode," to produce densely formed characters that come close to the quality of a daisy-wheel printer. Most printers achieve this as an option by making multiple passes on each line, considerably slowing the printer.

Dot matrix printers also lend themselves better to producing graphics, such as bar graphs, pie charts, and line graphs. In fact, when each dot in the matrix can be individually controlled by the computer, the graphics printing is superior to that of a letter quality printer.

Dot Matrix Printers—What To Look For

Print Quality. While most dot matrix printers have reasonable print quality, some cannot properly print the descenders of the lower case letters "y," "q," "p," and "g." Also, the particular shape of the letters and numbers differs from one printer to another. Manufacturers do not follow any standard in forming characters in the matrix. Carefully compare the readability of sample print-outs from different brand printers.

Print Speed. All manufacturers of character printers rate their machines in cps, which means characters per second. For dot matrix printers, a rating of less than 60 cps is considered slow, even though this is much faster than a good typist. Printers with speeds between 60 and 120 cps are medium speed, and those over 120 cps are fast. Some can even go up to about 300 cps. Dot matrix printers are faster than letter quality printers because the printhead can move across the paper without pausing. Use the rated cps only as a rough guide, since the actual performance depends on the type of printing and can vary widely. Remember, higher speed costs more money.

Paper Feeds. Tractor and friction feeds are standard on many printers, and both are necessary for business processing. Tractor feeds have pins or sprockets that match holes in the margins of the fanfold paper (or continuous forms). The tractor moves the paper evenly through the printer. Stock computer paper or preprinted forms can be purchased with the margins as tear strips to be removed after printing.

Most tractor feeds can be manually adjusted to allow for different paper widths. Some, however, allow only about a half inch of adjustment, which can be a problem if you want to run narrow forms such as mailing labels. Make certain the tractor feed is fully adjustable, or has an optional tractor attachment for narrow-width paper.

A friction feed holds a single sheet of paper against a roller while printing like a typewriter. Make sure this feeding mechanism is strong enough to handle the multiple part forms commonly used in business.

Print Formatting. Almost all accounting packages will format their standard reports up to 132 print positions across the page. This normally requires a wide (fifteen-inch) carriage. If you choose a printer with a small (nine-inch) carriage, you should look for one with a "compressed print" feature, which by a switch or software control allows you to change from printing 80 to printing 132 columns across an eight-inch sheet. Compressed print changes the horizontal spacing from 10 to 16.2 characters

all businesses. Every firm has its own characteristics so the system needs to be tailored to the operation. Two chapters are devoted to making the proper selection of hardware. The first explains the four basic components of the computer and the features to look for. The second chapter explains expandable computers, multi-user systems

all businesses. Every firm has its own characteristics so the system needs to be tailored to the operation. Two chapters are devoted to making the proper selection of hardware. The first explains the four basic components of the computer and the features to look for. The second chapter explains expandable computers, multi-user systems

Figure 7-12 Dot Matrix Compressed Print

per inch. The print then looks about the same size as newspaper type and serves to accommodate full-size reports on $8\frac{1}{2} \times 11$-inch paper. This feature is one way to avoid the cost of a larger printer.

Special print formatting is desirable if the computer is used for word processing. For example, boldface printing for headings and titles in text is done by the printhead making two or three passes over the phrase to make it darker than the rest of the text. Superscripting and subscripting, used in mathematical formulas, is done by controlling the vertical spacing of the paper. These and the following special print features can be found in some dot matrix printers. Look for them if you want, and can afford, something more than run-of-the-mill printing:

Dot Addressable Graphics	Expanded Print Mode
Emphasized Print Mode	Proportional Spacing
Double-Strike Print Mode	Compressed Print Mode

Software Compatibility.   The computer and its software, both the application software and the operating system, must be compatible with the printer. Your dealer is normally responsible for ensuring this compatibility, which is less a problem if you stay with the more popular brands like Epson or Okidata Microline. Hardware manufacturers and software publishers tend to make their products compatible with the best-selling printers. Be certain that your dealer will make the printer work properly with your computer.

Letter Quality Printers

At first glance letter quality printers look similar to dot matrix printers, except they are larger and heavier. They have platens, tractor feeds, and front panel controls much like dot matrix printers. The big difference is the output. The quality of the print can be superior even to that of expensive electric typewriters. Letter quality printers are used for office correspondence, proposals, legal documents, camera-ready copy, and other applications that require the best appearance. While they can also be used for accounting applications, they print slower and are more expensive than dot matrix printers.

Letter quality printers are sometimes called daisywheel or thimble printers. Each character in the alphabet and number set is positioned on the end of a "petal" of a wheel, which resembles a daisy flower. The wheel sits just behind the printer ribbon. When a certain character is to be printed, the wheel spins rapidly to position it under a small metal hammer. The hammer striking the petal transfers the character to the paper through the ribbon. A daisy wheel also can be changed easily for different type fonts, an advantage over dot matrix printers.

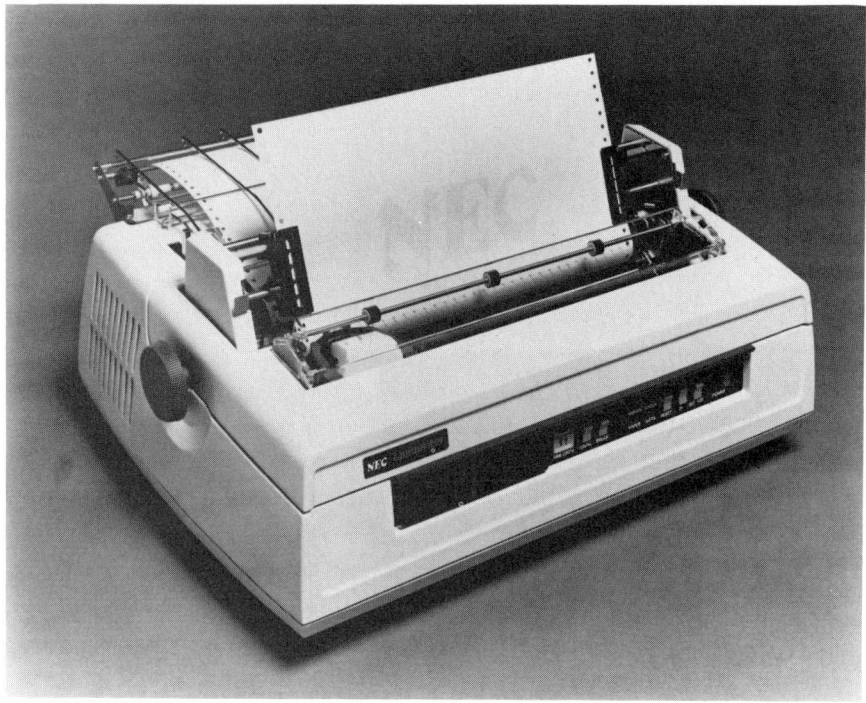

Figure 7-13   NEC 7700 Letter Quality Printer (Courtesy of NEC Information Systems, Inc.)

The better letter quality printers are capable of horizontal spacing to 1/60 or 1/120 of an inch. This provides another advantage over the matrix printers: micro-justification. For printing text with the right-hand margin justified, this feature allows for tiny adjustments to expand or compress the white spaces between the words, and between letters within words, for a neat, even appearance. Done line for line, it is similar to typesetting for books and magazines. Only the more expensive letter quality printers have this level of precision, and the word processing software must also support it.

Letter Quality Printers—What To Look For

Print Quality.   Predictably, print quality and prices vary from one printer to another. Better quality costs more. The more expensive printers generally produce a very well controlled, "heavier" looking text. These printers have a stronger hammer mechanism, which makes a better character impression on the paper. The NEC Spinwriters (Models 3500 and

Figure 7-14   Daisywheel Printwheel (Courtesy of Qume Corporation)

7700) and the Diablo (Model 630) fall into this category. These are heavy-duty printers designed to hold up under hours of continuous use. (Industry insiders sometimes call these rugged machines "bullet-proof" because they rarely break down.) Also, these printers are capable of all the special print formatting features found in sophisticated word processing programs, and they have optional tractor and sheet feeding devices often required in office situations.

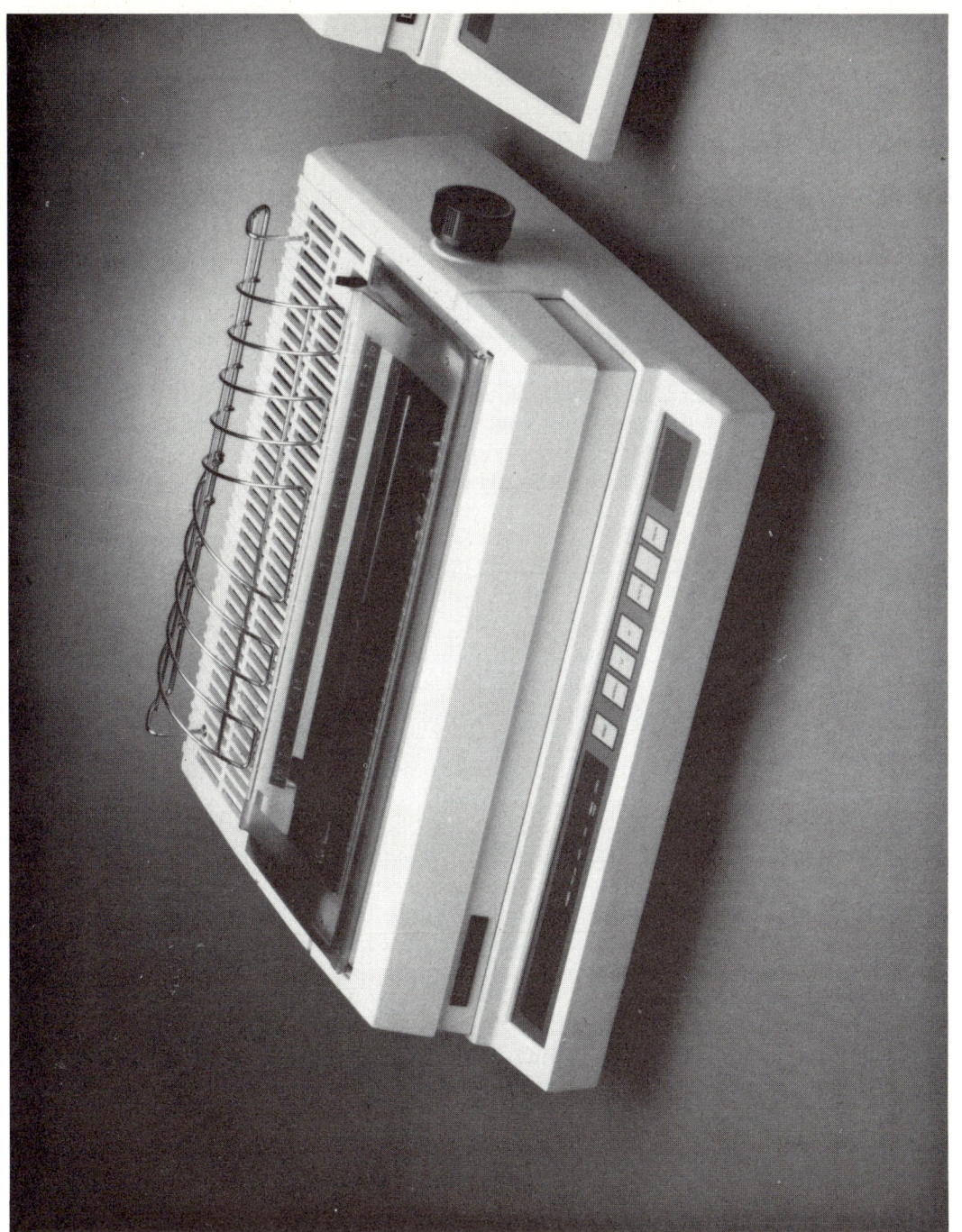

Figure 7-15 Diablo 630 Letter Quality Printer (Courtesy of Diablo Systems, Inc., A Xerox Company)

Type Fonts.   High quality daisywheel and thimble printers offer a choice of more than a hundred different type fonts, such as courier, pica, elite, manifold, courier legal, and pica legal, including foreign language characters. Each wheel or thimble contains up to ninety-six characters offering a full complement of letters, numbers, and special symbols. However, not all printwheels in all daisywheel printers are interchangeable with each other. Some less expensive daisywheel printers use only their own versions and thus offer a limited choice of type fonts. Ask to see a sample list of fonts before you decide.

Like printer ribbons, printwheels are considered supplies since they are made of plastic and deteriorate with usage. (The Diablo 630, however, can use a longer lasting metal wheel as well as plastic wheels.) Buying a popular brand printer allows you to replace these supplies more conveniently (and sometimes at lower cost) at stationery and office supply stores rather than through your computer dealer.

Print Speeds.   The trade-off for good quality print is slower print speed, usually even slower than a matrix printer. An extra fraction of a second is required to move the wheel to the correct letter position in addition to moving the printer carriage. Letter quality printer speeds range from twelve to eighty characters per second, with those above thirty cps considered fast. In actual tests, though, letter quality printers sometimes exceed their rated speeds due to a "logic seeking" feature which automatically eliminates unnecessary movement of the printhead. (Some dot matrix printers also have logic seeking.) If you plan to use your printer for more than a few hours each day, get a higher-speed printer.

Paper Feeds.   Most printers come with a hard rubber platen for feeding single sheets and a tractor feed for the fanfold paper. A tractor feed is essential for keeping continuous-form paper correctly aligned when printing multiple page documents. Therefore, tractor feeds are a must for most business applications. There are two kinds, standard and bi-directional. The main difference is that the bi-directional can feed the paper in reverse, or backwards through the printer, for superscripts, subscripts, special plotting, or graphics printing.

Software Compatibility.   Like any other peripheral, the printer must be compatible with the computer and its software. Your dealer should make sure the printer is connected properly and works with the computer. This is easier done, however, when you stay with popular printers like the Diablo and NEC Spinwriter.

Computer Hardware Checklist			
	Computer A	*Computer B*	*Computer C*
Main Processor			
Processor Chip			
8-Bit/16-Bit/32-Bit			
MHz Rating			
Memory Size			
Expanded Memory Size			
Number of Expansion Slots			
Number of Serial Ports			
Number of Parallel Ports			
Hard Disk Port			
Mutli-Color Display			
Multi-User: Number of CRTs			
Mass Storage			
Diskette Size			
Drive Capacity:			
Floppys			
Hard Disk			
Add-on Drive Units			
Hard Disk Backup:			
Removable Disk			
Tape Cartridge			
Work Stations			
Screen Size			
Resolution:			
Lines x Columns			
High Resolution			
Display Color			
Display Image			
Reverse Video			
Upper/Lower Case			
User Controls			
Tilt/Swivel			
CRT Emulation			
Detachable Keyboard			
Numeric Ten-Key Pad			
Auto Repeat			
Convenient Layout			
Printer			
Printer Type			
Print Quality			
Print Speed (CPS)			
Carriage Width			
Number of Print Positions			
Tractor Feed			
Friction Feed			
Adjustable Tractor			
Special Formatting			
Type Fonts			
Software Compatible			

Figure 7-16 Computer Hardware Checklist

CHAPTER
8

Computer Hardware: Beyond the Basics

This chapter discusses hardware considerations, beyond the four basic components described in Chapter 7, such as expandable computers, multi-user systems, and networking. All the hardware features described in the previous chapter apply to these systems as well. The final section on operating systems, system software, is included here because it usually is part of the hardware purchase.

SHOULD YOU BUY AN EIGHT-BIT OR SIXTEEN-BIT COMPUTER?

A dilemma facing nearly every small business computer buyer is: Which type of processor chip should be in the computer? The computers you are likely to consider use one of two types of microprocessor chips as the heart of the CPU, either "eight-bit" or "sixteen-bit." The eight-bit computers appeared a few years ahead of the sixteen-bit systems. The differences are such that each type of chip has somewhat different buying considerations.

Both kinds of chips are found in both single user and multi-user systems. They are also used in a wide price range of computers, from moderate to larger, more expensive business systems. Thus, neither chip is clearly in one category of computers.

The questions that generally arise are:

◢ Should you get an advanced, more expensive sixteen-bit microcomputer, or will an eight-bit machine serve as well?

◢ If you buy an eight-bit for your present needs will it be outdated in a few years?

◢ How long will you have to wait for the sixteen-bit software that meets your needs?

◢ Is the additional cost of the sixteen-bit system worth the increase in processing power?

Perhaps your first question is: What is a computer bit? To help your buying decision, a brief technical discussion is essential. Recall from the section on "How Data is Stored" in Chapter 4 that the smallest unit of computer storage is one character, or byte. Also remember that characters are single letters, numbers, or special symbols. This definition applies whether the character is stored on the diskette or in the computer's main memory.

Further, a single byte consists of a series of "bits." Recall from Chapter 7 that a bit (short for binary digit) is absolutely the smallest piece of information the computer manipulates. In fact, with one bit you can distinguish only two things: the condition of being On or Off. A good analogy is the common light switch, which is either On or Off.

The computer, then, recognizes, or "reads," characters by various On/Off combinations of the bits in a single byte. The characters are coded such that each can be written in an eight-position numbering scheme. These bits are stacked in the computer's main memory in such a way that eight of them make one byte. Thus, when the computer needs to move a character around, it accesses all eight bits of a byte at once.

Fundamental Differences

It follows, then, that a sixteen-bit computer has twice as many bits as an eight-bit machine. However, the sixteen-bit machine does not handle sixteen-bit characters. Instead, it processes *two* eight-bit characters at a time, while an eight-bit machine processes only *one* character at a time. Thus, the sixteen-bit system can "grab" twice as much data in a single pass as the eight-bit machine. Technically, this is the fundamental difference between the two processor chips. (This doubling effect is the same between sixteen- and thirty-two-bit computers, and thirty-two- and sixty-four-bit computers, which are the giant systems used for scientific research.)

What does all this mean to the user? These information handling differences create important buying considerations. In a word, sixteen-bit computers provide more processing power than eight-bit computers. Specifically, sixteen-bit systems offer the business user more speed, more memory, and more advanced software.

Processing Speeds. A sixteen-bit computer can cycle data through the CPU two to four times faster than a first-generation eight-bit machine. For example, some processing steps that take two seconds on a sixteen-bit chip might take as long as one minute on an eight-bit machine. In addition, the bigger machine needs to read information off the disk drives less often since it can have larger RAM memories in which to store the data and programs. This faster processing speed is essential in multi-user computers. (One advantage in speed may not be immediately obvious. The empty seconds can seem quite long and totally unproductive when the screen flashes a "Wait" message in order to catch up with your instructions.)

Eight-Bit Computers with Memory Banking

Generally, eight-bit computers are limited by their electronic circuitry to addressing 64,000 positions of main memory (or RAM) as mentioned. While it's more the exception than the rule, a few manufacturers have found a way to increase eight-bit memories to 128,000 positions. (The extra 64K memory is usually built in rather than being an add-on item.)

This is accomplished by "memory banking," in which the single eight-bit processor switches back and forth between two equal 64K memory banks. These banks are sometimes called "pages." Technically, the processor chip uses only one 64K bank at a time, but the speed makes it seem like it is utilizing both banks simultaneously. The switching is automatic and the user is unaware of the precise moment and frequency of occurrence. Thus, the effect is that the user has twice the normal memory capacity for an eight-bit machine. But the trade-off is a slower processing speed, especially in a multi-user machine.

Figure 8-1　Eight-Bit Computers with Memory Banking

More Memory. A sixteen-bit computer can take on a vastly larger main memory than an eight-bit system because of its ability to address far more memory locations, as mentioned in Chapter 7. This difference is similar to being able to call more telephones by adding more digits to the phone numbers. While almost all eight-bit computers are limited to 64K, the sixteen-bit machines can handle RAM memories up to one megabyte (1,000K). This larger dynamic memory means you can run larger, more sophisticated software packages. It also offers room to add more terminals in a multi-user system. (See Figure 8-1 for details on eight-bit machines with memories larger than 64K.)

Advanced Software. Since sixteen-bit machines can address larger memories, they can manage larger volumes of data at a time. They can also execute more advanced software packages, such as extended accounting, high-resolution business graphics, and the larger capacity electronic spreadsheets. Packaged software for a sixteen-bit machine can contain more program instructions, which allow more user-help menus and other features to be built into the program. For example, "housekeeping" tasks that the operator must do on an eight-bit computer can be done automatically on a sixteen-bit. Also, more application functions can be combined into one program, which avoids having to run several separate programs to complete one large task. These capabilities make sixteen-bit software more functional and easier to use.

Given all of the above, why doesn't everyone buy the more powerful sixteen-bit computer? Because using computers involves more than sheer processing power, and each type of chip has advantages and disadvantages.

Sixteen-bit machines are still fairly new, and the choice of software is still limited, although software writers are moving quickly to change this. Also, much of the current (1984) sixteen-bit software is actually converted eight-bit software, which does not take full advantage of the sixteen-bit chip performance. By contrast, eight-bit machines were first on the market and have available *now* a vast library of proven software. However, as the trend develops toward more sophisticated software, buyers will require the larger main memory that only a sixteen-bit machine can handle.

More power costs more. The sixteen-bit microprocessor chip costs the manufacturers only a few dollars more as electronic parts. The big cost difference is in the necessary electronics that surround the chip. Additional memory can add as much as 20 percent over the cost of an eight-bit system. Thus, sixteen-bit processors are not available in low-priced units.

How to decide? Besides price, your decision should be based on how the computer will be used. For most single user applications, such as word processing and electronic spreadsheets, an eight-bit machine is perfectly adequate. On the other hand, accounting applications often require a multi-

```
         8-Bit Computer                           16-Bit Computer

  Advantages
     Lower Overall Cost               Larger Main Memory
     Many Software Packages           Faster Processing Speed
     Mature Technology                Advanced Software
     Good For Single Users            Multi-User Computers
                                      High Resolution Graphics

  Disadvantages
     Trend Towards 16-Bit             Higher Initial Cost
     Incompatible with 16-Bit         Mostly 8-Bit Converted
     Runs Only Smaller Programs           Software Available
```

Figure 8-2 Eight-/Sixteen-Bit Computer Comparison Summary

user system running on a sixteen-bit computer. Generally, you should buy a 16-bit computer only under one or more of the following conditions:

◪ The software you need is currently available.
◪ You must run accounting applications.
◪ You need a multi-user computer.
◪ You need multi-tasking capabilities.
◪ You need sophisticated graphics.
◪ The other differences between an eight-bit and sixteen-bit system are not significant to you.
◪ You don't need compatibility with a previously installed eight-bit microprocessor.

Dual Processors

What if you still can't decide? One solution is to buy a system with both types of processors. Some manufacturers, such as Digital Equipment Corp., North Star Computers, Inc., Compupro, Inc., and Zenith Data Systems, offer computers with both eight- and sixteen-bit microprocessor chips. The two chips sit side by side in the CPU, and these computers are called "dual processor" machines. Dual processors eliminate the eight- or sixteen-bit decision dilemma by allowing you to run both kinds of software on the same machine. It is the best of both worlds, and offers the utmost in flexibility in choosing software.

With dual processors, one chip is the controlling unit, assigning "special tasks" to the other when needed. Also, this setup allows you to progress to sixteen-bit software without having to convert your eight-bit software library, and without having to change to another computer. Dual processor machines can also run both eight- and sixteen-bit operating systems. The Compupro, for instance, can even run both kinds of software simultaneously.

EXPANDABLE COMPUTERS

Almost all business computers allow for adding peripheral devices such as printers and hard disk drives. The multi-user computers can take on more terminals as well. These components are attached as separate units by cables to the main processor (CPU). See Chapter 4 under "Expandable Systems" for a description of expanding the computer's capabilities *externally*.

An expandable computer also allows adding more electronic capabilities *inside* the CPU enclosure. Expansion is typically done by inserting printed circuit boards in a special receptacle inside the CPU called a "bus" or expansion slot. Each printed circuit board is designed for a particular function, such as main memory, graphics, communications, or a peripheral interface. Thus, adding more memory can be as easy as inserting a board carrying all the required circuitry. Both single user and multi-user computers can be expanded in this way.

This method of expansion affects only the internal electronics of the computer. As an everyday user you may be totally unaware of any technical differences. Understanding these differences, however, may affect your purchase decision.

The electronics industry uses a variety of schemes for expandable computers, however, this section explains only two basic types: the bus-computer, and the single board computer with an expansion bus. These two types may be clearer when contrasted with the non-expandable computer, usually a single board computer without an expansion bus.

A single board computer has all its internal electronic circuitry attached to one printed circuit board. This board is the heart of the computer and contains the main memory, the interfaces to the peripheral devices, and the microcomputer chips (or integrated circuits). The average business computer contains dozens or even hundreds of integrated circuits. Many other electronic devices also use single board construction, such as radios, televisions, and stereo systems. When repairs are needed, a technician can simply remove and replace an entire board in the computer chassis.

One main advantage of the single board computer is that its lower production cost holds down the selling price. Many manufacturers of low-end personal and business computers choose this production design. Single board construction also appears typically in portable computers and all-in-one systems in which you need to add only a printer.

The main disadvantage of a single board computer is that it cannot be expanded the way a bus-type computer can (except in some cases by the manufacturer). You must accept the computer with its fixed internal capabilities. Also, repairs may cost more since a technician needs more time to replace defective parts on a "big" board than to replace the smaller, individual board in the bus-type system.

Bus-Type Computers

One kind of expandable computer has a series of internal receptacles called a "bus." Bus systems are of two types: a simple "motherboard" and a combination. A "motherboard" contains a row of receptacles to which *all* of the internal electronics are added by inserting printed circuit boards. This type usually needs a minimum of three or four boards to make a complete computer. The combination type uses a bus in addition to a single board, so that only *some* of the internal electronics are added as an option. Here the single board in itself is a complete computer and the open slots can be filled at a later time.

What is a bus? A single bus receptacle, which allows only one board to be inserted, consists of a row of small, uniform electrical contacts. In some computers these contacts number up to a hundred. When a circuit board is inserted in the bus, these contacts provide pathways for electronic impulses or "data" to travel from one part of the computer to another. For example, the bus creates an electrical route for digitized information to move from the memory to the microprocessor chip.

The electronics industry uses a number of different kinds of buses,

Figure 8-3 S-100 Bus Computer System (Courtesy of Compupro)

each with different physical dimensions, specifications, and numbers of electrical contacts. Because of these variations the STD bus, the S-50 bus, the VersaBus, and the Multibus are not interchangeable with each other. Some computers, such as the IBM PC, the Texas Instruments Professional Computer, and the Apple IIe, use their own unique bus design. Other manufacturers use an industry standard, the most popular of which is the S-100 bus.

The S-100 Bus.   The S-100 bus is physically larger than those in other bus computers such as the IBM PC or the Apple IIe. This larger board, allowing more room for electronic components, enables the designer to provide more functions to be built into the computer. In the S-100 architecture, the printed circuit boards have 100 gold-plated connectors (fifty contacts on each side of the board) that fit into the bus or connector sockets. By its design, the S-100 bus system can handle up to twenty-one boards, whereas the Multibus can only take on eight boards, and other bus designs even less. For this reason, S-100 computer systems are generally more powerful and have more capabilities than other types. Among the manufacturers using the S-100 design are Compupro, Cromemco, and Zenith Data Systems.

The main disadvantages of the S-100-type computer are its higher purchase price and the need for more dealer assistance for installation and upgrading. Also, it occupies more desk space. Still, the advantages of the S-100 bus computer are such that it is a strong candidate for the business environment. They are:

MODULARITY.   The S-100 bus system incorporates the module or building-block approach to configuring the system. You may add to or change the capabilities of the computer at any time. For example, you can upgrade a single user to a multi-user computer using the same enclosure and components. A technician can add new boards in a few minutes to a few hours, and remove existing ones even faster.

Modularity also means that as the technology changes, the S-100 bus system need never become obsolete. You can incorporate new memories and processor chips as they become available by exchanging a few boards. Instead of spending thousands for a whole new system, you can take advantage of new technology for a few hundred dollars.

CUSTOM CONFIGURATION.   Modularity also allows easier configuration of the system to suit the needs of the business. Some installations, for example, require two printers, a dot matrix for rough drafts and business reports, and a letter quality for final text. Other installations may require running both $5\frac{1}{4}$-inch and 8-inch floppy disk drives on the same system. These and other special requirements are best accomplished with the versatility of an S-100 system.

STANDARD BUS.   Most S-100 bus manufacturers now adhere to a standard known as the IEEE-696 (called "I-triple-E 696"), which was approved in December 1982 by the Standards Committee of the Institute of Electrical and Electronic Engineers. Most manufacturers (but not all) develop their products to these specifications for the S-100 bus.

For the computer owner, the IEEE standard means that S-100 board products from various manufacturers work together with a minimum of technical modifications. For instance, one may buy an S-100 bus system from one supplier, and use color graphics boards from another supplier. Because of the IEEE standards, the computer runs as though the graphics boards were original equipment. The standards also help assure that this bus will continue to be available on the market. When considering hardware, beware of products whose promotional materials do not mention the IEEE-696 specifications.

UPGRADE.   Suppose you want to add more main memory, data communications, or a hard disk to your computer. The compatibility of S-100 products makes upgrading easy. New boards need only be "dropped" into the system. In most cases, you simply buy one or two S-100 boards for a few hundred dollars. Occasionally you may need some help to adapt the existing operating system or application software, but these changes can be done by your dealer. The outstanding advantage of the S-100 upgrade capability is that you can substantially modify your computer without discarding your existing peripherals or application software.

Figure 8-4   S-100 Bus "All-In-One" System (Courtesy of Zenith Data Systems, Inc.)

Single Board + Bus Computers

The second basic design type is the single board computer with a bus for expansion. This combination type has most of the necessary electronics already built in. It usually comes complete with CPU, main memory, and peripheral connectors, without needing extra boards to make it operable. You need to buy additional boards only to *extend* its capabilities. While the manufacturers have designed this type to be the best of both worlds, it actually carries nearly all the advantages and disadvantages of the other types. For example, combination types generally are limited to only four or five expansion slots.

You can find many different types of buses from one computer brand to another. Some manufacturers use exclusive bus designs, while others use the S-100 type for broader market appeal. The IBM PC bus, for example, is a unique design, but the popularity of this machine stimulates other manufacturers to create add-on board products for it. This has the effect of a de facto standard. Zenith Data Systems, on the other hand, offers its computer with the S-100 bus, which accepts many board products already established in the market.

MULTI-USER COMPUTERS

The first true multi-user computers were large-scale mainframe computers developed in the early 1960s and still widely used today. Hundreds of terminals are attached to these machines, which have one giant CPU. These systems are called "timesharing" systems, and they offer a big advantage over the older punch card method of entering data into the computer. Using a terminal, each user has a direct connection to the computer. Though sharing it with others, the effect is of having the whole machine to oneself.

The concept of a number of individuals using a *microcomputer* simultaneously is the same as with larger mainframe computers, except on a smaller scale. Such microcomputers are called "multi-user" systems. In the world of micros, however, the term "multi-user" has different meanings. For example, some multi-user computers have only one CPU (or one microprocessor chip), while others have many CPUs (or multiple chips). Thus, we have three types of computers, of which the last two listed here are explained in this section.

Single Processor, Single User

Single Processor, Multi-User

Multi-Processor, Multi-User

SINGLE PROCESSOR, MULTI-USER SYSTEM

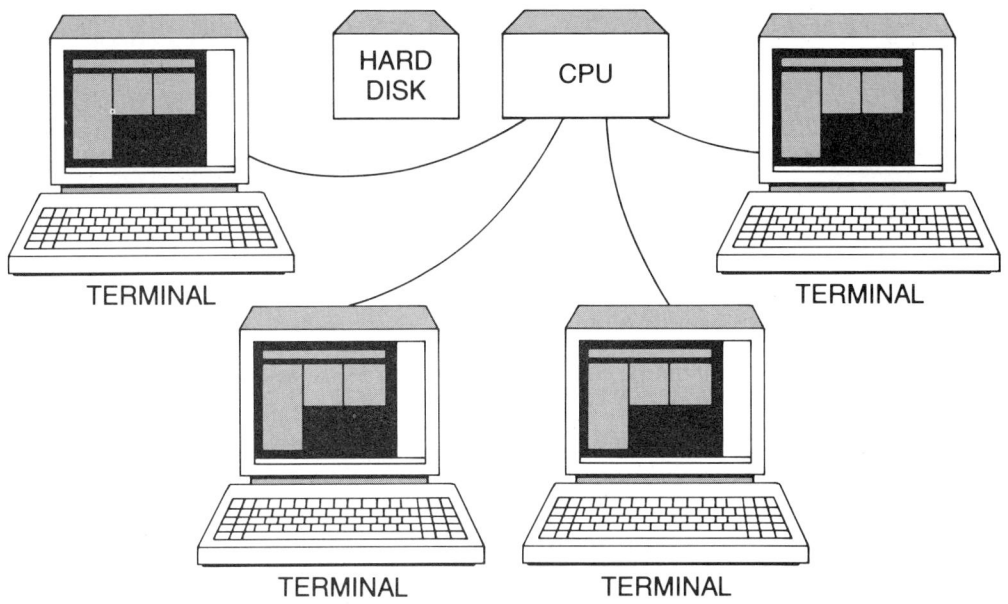

MULTI-PROCESSOR, MULTI-USER SYSTEM

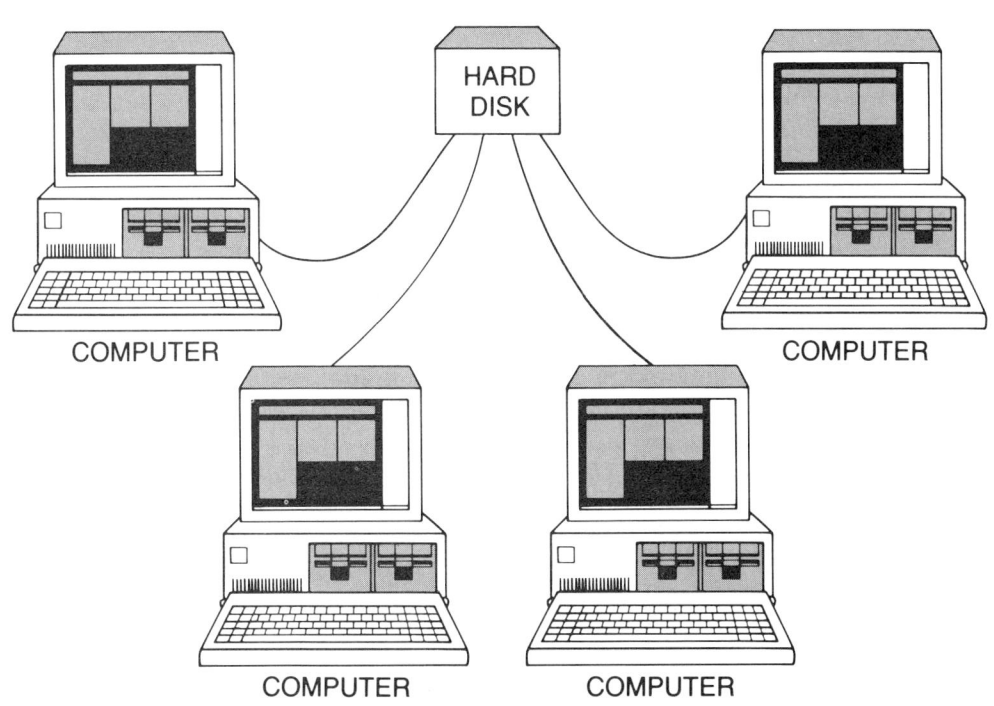

Recall from Chapter 4 that a single user computer executes only one program from one user at a time. (The exception to this is a single processor, single user, "multi-tasking" computer.) By contrast, a multi-user microcomputer can run many different computer programs at the same time, similar to a large timesharing system.

Single Processor, Multi-User Computers

Some multi-user computers, such as the Altos 586-10, have only one CPU or microprocessor chip. Yet several users can share the CPU, including the main memory, because the operating system automatically allocates a portion of the main memory to each user. The computer can thus process two or more programs side by side. Users also share external components such as disk drives and printer. Through separate terminals each user can maintain and work from individual data files. The effect is as if each user has his or her own computer.

One strong advantage of this type of system is the easy sharing of all the data files stored on the disk, especially on a system used for accounting. For example, several employees can access one set of inventory or accounts receivable records as their jobs require. Also, a single update to the files is immediately available to all other users. Here the accounting information remains in place on the disk drive, rather than being passed around from one work station to another, as in a networking system. Multi-user computers also can share expensive peripherals, such as hard disks and letter quality printers. Compared to networking, a single processor, multi-user system usually costs less per terminal.

But the single processor, multi-user computer has two inherently weak characteristics. First, if the central processor goes down, no one can use the system, since the attached terminals have no processing power of their own. When the CPU isn't running, the entire machine is virtually useless.

Second, when one microchip is serving a number of users at the same time, the system responds more slowly at each terminal. It seems like a short time, but responses of three seconds or more after every keyed entry can make the average user feel impatient. This delay caused by an increasing number of users is called "system degradation," and even the largest computers suffer from it.

Multi-Processor, Multi-User Computers

A multi-processor, multi-user computer looks quite the same as a single processor type: a number of terminals all connected to each other, or to a central "box." The main difference is that each terminal has its own CPU. In other words, a multi/multi system is a group of individual computers linked together, so that each person has his own "local" processing power. This arrangement is called "networking," and most such systems

Figure 8-6 Altos Multi-User Computer (Courtesy of Altos Computers)

are made of complete computers (including floppy disk drives) that are electronically tied together. Without the common linkage, each unit is simply a single processor, single user computer.

Instead of sharing files (or the company data base) as in a single processor, multi-user system, network users swap data files from one work station to another. The exchange occurs by placing a "call" to another user's computer for the desired file. Like calling someone on the telephone, a user "dials up" a specific computer in the network. You can even send messages back and forth in-house like a telegram service.

Networking, however, does not use ordinary telephone lines between computers. Instead, the units are attached by special cables unique to the network. (Using phone lines is called "data communications" or "telecommunications" and requires using modems.) Because of the cabling requirement, networking is limited to short distances between work stations, such as in the same office building. For this reason networking is often called "LANS," for Local Area Networking System.

Unfortunately for the beginning buyer, the computer industry offers a confusing array of networking variations; too many to detail in this book. However, a brief mention may help. Some networking systems are simple "node to node" connections, while others allow sharing of expensive peripherals as with a single processor, multi-user computer. Other networking systems connect to a host computer, such as a large corporate mainframe computer or a local minicomputer.

Still another type is the "supermicro," where each work station uses its own CPU, but all the CPUs are contained in one enclosure. Each user still has individual processing power. In this design the microprocessor chips are physically located in the main cabinet (along with a hard disk) instead of in each terminal. The total system capabilities here are between those of a large microcomputer and a traditional minicomputer. Molecular Computer and the OSM Zeus systems are examples of this type.

Regardless of design variations, the main advantages of multi-processor, multi-user computers are as follows:

◪ Downtime risk is greatly minimized, since each work station as a self-contained computer will function even when the others are not working.
◪ No time lapse or response degradation, regardless of the number of users on the system, as with a single processor, multi-user computer.
◪ Easy to add additional work stations. In most cases networking can be adapted after single user computers are in place.
◪ Allows distances up to 4,000 feet between work stations, an advantage over single processor, multi-user computers limited to 100 feet.
◪ Maximum number of work stations (e.g., sixty-four) four times higher than the maximum number (e.g., sixteen) in a single processor, multi-user computer.
◪ Can share printer and hard disk among users.

The main disadvantages are:

◪ Higher costs per work station than with a single processor, multi-user computer.
◪ Requires special communications software, which is currently limited.
◪ Currently, no standards exist. So-called standards work only on a few brands.
◪ Networks have not yet proven suitable for highly interactive processing such as accounting.

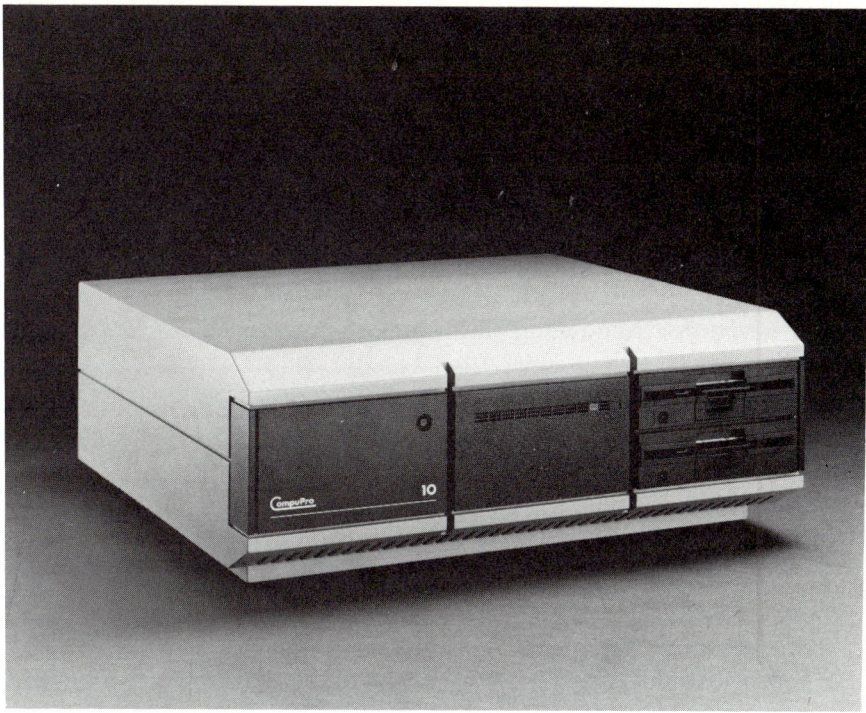

Figure 8-7 Compupro Multi-User Computer (Courtesy of Compupro)

◪ Not all of the popular software packages are designed to work on networking systems.

In conclusion, the single processor, multi-user computer has the edge for supporting an interactive accounting package in a business environment. However, industry observers expect the disadvantages of networking for such an application to be overcome. Given the many variations of multi-user systems, only the primary considerations are outlined here. Your application needs and your business plan must determine your final choice.

In summary, obtaining answers to the following questions should help with your system selection:

1. How many people will need to use the system at the same time?

2. Will the software you need work on a multi-user system?

3. Do the data files need to be shared in an interactive way?

4. Which hardware components need to be shared between users?

5. Will the system provide an acceptable level of machine failure protection?

6. What levels of data protection do you need?

7. How easy is it to add more work stations?

OPERATING SYSTEMS

The operating system for your computer is usually one of the last items to consider in your purchase. Although the operating system is a software item, it is a necessary and integral part of the computer, and each operating system is a special version customized to run on one brand of computer. Every hardware manufacturer supplies an operating system, generally as part of the computer purchase.

The complex and often confusing story of operating systems stems from the way the microprocessor industry evolved. In the "old days" (before microcomputers), every manufacturer developed its own proprietary operating system to run on its computers. The buyer took whatever operating system that came with the computer (and computer company) he or she chose.

Today a number of independent software developers, who are not associated with manufacturers, offer operating systems which run on many different microcomputers. Earlier, these emerging operating systems were left solely to the dynamics of the marketplace. No single company or agency had enough influence to set any lead in the industry. Now the consumer faces the two-edged sword of more choice among operating systems, but more to think about before buying.

Operating Systems Defined

Generally, operating systems serve the same purpose in all computers. While the user works with the application software, sometimes he interacts with the operating system directly. How it is used will be explained in a moment, but first the question: What is an operating system?

The operating system is a crucial set of programs that direct the internal functions of the computer according to what the user wants to do. Its main purpose is to provide a way to control the resources of the computer. More precisely, the operating system is the "connection" between the central processing unit, the peripherals, and the user's application program. The operating system helps the user in three general ways:

1. It loads and executes user programs.

2. It organizes data and programs, and reports the status of the disk drive units. For example, it tells what files are on a disk, how much disk space they occupy, and how much unused space remains.

3. It takes care of thousands of small tasks involved in transferring information from the main processor to the computer's peripherals, such as disk drives, printers, and terminals.

The operating system helps the user do some of the important "housekeeping" chores while running the computer. Below are sample commands from CP/M, one of the popular operating systems. The computer performs the described function when the operator enters the command.

DIR — The "directory" command lists on the video screen the names of all the files stored on the disk.

TYPE — The "type" command displays the contents of a file on the video screen.

ERA — Erases or deletes a file from the disk.

STAT — Gives the status and the amount of space occupied by the files on the disk.

COPY — Allows the user to make identical copies of the diskettes.

Not only do operating systems vary among machine-specific versions, they also are of different types. For example, different operating systems are offered for eight- and sixteen-bit computers, and for single user and multi-user computers. In addition, "single tasking" and "multi-tasking" computers have different operating systems. (Either of which can run on single user computers. Multi-tasking here is different from multi-user, and these operating systems are discussed later in this section.)

Microcomputer operating systems are groups of programs on floppy disks that can be removed from the computer. In small computers the operating system is sometimes referred to as the "DOS" (pronounced "D-O-S" or "doss"), which means disk operating system. More often, operating systems are referred to by their trade names, such as "CP/M" or "MS-DOS."

Using an Operating System

How do you use an operating system? When you first turn on the computer the main memory is activated but "empty." That is, nothing can happen until the memory has a computer program to make it useful. When you insert a diskette that contains the operating system into the drive unit, a copy of the system program is "written" into a portion of the main memory. This loading of the operating system software into the main memory is called "booting up" the system. On some computers this loading is automatic, while on others you must enter some simple commands through the keyboard.

Loading the operating system is a prerequisite to running any application program, be it word processing, accounting, or anything else you have in mind. Once the operating system is in the RAM memory, the computer is ready to accept the application program, which can come from the same disk as the operating system or another disk.

The operating system controls the computer when you are not running any application program. When you want to run a program, you instruct the machine to load it in memory alongside the operating system. Then the operating system recedes into the background and becomes "invisible" while your program moves into place. When you finish your task and exit from the application, control of the hardware reverts back to the operating system, and it indicates it is ready for the next task.

In many cases the staff will not need extra training in how to use the operating system because some application programs duplicate some of the functions found in operating systems. For example, WordStar, a popular word processing program, allows you to copy, delete, and rename data files more easily than doing the same things with the CP/M operating system.

The Compatibility Problem.   Suppose you want to play an LP record on your friends' stereo system. You just turn it on, put the record on the turntable, and activate the tone arm. You can play audio cassettes the same way because they are compatible from one brand of machine to another. They all play at exactly the same speed. Unfortunately, this kind of compatibility does not exist with small computers (or even big ones for that matter). With a few exceptions, a number of conditions must be met for you to run your computer software on a machine other than your own.

PROCESSOR CHIP.   The CPU's processor must be the same, since each type of chip contains a different instruction set (built-in codes that recognize computer program instructions). For this reason, programs for the Apple IIe computer (using the 6502 chip) do not work on other eight-bit machines, except those that have the same 6502 chip. Also, the memory addressing schemes are different among the chips.

DISK DRIVES.   Three conditions must exist for floppy disk drives to be compatible. First, the physical dimensions must be the same. The most popular sizes are 3 1/2-, 51/4-, and 8-inch. Second, the recording density must be the same, either single or double. Most machines can switch between the two. Third, the recording format must be identical. (See "Recording Formats," Chapter 7.)

OPERATING SYSTEMS.   The operating systems must be the same in order to run programs and data from one machine on another. The two most popular operating systems, CP/M and MS-DOS, are not compatible. Also, sometimes different versions of the same operating system are not compatible with each other. For example, some programs written to run under CP/M-80, version 2.2, will not work under earlier versions of CP/M.

PRINTER.   Even if all of the above are harmonious, the printer must also be compatible. For example, if you have an IBM PC and you want to run your program and print its output on another IBM PC, the printer must work the same way as yours. Remember that the application software *and* the operating system are both tailored to the computer hardware. If the printer software on your application program disk (called a "driver") is different, the program will not print correctly even though everything else is the same.

The compatibility problem is critical but not insurmountable. You may bypass the disk compatibility problem by transmitting data between different machine brands using modems and telephone lines or direct hardwired connections. (Portions of this book were written and edited this way on two incompatible machines situated miles apart.) Everything else, though, must still be compatible. These methods are not as convenient as swapping diskettes from machine to machine, but they do allow an outside salesman, for example, to travel his territory with a different make machine than you have back home in the sales department.

Also, greater flexibility exists if you need only to process your data files (not your programs) on another computer. If two machines each have their own program (such as WordStar or Lotus 1-2-3), but each program is configured differently, you can still create the data files on one and process on the other. This is one reason to keep diskettes for your data separate from your program diskettes.

Finding good application software that is compatible with the popular operating systems is not a problem—good software draws attention and acceptance from satisfied users. On one side, leading software publishers offer their products under more than one popular operating system. On the other side, hardware manufacturers give you a choice of operating systems with their equipment. Why? Both publishers and manufacturers recognize they will miss a large market share by limiting their products to one operating system. IBM, for example, offers its Personal Computer with a choice of three widely accepted operating systems: CP/M-86, MS-DOS, or the UCSD-p System.

Operating System Sources

Most of the popular operating systems come from independent software suppliers. These are companies like Digital Research, Inc. (Pacific Grove, California) and Microsoft Corporation (Bellevue, Washington), whose only products are software for a broad commercial market. In addition to operating systems, they produce programming languages, utilities, and some application packages. Normally you do not buy an operating system directly from these firms. Instead, a computer manufacturer arranges with them to distribute the operating system that the manufacturer has customized for its hardware. Because you buy the operating system from the hardware manufacturer, you are certain it is compatible with your system.

Besides Digital Research and Microsoft, a third software firm, SofTech Microsystems, offers a unique operating system, called the UCSD-p. At least twenty other firms have developed operating systems for microcomputers, including Bell Laboratories (UNIX), Digital Equipment Corporation (RSTS, RT-11), Phase One Systems (OASIS), and Ryan-McFarland (RM/COS). The most popular products, though, come from Digital Research and Microsoft.

Digital Research, Inc.   Perhaps the closest the microcomputer industry comes to a standard disk operating system is one called CP/M, which means Control Program for Microcomputers. Digital Research now offers an entire family of operating systems under that trademarked name. Because CP/M was one of the earliest operating systems available and was easily adaptable to many different kinds of hardware, it became a de facto standard in the industry. The following is a brief description of some of the operating systems available from this company:

1. **CP/M-80 and CP/M-86** are both written for single user computers. CP/M-80 is a general purpose, hardware-independent, modularized operating system created for three particular eight-bit microprocessor chips: 8080, 8085, and the Z80. CP/M-86 is a later version of CP/M-80, but is designed for the 8086 and 8088 sixteen-bit microcomputers. Only the data file structures are compatible between these two operating systems.

2. **CP/M Plus** is also written for eight-bit computers but is easier for computer novices to use. For instance, it includes a "Help" command to explain the various system commands. This system is compatible with all other eight-bit operating systems from Digital Research. Also, CP-M Plus allows users to access additional banks of memory in eight-bit computers. (See "Eight-Bit Computers with Memory Banking," Figure 8-1.)

3. **Concurrent CP/M-86** is a real-time, multi-tasking operating system for single user microcomputers based on the 8086, 8088, 68000, and Z8000 chips. Multi-tasking allows a user to run more than one job simultaneously on a sixteen-bit single user computer. This operating system has the same basic commands as CP/M-86, and the file structures are compatible with all other Digital Research operating systems.

4. **MP/M-86** is a multi-user, multi-tasking operating system for the 8086, 8088, 68000, and Z8000 sixteen-bit microprocessor chips. Multi-user operating systems involve a higher order of sophistication, but the command structure is similar to the other CP/M operating systems. This software is commonly used in a multi-user computer running accounting applications.

5. **CP/NET** is a hardware-independent microcomputer network operating system. Recall that networking means attaching several computers

to a common communications schema. Networking allows you to transfer data from one computer to another while sharing peripherals such as hard disks and printers.

Microsoft Corporation. The next two operating systems are among those offered by Microsoft Corporation. This company became popular because its MS-DOS software is the leading operating system for the IBM PC, which was introduced in late 1981.

1. **MS-DOS** is a single user operating system for sixteen-bit microcomputers. It is sometimes called PC-DOS, by IBM, and Z-DOS, by Zenith Data Systems, and there are minor differences between these and the standard MS-DOS. This operating system is designed to run on the 8086 and 8088 processors. Its features and capabilities are comparable to Digital Research's CP/M-86, although it is considered easier to use.

2. **XENIX** is a multi-user, multi-tasking operating system for sixteen-bit computers. It is similar to UNIX, which was developed earlier at Bell Laboratories. This operating system, derived under a license from American Telephone and Telegraph, incorporates features that make it more suitable for business use. It runs on the 8086, 68000, and Z8000 microprocessor chips. All UNIX-type operating systems require more disk storage for their programs than the others, and are best suited to large multi-user systems.

SofTech Microsystems. UCSD-p System is a single user operating system from SofTech Microsystems of San Diego, California. While not as popular as the others, it is worth noting because it is designed to be "portable" from one machine to another. Programs that run on an eight-bit computer, for example, can run on a sixteen-bit computer if both use the p-System.

Beyond the popular operating systems, some producers of small business computers have chosen to provide their own proprietary operating system. For example, Apple, Cromemco, DEC, North Star, and Radio Shack all provide operating systems under their own brand name. When you choose a computer with a proprietary operating system, you are thus limited to running programs that are compatible with it alone. Some manufacturers write their own software, not as an improvement over the others but just to be different. So as not to restrict consumers unduly, almost all manufacturers now offer a choice of operating systems that usually includes at least either CP/M or MS-DOS.

Operating Systems—What To Look For

Operating systems seem confusing because they are. Properly interfacing many different brand computers with many different software products

Operating System Summary

	Single User	Multi-User	8-Bit	16-Bit	Micro-chip	Multi-Tasking	RAM Req'd	File Lockout	File Security	Device Indep.
CP/M-80	X		X		Z80 8080 8085	No	8K-12K	No	No	Yes
CP/M-86	X			X	8086 8088	No	56K	No	Yes	Yes
CP/M Plus	X		X		Z80 8080 8085	No	16K-32K	Yes	Yes	Yes
Concurrent CPM	X	X		X	8086 8088 68000 Z8000	Yes	128K	Yes	Yes	Yes
MP/M-86		X		X	8086 8088 68000 Z8000	Yes	64K	Yes	Yes	Yes
CP/NET		X	X		Z80 8080 8085 8086 8088 68000 Z8000					
MS-DOS	X			X	8086 8088	No	12K-25K	No	No	Yes
XENIX		X		X	8086 68000	Yes		Yes	Yes	Yes
UNIX		X		X	8086 68000	Yes	80K-200K	Yes	Yes	Yes
UCSD-p	X		X	X	Z8000 Et.Al.	Yes	64K	No	No	Yes

Figure 8-8 Operating System Summary

makes operating systems a complex subject. In addition, no one particular operating system stands clearly superior over the others to make your choice any easier.

The specific differences between operating systems are important to hardware and software suppliers, programmers, and technical users. Generally, these differences are not as critical to the day-to-day business user. Even clerical and administrative people can get by knowing only a few simple commands. In fact, you can live with almost any operating system if it supports the applications you need. Thus, choose first the computer application, then the operating system.

After assessing your requirements, your computer dealer should help you decide on an operating system. Some guidelines may help:

First, you should get an operating system that allows you to change hardware options easily without worrying about how it "communicates" with them. This is called "peripheral-independent" software. Any such changes should be easy for the dealer to handle without excessive service costs.

Second, if you need a multi-user system, make sure the operating software has a "file lockout" capability, especially for accounting applications. As explained in Chapter 6, this feature prevents irreparable changing of a data file, such as an inventory record, if it is accessed at the same instant by two users.

Third, while some operating systems are easier to use than others, they may not be sophisticated enough for your ultimate needs. Either pick an easy one that is compatible with a more advanced version and upgrade later, or start with the sophisticated system that meets your future needs as well.

Once you begin to use an operating system, though, it can become the tie that binds. Because you must process your accumulated data files under any new system, there is a resistance to change—even if a new operating system appears to be a worthwhile improvement. It is much easier to change to a different spreadsheet or word processing program than to change operating systems. Thus, it is best to buy one operating system and stay with it. Pick a best-seller, like the CP/M or MS-DOS product lines, since they are established, supported, and offer an upgrade path to the advanced operating systems.

CHAPTER

9

Risks and Reliability

Risk is the threat or possibility of suffering harm or loss. Like any piece of business equipment, a small business computer is subject to risks such as physical damage, theft, and misuse, either deliberate or accidental. This chapter outlines the precautions that minimize these risks.

The small business computer presents unique risks. Chief among these is the rapid, total loss of data. Computers have been known to lose or destroy in seconds what took hours or days to create. With its electronic speed, once the computer is instructed to eliminate information on the surface of the diskette, no human can stop it. Furthermore, the destruction is total. When it's gone, it has completely vanished without a trace.

While these risks can never be totally eliminated, you can protect yourself against such losses and keep your equipment highly reliable at minimum expense.

UNAUTHORIZED USE OF THE COMPUTER

Ensuring that only authorized persons use the computer can be handled in several ways. You can restrict physical access to the computer through traditional in-house security measures such as locked doors, burglar alarms, etc., but most small businesses set the system in an open office environment so the staff can have free access to it. If security is critical, however, you may isolate the computer by putting it in a separate room or enclosure open only to authorized persons.

Another possible solution is to use a computer designed to be turned on only with a key switch, similar to an automobile ignition switch. The keys can be restricted to authorized users.

Perhaps the most common and practical security measure is to restrict access to the floppy disks containing sensitive business information, rather than the computer itself. The data files can be removed from the computer site at the end of the day and stored under lock and key in a fireproof, waterproof vault, or even secured in an ordinary filing cabinet. Securing sensitive files away from the computer also allows users to continue using the hardware for other purposes.

In a multi-user system access may also be restricted through user passwords. Automated Teller Machines (ATM) at banks employ a similar password security when they require customers to enter a personal identification number known only to themselves and a few bank officials. Some computer operating systems, like the bank ATMs, hide the password from onlookers by not displaying it on the terminal. Once the user has properly "signed on" and has been accepted by the computer, he is free to use the machine. Another level of password security permits some users to gain access only to certain confidential data and programs such as payroll, while allowing other users free access to other files.

Another approach is to design software so that the computer records the user's identification. As changes are made to the company's operating or financial information, the computer automatically records the user's password, along with the transaction data, in a special file called an audit trail file. This record allows tracing back over any time period to find who did what in making changes. Audit trails are typically developed only when a piece of information is altered, such as an inventory balance, or a general ledger journal correction, or a customer credit limit.

Audit trails also add security against computer crimes. Unscrupulous but computer-knowledgeable people have been known to enter a computer and order expensive equipment sent to unauthorized locations, or transfer funds to fictitious creditors. Audit trail files can record their identity without their awareness. Since keying in an acceptable password can only be done by someone who knows the computer and how it works, audit trails also help investigators narrow the list of possible suspects.

ACCIDENTAL LOSS OF DATA

The accidental loss of data is the most likely risk with any computer. People fear it most because of the huge cost in person hours to recreate the lost data. The three most frequent causes of data loss are electrical power failures, physical damage to the computer or media, and operator error.

Power failures, even for a split second, can create a voltage peak that gaps across the disk drive recording head. The gap leaves an electronically meaningless impulse on the disk's surface, rendering it ineffective. While a voltage interrupt may destroy only a portion of the disk's information, it can make obtaining the data from the disk very difficult, since "reading" it is a continuous operation. Some solutions to these power supply problems are described in a later section in this chapter.

Like any piece of equipment, disk drives face the possibility of physical damage, ranging from a spilled cup of coffee to outright malicious intent. Even relocating the hardware to another part of the office or down the street can result in damage if the drive heads are not properly "locked" in place, which is a small job for a technician. Replacing damaged equipment, however, is often easier than restoring the resulting lost data files.

Operator error is certainly the most common cause of accidental loss of data. He or she can absentmindedly key the wrong instructions and—zap!—it's all gone. Even with the proper safeguards built in, people make mistakes. Office confusion, incorrect procedural instructions, or simply lack of proper training are the usual causes.

Therefore, to protect your firm's valuable information you must provide "backups" to all your data and computer programs. A backup is simply an identical copy of the original disk or diskette. The backup copy is created on a routine basis and stored in a safe place away from the computer site. Typically, at the end of the day the computer operator will stop all processing and execute the copy procedure.

Let's look at the true value of a diskette to illustrate why the backup concept is important. An eight-inch quality diskette (single side, double density) costs about $6.00, but with the stored data, it may be worth hundreds of dollars. For example, a typist who averages fifty wpm (with

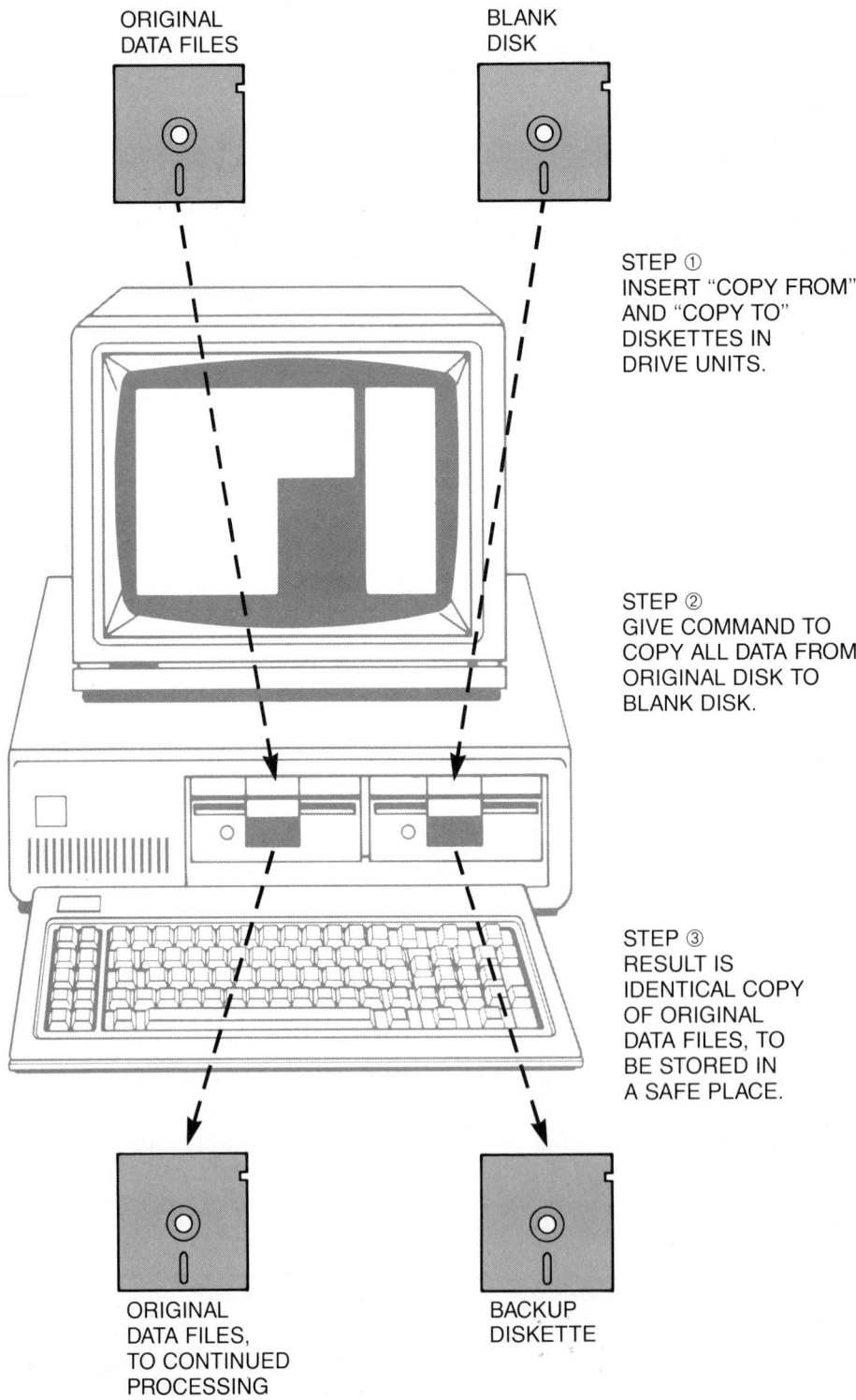

ORIGINAL
DATA FILES

BLANK
DISK

STEP ①
INSERT "COPY FROM"
AND "COPY TO"
DISKETTES IN
DRIVE UNITS.

STEP ②
GIVE COMMAND TO
COPY ALL DATA FROM
ORIGINAL DISK TO
BLANK DISK.

STEP ③
RESULT IS
IDENTICAL COPY
OF ORIGINAL
DATA FILES, TO
BE STORED IN
A SAFE PLACE.

ORIGINAL
DATA FILES,
TO CONTINUED
PROCESSING

BACKUP
DISKETTE

Figure 9-1   Floppy Disk Backup Method

an average word length of six letters) can enter 18,000 characters per hour. The capacity of the disk is 600,000 characters, but the data files should not exceed 80 percent, which is 480,000 characters. The typist would require about twenty-six hours to reach the 80 percent mark, and the cost at $9.50 per hour is $247.00. Therefore, the main purpose of the backup disk is to save the time and cost of having to re-enter all the data should something happen to the original.

The backup method is quite simple with floppy disks. Using a second disk drive, you instruct the computer to copy all the information from the first disk onto a second blank disk (or a previously used "scratch" diskette). This procedure takes less than five minutes, even with a full disk. (This ease of copying is one good reason for having two disk drives in any business computer system.)

With a hard disk you must provide backups either with several floppy disks, with a magnetic tape cartridge, or with a removable hard disk (which is preferable). Tape cartridges and hard disk packs generally have a storage capacity from 5 million to 20 million characters (five to twenty megabytes). Whatever you are using for backup should have roughly the same storage capacity as the total of all the files you want to copy. This one-to-one copying can be done in a reasonable period of time, often less than ten minutes.

How often should backup copies be made? The answer depends on how much time and expense you can afford in recovering from an accidental loss of data. When you experience deleted files on your computer you recover by re-entering all the data since the last backup was made. This could be anywhere from a few minutes to a few hours of data entry. Thus, the less time you can afford to lose, the greater the need for more frequent backup procedures.

Frequency of backup can also depend on how often the information changes. Accounting information changes daily and therefore demands more frequent backups, while computer programs may change only occasionally as new versions arrive. Most computer installations make complete copies of all data files at least once a day.

PHYSICAL ENVIRONMENT

Many so-called computer failures are caused by conditions in the physical environment that could have been avoided. With a few simple precautions, computers can operate almost indefinitely without any problems. The computer will never tell you that it's too hot or humid, or that a speck of dirt is causing the disk drive head to misread. It will simply react in other ways and thus force you to discover the environmental problem. Although the new small computers do not need the specially controlled environments the larger systems do, some special precautions are still necessary. Obviously, you should not place your system in a garage or in the middle of a manufacturing plant where dust and dirt are excessive.

Environmental Threats

Computers are sensitive to extreme temperature and humidity conditions. Most will operate satisfactorily under the same room conditions suitable for office personnel. The typical temperature range for microcomputers is fifty to eighty-five degrees Fahrenheit with 20 percent to 80 percent relative humidity. Excessive heat build-up within the internal circuits is a threat to continued operation. Higher temperatures can create "glitches" in the computer and shorten the life of the electronic circuits. (A glitch is a temporary electrical malfunction in the computer's components.) If air-conditioning is unavailable, then a portable electric fan will help keep the system cool. Many quality systems have small electric fans built in to reduce heat build-up.

Dust attacks computers, especially the disk drives and diskettes. The inside of the black diskette jacket is lined with a special material to help trap dust particles as the disk rotates in the drive unit. When not in use the diskettes should be immediately returned to the paper envelope supplied, and they should be stored in plastic or metal boxes when the computer is shut down. The computer should be located in a relatively clean area away from dust and smoke. Particles of smoke have the same effect as dust, so "no smoking" around the computer site is a wise policy. As an extra precaution, dust covers can be used to cover the equipment when not in use.

Care of Diskettes

Improper handling of the diskettes is probably the most common source of computer malfunction. Diskettes should be treated as delicate instruments and not abused. Here are the basic Do's and Don'ts in caring for your diskettes. The Do's first:

◤ Handle with care. Insert the diskette in the drive unit without bending or scratching it.

◤ Use only a felt tip pen to label your diskettes. Pencils leave traces of graphite, and ballpoints may indent the disk surface.

◤ Keep the disks free from dust, liquids, and smoke.

◤ Store the disks in a metal box to minimize the effects of magnetic fields.

◤ Keep backup diskettes away from the computer site where they won't be handy to use.

◤ Buy quality disks—the extra cost is cheap insurance against potential problems of disk reading and recording.

◤ Accurately identify diskettes with labels, which may include program and file names, date of origin, disk density, and disk library number.

◪ Keep the disks away from magnets and magnetic fields such as computer cabinets, video screens, power lines, and desk-top paper clip holders.

The Don'ts:

◪ Don't touch the magnetic surface of the diskette. Contamination can cause reading/writing errors.

◪ Avoid exposing diskettes to airport metal detection devices and postal X-ray machines.

◪ Do not bend or fold the diskettes. Don't attach notes with paper clips, which may damage the disk's recording surface.

◪ Do not use chemicals or solutions of any kind to clean the diskettes.

◪ Don't expose the disks to excessive heat or sunlight. Disks can typically be stored only in temperatures of 40 to 125 degrees Fahrenheit.

◪ Do not leave the diskettes in the machine when turning the power On or Off. Transient drive head voltages may alter the stored information.

◪ Never insert or remove a disk when the disk drive unit is "active," i.e., when the drive light is on.

◪ Don't allow your diskettes to get too full of programs and data files. Frequently check the file status of your most active disks and keep the total space used below 80 percent of capacity.

◪ Don't attempt to use the other side of the diskette. They are designed to be inserted in the drive only one way.

Power Supply Threats

To operate reliably, any computer and its peripherals depend on a constant "clean" electrical current. Although you can plug your system into any standard wall outlet like a typewriter or adding machine, it is much more sensitive to voltage changes than other equipment. As mentioned earlier, a split-second voltage fluctuation can render disk files unreadable—even without the operator being aware of it at the time. Various surges, spikes, dips, and line "noise" can play havoc with programs and circuitry, while a sustained power failure will blank out all the programs and data in the computer's main memory.

Only extremely expensive equipment is an adequate guard against total electrical power failures. Special power generators or battery backups (called "UPS," for un-interruptable power supply) are costly for the average small computer installation. The UPS devices at best only sustain power for a few minutes while you properly shut down the system. Thus, backup diskettes are the only realistic safeguard against this event. Several measures, however, can be used against less critical electrical power fluctuations.

Power line fluctuations are caused by anything from the electric utility company to electrical devices attached to the same circuit in your office or plant. Electric motors used in heavy industrial equipment, air-conditioning and furnace units, even refrigerators draw a large amount of current during startup. These can be an unpredictable source of voltage changes within your own office. Therefore it's best if the computer system is plugged into a circuit that runs from the building's fuse box separately. The power line must be electrically grounded, and the computer and all of its peripherals should be connected to the same set of wall outlets.

Other devices to help protect against excessive power changes include voltage regulators, but these can cost up to about a thousand dollars. A voltage suppressor is useful to clip the sharp, sudden current increases called spikes, but offers no protection against current dips or brownouts. They cost about $35 to $125. A noise filter protects against minor fluctuations only and is the least expensive item, about $30.

Static Electricity

Static electricity is the most random and perhaps the most difficult to control environmental threat. Walking across a carpeted floor and touching the computer can send a thousand-volt static electric shock through the system. Atmospheric static electricity is at its highest when the weather brings cool, dry winds. Either source can cause the computer to do strange things. One solution to dry air is to install a room humidifier. The static from floor surfaces can be minimized by installing a hard-surfaced floor or antistatic mats. Overall, the worst part of static electricity is the difficulty it causes in diagnosing hardware problems since it occurs inconsistently.

Radio Frequency Interference

Any computer, large or small, can inadvertently act as a radio transmitter or receiver. This is known as Radio Frequency Interference (RFI), and it can affect the performance of television sets, radios, and other electronic appliances. Signals can also be received, which will create problems if the interference is strong. The receiving parts of the computer are usually the peripheral cables, but it can be any component not protected by metal shielding. The cables act like antennas and this is why short cables are recommended. For computer enclosures, a metal shelf or desk will help block the radio emissions. A power line surge suppressor with a noise filter, mentioned above, will also help.

LEVEL OF REQUIRED RELIABILITY

The first three sections of this chapter discuss what you as the owner can do to minimize the environmental risks to your computer. The next two sections deal with what level of reliability you require, which includes servicing and repairs, and how to decide what you should do.

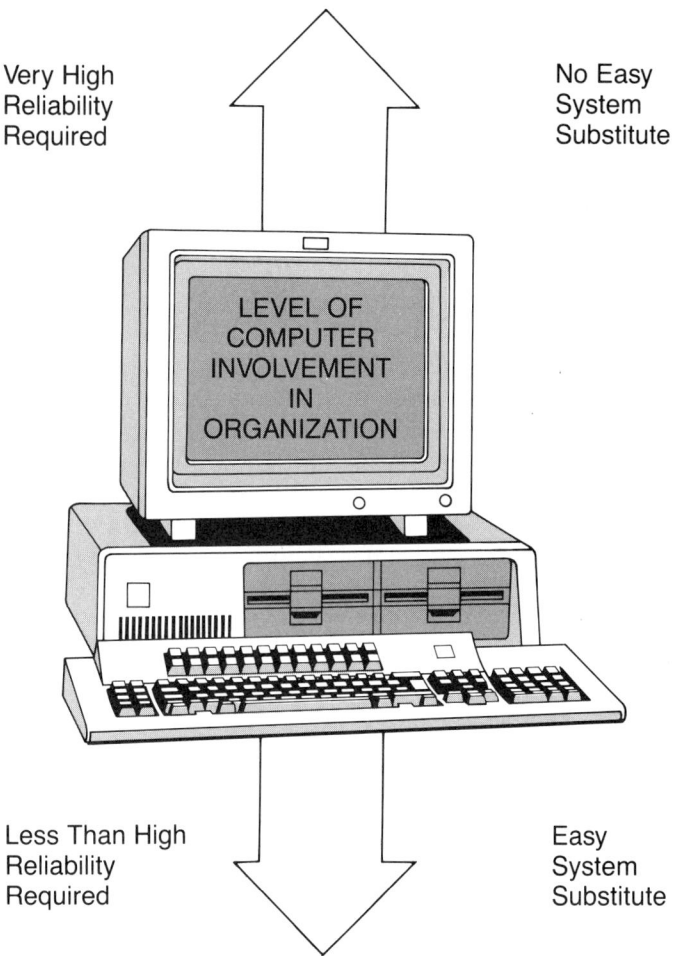

Very High
Reliability
Required

No Easy
System
Substitute

LEVEL OF
COMPUTER
INVOLVEMENT
IN
ORGANIZATION

Less Than High
Reliability
Required

Easy
System
Substitute

Figure 9-2   Level of Required Reliability

When thinking of purchasing a computer, businesspeople justifiably ask: "How reliable is this equipment?" Computers are high technology and, compared to other modern machines, they are very reliable. Many systems run problem-free, and averages are better than 95 percent reliability. Nonetheless, a business can still suffer when the machine is not operating that 5 percent of the time. How to resolve the downtime problems and the related costs depends entirely on how dependent your business is on the computer. Some businesses demand the ultimate in reliability, that is, no loss in service greater than just a few minutes, while others might go for days without any severe impact. Thus, the solution to the reliability factor lies in the answer to the question: "How long can you afford to be without your computer?"

Very high reliability is required when your business is dramatically affected by the loss of a computer's operation for more than a few minutes. A good example with a larger computer is an airline's reservation system, which uses terminals in airports all over the country connected to one giant computer. Their business literally stops when their computer isn't running, because there is no easy substitute. The airline's answer to its reliability requirement is to have a second giant computer on-site in case the first one breaks down. An automatic switchover is made in seconds and it's business as usual. This need for immediate backup, however, is not limited to large corporate businesses.

Any size business that cannot afford to have the computer down for sustained periods, and that has no easy substitute, will need to take the same measures as the airlines. For example, a wholesale distributor taking orders over the telephone and entering them directly into the computer might need a second on-site computer for backup. On the other hand, in a firm where there is less dependency on the machine, and a substitute is easily available, reliability is less important. For instance, if a computer-based word processing system doesn't run, you can easily shift to an ordinary typewriter and some of the work will still get done. Or a building contractor who uses a computer for cost estimating can switch to a hand calculator while his system is out for repairs.

Consequently, you will have to decide at what point on the reliability spectrum your business is. The answer lies in the level of computer involvement in your firm's activities. Is it at the heart of your operation, or somewhere on the periphery? The reliability support you need can be found in a number of hardware backup and maintenance choices described in the next section.

LEVEL OF HARDWARE MAINTENANCE

Fortunately, a range of maintenance possibilities exists, from very high reliability needs to low reliability needs. Each has its own set of considerations, and the costs are successively lower going from the highest level to the lowest. Thus, the challenge is to optimize the performance you would like from your system with the costs you can afford for the service. In ranking order the five choices are:

1. On-Site Backup Computer
2. On-Site Backup Peripherals
3. On-Site Field Maintenance:

    A. Service Contract
    B. Time and Materials Repairs

4. Off-Site Backup Computer

5. Off-Site Repair by Dealer or Manufacturer

The first choice is a second on-site backup computer like the airline system. This means paying for two complete systems, but computers are now so inexpensive that this is no longer considered an extravagance. And the second computer doesn't have to sit idle waiting for the first to break down. In the case of the wholesale distributor who enters phone orders all day, the second system can perform other functions, like word processing and financial planning. The risk is greatly minimized since it is highly unlikely that both computers will fail at the same time. This also means you can opt for the low-cost carry-in repair service and eliminate the need for a field maintenance contract.

Peripheral devices are actually more prone to failure than the central processing unit. Components with mechanical moving parts, such as disk drives and printers, have a greater frequency of repair than the electronic circuits, which are solid-state. If you choose to have on-site backup peripherals you simply exchange or "swap out" the unit in need of repair for the backup unit. In the event you want to protect against failure of the electronic circuit boards and you have a bus-type computer (see Chapter 8), you can buy additional printed circuit boards. To install these, however, requires someone with a technical capability.

Field maintenance service can have a number of options depending on the service contractor. Generally, under a service agreement, for a fixed sum per month the contractor agrees to be on call and make on-site repairs (or replacements) regardless of the actual cost per call. It's like buying an insurance policy. The agreement is usually available from the hardware vendor for a twelve-month period, renewable annually.

Field maintenance contracts will often specify different levels of service in response to various customer needs. For example, the service on-call response time (how quickly they call you back or send someone out) can be shortened from twenty-four to four hours if necessary. The hours of service availability can be changed from eight to sixteen, or to twenty-four hours each day. The work week can be extended to include weekends and holidays. A premium is charged for each additional level of service required and is figured in the monthly charge. Some service firms will provide maintenance contracts for customer carry-in repairs, as well as non-contract on-site service calls.

An off-site backup computer can be arranged in a number of ways. You can agree with another computer owner to back up each other; that is, you use their machine when yours is down, and vice versa. This form

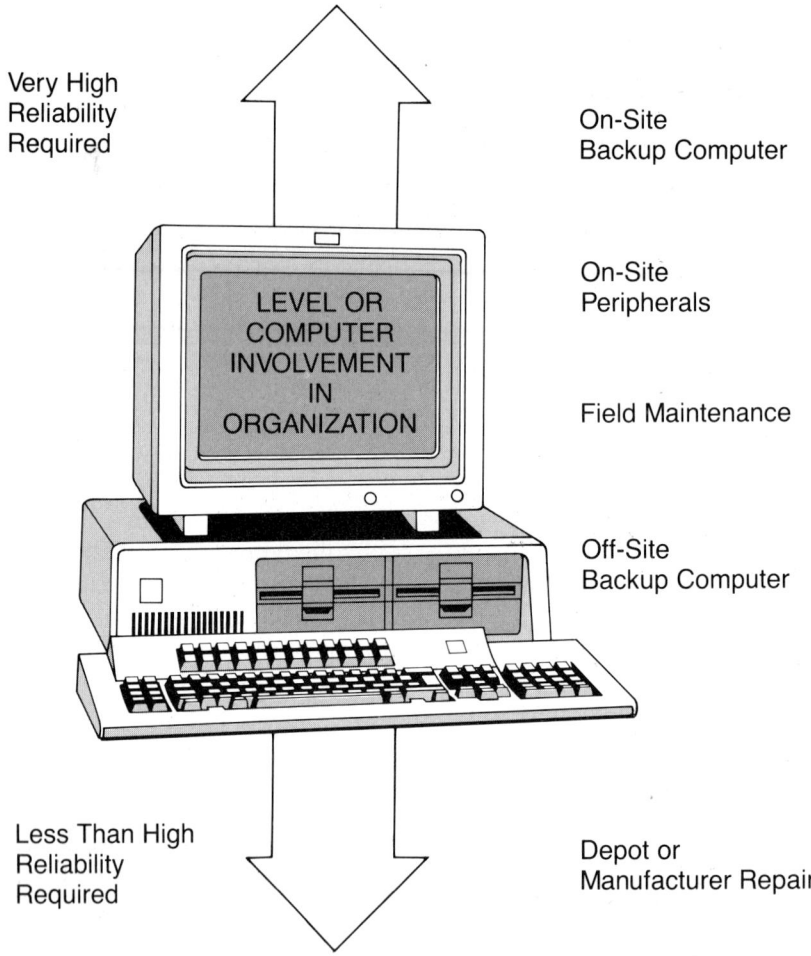

Very High
Reliability
Required

Less Than High
Reliability
Required

On-Site
Backup Computer

On-Site
Peripherals

Field Maintenance

Off-Site
Backup Computer

Depot or
Manufacturer Repair

LEVEL OR
COMPUTER
INVOLVEMENT
IN
ORGANIZATION

Figure 9-3   Level of Hardware Maintenance

of backup works best when both firms are near each other, are in non-competing businesses, and have nearly the same computer configurations and operating systems. This form of backup can also be provided by your dealer. You might ask to use the dealer's demo machine or some other system he has set up for this purpose. Off-site backup is another good reason for making backup diskettes, which are portable from one computer site to another.

The last and least expensive alternative is carry-in dealer or manufacturer repair. You simply pack up your ailing computer and take it in to a repair depot like you would a toaster or television set. While this is the lowest-cost option, it's also the slowest turnaround, which can be anywhere from a few days to a few weeks. You may find a repair service that rents or loans a replacement until yours can be returned. If so, this arrangement can be the next best thing to the first choice of the on-site backup computer.

CHAPTER
10

The Computer as an Investment

You're probably considering buying a computer because you believe it can save you money. Certainly the most compelling reason for doing so is simply that it is profitable. Reducing operating costs, increasing productivity, and improving management decision information will contribute to your firm's financial vitality. These tangible and intangible benefits were discussed extensively in Chapter 2, but some issues remain:

- How do the tangible benefits translate into total dollar savings?
- When does the computer pay for itself?
- What are the after-tax costs of the system?

This chapter answers these questions by calculating the benefits that can be measured in dollars. The two sections here show how to estimate the total dollar savings of the tangible benefits and the after-tax savings of the computer installation. Thus, this chapter provides an investment point of view on your computer purchase.

The examples in this chapter only suggest a possible cost/benefit analysis and are not intended to serve as final investment advice. Obviously each computer purchase has its own variables and circumstances. You should review your situation with your tax attorney or CPA to gauge the validity of your computer investment.

Case Investment: Sampson Electric, Inc.

A hypothetical firm, Sampson Electric, is used as an example with the following background information:

Annual Sales	$4,500,000
Product	Solenoids
Employees	28
Current System	Manual
Inventory Value	$400,000

Sampson Electric is seriously considering the purchase of a multi-user computer system. Briefly, they need a computer with three work stations, 384K of main memory, a twenty megabyte hard disk, and a letter quality printer. The hardware costs total $18,190. (Refer to System C in Figure 11-2 for configuration details.) Sampson Electric will also require word processing and accounting software, and a number of dealer services upon installation. The software costs are $3,990 and the dealer services amount to $4,170. (See System C in Figure 11-4 for details.)

Additional costs are anticipated for legal and consulting fees ($2,000), electrical contracting for a separate power line ($450), and computer furniture ($1,200) for a total "other" cost of $3,650. All of these items are included in the one-time purchase cost summary below.

The recurring cost for hardware maintenance of $275 per month is $3,300 a year, except that the three-month warranty applies the first year, for a lesser charge of $2,475. (See "Maintenance Contracts," System C, Chapter 11.) Special computer paper stock runs $450, and insurance is $255, which makes up the $705 total annual operating cost. (See "Operating Costs," Chapter 11.) All these figures are included in the system recurring costs below.

Thus, the system expenses for the first year are summarized as follows (Note: This section of the analysis assumes full cash payment for the system. The financing aspects are included in the last section of this chapter):

One-Time Purchase:

Hardware	$18,190
Software	3,990
Services	4,170
Other	3,650

Recurring Costs:

Hardware Maint.	$ 2,475
Software Maint.	—
Operating Costs	705
TOTAL SYSTEM COST	$33,180

The next section will show that Sampson can indeed save $11,120 over the total system cost by the end of the first year of operation. (Total first year savings of $44,300 minus total system cost of $33,180 equals $11,120.) Briefly, this is accomplished by improved controls in the accounting functions, and a reduction of operating expenses.

Also, the total system cost is well within the 1 percent rule, which is: The total annual system cost should not exceed 1 percent of the firm's gross income. By this rule, Sampson could spend up to $45,000 a year. (See "One Percent Rule," Chapter 4.)

TANGIBLE COST SAVINGS

Four distinct areas of tangible cost savings for Sampson Electric will be shown here. They are: accounts receivable, inventory control, accounts payable, and selected operating expenses. Because these areas were explained in Chapter 2, they will only briefly be mentioned here. (See "Reduce Operating Costs," Chapter 2.) The resulting savings in each of the four areas are summarized at the end of this section.

Accounts Receivables

One of the largest potential savings for Sampson Electric is lowering the amount of outstanding receivables. This is achieved by reducing the collection period. The computer is expected to speed up the invoicing operation and provide better control over past-due accounts, thus cutting the collection period by an estimated seven days. Sampson has an average of $924,800 in outstanding receivables, which take an average of 75 days to collect. The annual cost of borrowing $924,800 at 15 percent interest is $138,720. This seven-day reduction saves an annual interest charge of $12,940 (7/75 = 9.3% × $138,720 = $12,940).

By better tracking of delinquent accounts, Sampson can expect some savings in reducing bad debts. Some businesses have achieved cutting such losses by 20 to 50 percent. Sampson currently averages $27,000 a year in bad debts and has estimated recovering 15 percent by computerizing, thus resulting in a savings of $4,050.

Another area of potential savings (or income) in accounts receivable is applying a finance charge on past due accounts, which Sampson has never done. Even though they expect to reduce the collection period, some customers will remain delinquent. In this case, the average collection period will be cut to sixty-eight days, and with terms of net thirty, thirty-eight days of sales are overdue. The income here would amount to thirty-eight times Sampson's average daily balance, times the finance charge. Therefore, thirty-eight days overdue times $12,330 average daily sales times 12% finance charge equals $56,220 annual income. If only 6 percent of the delinquent customers pay the finance charge it would amount to $3,510 a year.

Inventory

Improved inventory control is another area of potential large savings for Sampson Electric. The computer is expected to help reduce inventory overhead and improve sales in several ways.

Slow Moving Items.   Money can be saved by pinpointing the slow-selling stock and eliminating it from inventory. This reduces inventory overhead costs. Additional savings are made by not continuing the purchase of these items once they are known.

Lost Sales.   Inventory shortages mean lost profits. More sales can be achieved by improved restocking of frequently depleted products. Thus, the computer helps avoid out-of-stock conditions by tracking items that should be continually inventoried.

Best-Sellers.   Profits can be increased by better tracking of high margin, high turnover inventory items. Also, Sampson can expect to identify market trends and customer buying habits more accurately than before.

Many variables of inventory prices, gross margins, handling costs, and inventory turnover can be used in determining the total potential inventory savings by using a computer. Many businesspeople, however, have an intuitive feeling for what percentage of their inventory value can be saved. It's been heard, "If I had current inventory figures, I know I could save 20 percent." At least rough estimates can be made by comparisons with other companies in the same industry.

Sampson Electric already has good controls on their inventory, but believes an additional 4 percent savings could be achieved. Thus, an inventory of $400,000 would result in an estimated savings of $16,000.

Accounts Payable

Computerized payables indicates how much is owed suppliers. It helps decide who to pay, when, and how much, based on financial conditions.

Sampson Electric expects to save money by taking greater advantage of vendors' payment discounts. Their payables average $35,000 a month, and half the suppliers offer a 2 percent discount for prompt payment. This would result in a savings of $350 per month or a total of $4,200 a year ($35,000 payables/mo. × 50% offered × 2% discount = $350/mo., or $4,200 cash savings/year).

Operating Expenses

Savings in the accounting functions is not, of course, the only source of cutting costs and improving revenues. Many firms have operating expenses in their business that can be minimized or eliminated by installing a computer. Some examples:

Bookkeeping Fees	Outside Service Bureau
Plant Overtime	CPA, Auditing Fees
Office Overtime	Collection Agency Fees
Temporary Help	Direct Mail Services

Sampson Electric figures it can save on auditing fees, temporary clerical help during physical inventory, and direct mailing services (by using the word processing program). Totalled, these estimated out-of-pocket costs come to $300 per month or $3,600 a year.

Total Net Savings

Let's recap the estimated annual savings in summary form. Remember, the figures here represent only the first year savings and computer expenditures:

Accounts Receivable:	
Shorten Collection Period	$12,940
Reduce Bad Debts	4,050
Apply Finance Charges	3,510
Inventory Control:	
Reduce Inventory	
Minimize Overhead	
Improve Sales	16,000
Accounts Payable:	
Vendor Discounts	4,200
Operating Expenses:	
Reduce Services	3,600
Total Savings	$44,300
System Cost	33,180
NET SAVINGS	$11,120

For many firms, these accounting functions and expense items can yield direct cash savings when converting from a manual system to a computer. Other areas can have cost-saving potential as well, such as eliminating outside data processing services, minimizing new staff hires, and adding other accounting modules. These areas are covered in Chapter 2.

AFTER-TAX SAVINGS

The foregoing showed that the computer system could pay for itself in less than a year. This section analyzes the system cost and the effect of income taxes over a five-year period. Extending the analysis over the expected life of the computer will reveal the true costs of ownership. It will be demonstrated that the average monthly cost is $495, and the overall savings is approximately 55 percent of the total amount invested.

This analysis is based on a number of factors, all of which are variable and subject to change. For instance, the system can be leased instead of financed by borrowing as shown here. (See "Rent, Lease, or Buy?" in Chapter 11.) Also, interest rates can change, the down payment can be larger, and certainly the system cost will be different for each buyer. In addition, other methods of depreciation could be used, such as straight-line or declining balance, instead of the ACRS method used here.

It's known that even the IRS tax laws change from time to time. For example, now you can deduct up to $5,000 of your purchase as a business expense instead of using the investment tax credit or depreciation. By 1986, this provision will be increased to $10,000. Because of these changes you should review your situation with your tax attorney or CPA.

A few notations about the factors used here should be helpful. First, the Accelerated Cost Recovery System (ACRS, part of an IRS law passed in August 1981), allows a faster depreciation write-off for capital equipment including computers. ACRS permits 15 percent depreciation the first year the computer is placed in service, 22 percent the second year, and 21 percent for each of the remaining three years. Thus, the system can be fully depreciated in five years. The ACRS depreciation here is based on a system cost of $30,000, which includes the software.

Second, the Investment Tax Credit (ITC) of 10 per cent is allowed on new or used equipment the year it is placed in service. This is a direct reduction of the tax liability. It also is based on the $30,000 system cost, and is applied only in the first year as Figure 10-1 shows. In this case, the ITC has the advantage over the $5,000 expense deduction mentioned earlier.

Third, as indicated earlier, the hardware maintenance is $275 per month, but shows a lesser amount the first year due to the first three months under manufacturer warranty when no charge is incurred. Also, the effect of any state or county sales tax is not included in this analysis.

Five-Year System Cost and Tax Analysis

	Year 1	Year 2	Year 3	Year 4	Year 5	Total
Cash Payments						
Down Payment	$ 3,000	$ —	$ —	$ —	$ —	$ 3,000
Principal	3,920	4,550	5,284	6,129	7,117	27,000
Interest	3,784	3,154	2,420	1,575	587	11,520
Hardware Maintenance	2,475	3,300	3,300	3,300	3,300	15,675
Software Maintenance	—	1,000	1,000	1,000	1,000	4,000
Other Expenses	705	700	1,200	800	900	4,305
Total	$13,884	$12,704	$13,204	$12,804	$12,904	$65,500
Tax Deductions						
Depreciation	$ 4,500	$ 6,600	$ 6,300	$ 6,300	$ 6,300	$30,000
Interest	3,784	3,154	2,420	1,575	587	11,520
Hardware Maintenance	2,475	3,300	3,300	3,300	3,300	15,675
Software Maintenance	—	1,000	1,000	1,000	1,000	4,000
Other Expenses	705	700	1,200	800	900	4,305
Total	$11,464	$14,754	$14,220	$12,975	$12,087	$65,500
Taxed Savings						
Tax Credit	$3,000	$ —	$ —	$ —	$ —	$ 3,000
Federal	4,585	5,902	5,688	5,190	4,835	26,200
State	1,146	1,475	1,422	1,298	1,209	6,550
Total	$8,731	$7,377	$7,110	$6,488	$6,044	$35,750
Summary						
Cash Payment	$13,884	$12,704	$13,204	$12,804	$12,904	$65,500
Tax Savings	8,731	7,377	7,110	6,488	6,044	35,750
True Cost/Year	$ 5,153	$ 5,327	$ 6,094	$ 6,316	$ 6,860	$29,750
True Cost/Month	$ 429	$ 444	$ 508	$ 526	$ 572	

Figure 10-1   Five-Year System Cost and Tax Analysis

The following factors are used for the System Cost and Tax Analysis (Figure 10-1) for Sampson Electric:

Investment:
Total System Cost	$33,180
Less Recurring Costs	3,180
Investment Amount	$30,000

Financing:
Down Payment	$ 3,000
Amount Financed	27,000
Months Financed	60
Interest Rate	15%
Monthly Payments	$ 642

State Tax Bracket	10%
Federal Tax Bracket	40%
Depreciation Method	ACRS
Residual Value	-0-
Investment Credit	10%

CHAPTER
11

What Does It Cost?

If you pay much attention to the advertising splash by manufacturers from Radio Shack to IBM, you've heard that small computers cost anywhere from $300 to $30,000. In spite of this price range, almost all claim to be "business computers." Treat this claim with some skepticism.

The question remains: How much should you pay for a bona fide business computer? This chapter provides some cost guidelines for hardware, software, and other important aspects of your purchase.

To begin, a few quick rules: First, no home computers. These small computers cost as little as a few hundred dollars, but they are not designed

206 Manager's Guide to Small Computers

for a business environment. Second, no "just announced" computers. The prospect of buying the latest technological innovation may be tempting, but state-of-the-art equipment may not be the best value for your business, nor the most reliable. Third, hold your expenditure within the 1 percent rule from Chapter 4: "The total annual system cost should not exceed 1 percent of your firm's gross income." The annual system cost includes the hardware and software purchases amortized over five years, plus annual maintenance cost. With the capabilities and prices of current small business computers, it should be easy for you to stay within the 1 percent guideline.

Your total system cost depends on many variables. The main ones are what you want the computer to do versus what is on the market at what price. Nearly everyone assumes the computer hardware will be the largest portion of the total system cost. Some people expect it to be the *only* system cost. In fact, the list price of the hardware is only the beginning of the system purchase. Commonly, the hardware is less than 30 percent of all costs during its useful life. Other costs, such as software packages, program modifications, field maintenance, and dealer support services, can well exceed the cost of the hardware over time, especially if the system is used for general accounting purposes.

Before you complete your purchase, work out a budget for the system's entire lifespan. Even though the figures will no doubt change, the budget will help you decide if you can truly afford the system after its initial purchase. Estimating total costs from the beginning helps you avoid cash flow problems. Also, you should always anticipate software changes or new programs to be added during the life of the system. Even with the shrewdest, most careful planning, you will invariably need to change computer programs to fit new business circumstances.

For example, one company installed a well-designed computerized solution to an inventory control problem. The computer kept better-than-before records on inventory issues and receipts, and gave accurate, up-to-the-minute inventory status. Soon customer service improved and orders increased. Unfortunately, customers also took for granted the accuracy and delivery of the new computerized system, began relying on its prompt service, and eventually placed orders less frequently. The computer installation was so successful it had a negative effect on the buying habits of the company's customers. For all its sound planning, management still had to make adjustments after the installation.

Other conditions, external to any company, can also force management to buy new software or modify the old. Unforeseen events, such as mergers and acquisitions or new government regulations, can require substantial software changes. One commonly changing variable, for example, is payroll withholding tax tables.

In estimating the useful life of the computer, some businesspeople

---

System Cost Considerations

Purchase Costs	*Recurring Costs*
Hardware	*Hardware Maintenance*
Central Processing Unit (CPU)	On-Site Maintenance
Floppy Disk Drives	Carry-in Repairs
Hard Disk Drives	Equipment Rentals
Work Stations (Terminals)	
Printers	
Communications (Modems)	
Software	*Software Maintenance*
Application Software	Software Modifications
Operating System Software	Software Updates
Dealer Services	*Operating Costs*
Systems Analysis	Computer Supplies
System Integration	Diskettes
Computer Installation	Printer Paper
Staff Training	Printer Ribbons
Program Modifications	Printed Forms
Data Conversion	Telephones
Other Costs	Insurance Premiums
Consultants' Fees	Interest Expense
Lawyers' Fees	Staff Re-Training
Financing Charges	
Site Preparation:	
Surge Protectors	
Electrical Work	
Computer Furniture	
Telephones	
Security	
Pre-Printed Forms Master	
Freight, Sales Tax	

Figure 11-1   System Cost Considerations

---

believe it will last forever. Or that the owner will later recover a major portion of the purchase price by selling it as a used product. Both notions are unrealistic, given the nature of the technology and how the computer industry operates. Generally, a computer system gives a worthwhile return on the investment for three to seven years. If the equipment has not then worn out, it will be out-of-date and perhaps unrepairable. Maintenance on the machine may become too expensive and spare parts will probably be difficult to find. For these reasons, a five-year-old computer has little resale value. Therefore, the financial amortization of the system and the budgeting for new, replacement equipment should be within this range.

This chapter does not tell you exactly what your computer system will cost, but it does show you what to expect. The list in Figure 11-1 shows typical cost considerations for buying and maintaining the system.

Use the list to decide which items apply to you. This chapter will also help you understand some of the differences between more- and less-expensive computer systems. Its main purpose, though, is to help you develop realistic cost expectations. First-time buyers often have financial trouble when they invoke the new computer technology, because they do not know what to expect.

The next section of this chapter deals with the costs of the computer purchase, followed by another on the system recurring or on-going costs. The last two sections address the questions: Should you rent, lease, or buy? and Should you buy the technology available now, or wait for new developments later?

SYSTEM PURCHASE COSTS

This section deals with all the one-time costs at the time of purchase. These include hardware, software, dealer services, and other, or "hidden," costs. Example prices provided are industry figures for the year 1984.

Hardware

As part of any system, hardware costs usually come to mind first in pricing a computer. Generally, the hardware is the major portion of the initial purchase. People often wonder what they get if they spend more money. What is the difference between a $3,000 computer and one costing $12,000? All computers function largely the same, but a higher-priced system typically offers higher performance and more features. Computers parallel many consumer items, such as television sets, stereos, and videotape recorders, in that lower-priced units provide the basic functions, while higher-priced units offer features that extend the product's utility. The list below shows some of the features that add to the cost of any basic computer system while increasing its usefulness.

> MAIN PROCESSING UNIT
> > Dual Processors
> > Larger Main Memory
> > Internal Expansion Slots
> > Extra Peripheral Connectors or Ports
> > Hard Disk Connector or Port
> > Multi-user or Networking Capability
> PERIPHERALS
> > Larger Floppy Disk Capacity
> > Multi-color Video Display
> > High-Resolution Graphics Display
> > Letter Quality Printer
> > Higher-Speed Printer
> > Hard Disk Drive

Hardware Purchase Examples

System A: Single User Computer

8-Bit Processor Chip
64K Bytes Main Memory
Dual 5-1/4″ Floppy Disk Drives
    (320K Bytes Storage per Drive)
12″ Monochrome Video Screen
    (80 Columns Wide × 24 Lines)
Detachable Keyboard
1 Serial Connector for Printer
Printer Hook-up Cable
1 Serial Connector for Modem
CP/M Operating System Software....................................$2,495.00
Dot Matrix Printer, Serial Connector
    (80 Columns Wide, 160 Char/Sec)................................ 830.00

                                System A Total $3,325.00

System B: Single User Computer

16-Bit Processor Chip
256K Bytes Main Memory
Dual 5-1/4″ Floppy Disk Drives
    (400K Bytes Storage per Drive)
13″ Color Video Screen
    (80 Columns Wide × 24 Lines)
Detachable Keyboard
1 Serial Connector for Modem
1 Parallel Connector for Printer
Printer Hook-up Cable
Color Graphics Capability
5 Internal Expansion Slots
MS-DOS Operating System Software....................................$3,495.00
Full Character Printer, Parallel Connector
    (132 Columns Wide, 55 Char/Sec)................................ 3,195.00

                                System B Total $6,690.00

System C: Three Terminal Multi-User Computer

8- and 16-Bit Processor Chips
384K Bytes Main Memory
Dual 8″ Floppy Disk Drives
    (1200K Bytes Storage Per Drive)
3 Video Work Stations Each With:
    12″ Monochrome Screen Display
    80 Columns Wide × 24 Lines
    Detachable Keyboard
    Terminal/Printer Hookup Cables
9 Serial Connectors for Peripherals
12 Internal Expansion Slots
MP/M Multi-User Operating System....................................$11,500.00
Hard Disk Sub-System (20 Million Bytes)...............................3,495.00
Full Character Printer, Serial Connector
    (132 Columns Wide, 55 Char/Sec)................................ 3,195.00

                                System C Total $18,190.00

Figure 11-2   Hardware Purchase Examples

To help illustrate the costs of a computer, Figure 11-2 shows three sample systems. They provide a cross section of typical microcomputer hardware purchases. All may be used in a business environment, but each for a different purpose. The cost of the operating system (system software) is shown here, since it is usually included with the hardware purchase. (Application software and other costs are shown in Figure 11-4.)

System A in the figure is a basic single user computer for word processing, financial planning with an electronic spreadsheet program, and a single accounting function, accounts receivable. The system is meant for a very small business in which a dot matrix printer is sufficient, thus keeping costs low.

System B is also a single user computer. Five major differences justify doubling the price over System A. System B uses a more powerful sixteen-bit processor chip, whereas System A has the traditional eight-bit chip. System B also has 256K bytes of main memory, four times that of System A. System B also has color graphics and internal expansion slots by which to add more memory and other capabilities. Finally, for word processing it comes with a high-quality, high-speed, full-character printer. Together these account for the major difference in the price over System A.

Neither of these first two systems can be converted into a multi-user system. However, both A and B can be used for data communications, and System B has provisions for networking.

System C is a multi-user computer with three work stations. It also comes with both the eight- and sixteen-bit processor chips, which greatly extends its versatility. It is not limited to one group of software packages, but runs both eight-bit and sixteen-bit software with no hardware changes. Its 384K bytes of main memory is substantially larger than system B. Although it has no multi-color or graphics capabilities, it does have twelve internal expansion slots for future use. It also comes with a hard disk, which holds 20 million bytes of characters, or about sixteen times as much as the 8-inch floppy disks attached to the system.

Although it has the same high-quality, full character printer as System B, System C can accept a second printer, which saves other users from having to wait for the main printer when it's busy. System C is a true multi-user business computer as described in this book. This system is configured primarily for accounting functions but also can be used for word processing and data communications.

When pricing a computer system, you face a number of choices on hardware features and capabilities. When given a choice, what options do most buyers usually take? Most select the following three features for their first computer purchase.

First, dual disk drives. You should have two disk drives, at least one of which uses removable media. Aside from capacities, it doesn't matter whether they are $5\frac{1}{4}$-inch or 8-inch, or even a combination of one or the other with a hard disk. What matters is that you are able to copy from one disk drive to another to make backup diskettes. Also, a second drive allows you to separate the program disk in one drive from the data files in the other, which makes operation easier.

Second, for visual ease and operator comfort almost all buyers choose the larger video screen, measuring either twelve or fourteen inches. The majority of terminals sold also have keyboards that are detachable from the screen enclosure, which is another user convenience.

Third, if the computer system is to be used for medium to heavy word processing, a heavy-duty printer capable of using all the word processing features has proven to be a popular choice.

Software

Applications software packages can make up as much as 30 per cent of the initial system cost. Compared to custom software, packaged software for microcomputers is a bargain. Customized software can cost from $10,000 to $75,000, while packaged software with many of the same capabilities (or more) costs from $200 to $3,500. The majority of application packages available for word processing, spreadsheets, and data base systems cost $200 to $700 each. The relatively low cost for a sophisticated software package is achieved through wide distribution in the marketplace.

Figure 11-3 shows the price ranges for the popular types of application software. These prices are for the basic package and do not include supplemental packages, like spelling checking or grammatical correction for word processing, which may cost almost as much as the initial package itself.

The general price range for accounting software is $400 to $1,200 per module, which is a single function such as accounts receivable or inventory. Many software suppliers and dealers offer price discounts when you buy more than one module at a time. These prices do not normally include any dealer service, such as installation and training.

Figure 11-3 also shows the general price ranges for computers and peripherals. The computers here are the all-in-one type, which means the video screen, the disk drives (typically $5\text{-}\frac{1}{4}$ inch, holding 300 to 400K bytes of information), and the keyboard are sold as one unit. The video screens in these systems are usually twelve-inch, single color display.

Dealer Services

Dealer services can amount to 20 percent of the total system purchase and are a significant consideration. Higher costs apply when the system is used primarily for accounting. The services mentioned here play such an important role that they are discussed further in Chapter 9, "Level of Required Maintenance"; Chapter 12, Section VII, "Vendor Services"; Chapter

System Component Price Ranges	
All-In-One Computers	
8-Bit CPU—64K Memory	$1,800 – $3,000
16-Bit CPU—128K Memory	2,500 – 3,800
16-Bit CPU—256K Memory	3,200 – 4,500
Disk Storage Devices	
Dual 5-1/4″ Floppy Disk Drives	$ 700 – $1,200
Dual 8″ Floppy Disk Drives	1,200 – 2,200
Hard Disk—5 MB	1,800 – 2,500
Hard Disk—10 MB	2,500 – 3,200
Hard Disk—20 MB	3,200 – 4,500
Work Stations (Terminals)	$ 500 – $1,200
Printers	
Dot Matrix (80—160 cps)	$ 350 – $1,000
Dot Matrix (120—240 cps)	850 – 2,200
Letter Quality (12—35 cps)	900 – 1,600
Letter Quality (35—80 cps)	1,800 – 3,500
Data Communications	
Modem—300 Baud	$ 125 – $ 300
Modem—300/1200 Baud	450 – 800
Application Software Packages	
Word Processing	$ 250 – $ 500
Electronic Spreadhseets	200 – 500
Data Base Management	300 – 700
Accounting (per Module)	300 – 1,200
Communications Software	80 – 200

Figure 11-3   System Component Price Ranges

14, "Selecting a Vendor"; and Chapter 17, "Hardware and Software Installation." The following is a description of the six basic services a dealer may offer.

Systems Analysis.   Systems analysis is a small-scale study to find the best computer system to solve the problem. It is a detailed effort to match hardware and software to the application. In some cases a technical person does the study, but more often it is joint effort with the salesperson. The result of this study is usually a written set of specifications, or a request for proposal as described in Chapter 12. Systems analysis takes from a few hours to a few days, depending on the complexity of the problem. Hourly rates for systems analysis can be as much as $75, although you can expect an estimate of the total cost in advance.

System Integration.   System integration is the dealer's preparation of the computer just before delivery. It includes assembling, testing, and connecting mixed brand-name components such as printers and hard disk drives. It is similar in concept to automobile dealer preparation.

Installation.   The physical installation of the system is another important dealer service, since few businesses are able to handle it themselves. Installation normally includes delivery of the equipment, setting it up, testing the system, and installing the application software packages. The first-time buyer is better off paying to have the system professionally installed because the dealer bears all the responsibility. The cost of on-site installation by the dealer can vary from no charge when included with the system purchase to $200 or more. The cost also depends on such variables as the number of physical components to be installed and the work involved, such as laying cables for remote terminals. It may even include a mileage charge from the dealer's store to the installation site.

Training.   Your system purchase should include training for your staff and key operators. This training should include basic operation of the computer equipment as well as how to use the various applications programs. Training at your location can cost as much as $65 per hour, but dealers usually charge a flat sum for a fixed number of hours. A lower-cost option is to have your staff attend dealer seminars, which range in price from $10 to $35 per hour. Sometimes the training is included with the cost of the system. Even as an additional expense, training is usually a good value because it's an efficient way for your staff to begin using your system.

Program Modifications.   The cost of program modifications, such as making changes to the programming code in your accounting package, vary widely depending on what you want done. Only rarely can significant changes be made for less than a few hundred dollars. Extensive changes can cost several times the price of the original accounting module. For example, you can easily pay $3,000 for an accounting package and $8,000 for major changes. If you need this service, always ask for a written proposal describing the modifications and showing the costs.

Data Conversion.   This is the one-time task of transferring data from its present system (such as a manual set of books) into the new computer during installation. It involves at least several hours of keying in the required information, such as account balances or inventory part numbers and descriptions. Entering this data is normally a clerical-level operation. Some companies elect to pay their existing staff overtime for the work, while others choose to use temporary help. The true cost of the conversion is hard to estimate because it is difficult to know how long it will take. Yet rough estimates are better than nothing, and this cost is often overlooked in installing the system. Other aspects of data conversion are explained in Chapter 17.

To sum up, all costs for dealer services are at best estimates, except for integration, installation, and initial training. All services should be specified in the vendor's proposals. The costs may be fixed if the proposal becomes a formal agreement. Figure 11-4 shows the cost of packaged

Total System Purchase Examples			
Computer System	**_A_**	**_B_**	**_C_**
Hardware			
Single User	$3,325	$6,690	
Multi-User			$18,190
Packaged Software			
Word Processing	495	495	695
Spreadsheet	275		
Data Base		695	495
Accounting	495		2,800
System Cost	$4,590	$7,880	$22,180
Dealer Services			
Systems Analysis		350	720
System Integration			150
Installation		75	125
Training/Seminars	190	365	1,400
Program Modifications			1,500
Data Conversion			275
Total	$4,780	$8,670	$26,350

Figure 11-4   Total System Purchase Examples

software and dealer services in addition to the hardware from the three earlier examples.

Other Costs

The purchase price for the hardware, software, and dealer services are normally paid directly to the vendor. The buyer often pays other fees for third-party services. For example, you may hire a consultant to do the initial systems analysis and oversee the installation. A consultant should provide you with an overall estimate for his work. Time is billed hourly or daily, and may range from $150 to $500 per day. You may also want to hire a lawyer to assess the legality and fairness of the contracts between you and the vendor. Normally this involves only a few hours work, but may still cost several hundred dollars.

Site preparation can involve a number of items often referred to as the "hidden" costs of the system. These can include accessories, such as electrical power surge protectors, line conditioners, and extra-long hookup cables for the computer peripherals. You may want special computer furniture to reduce worker fatigue and provide a pleasant work setting. The site may be improved with specially placed sound absorption materials and extra telephones for the operator convenience. The existing electrical power may be unsuitable for the computer, requiring that you hire an electrical contractor to run a separate power line to the computer site. Planning and preparation for these items are discussed further in Chapter16.

Still other costs may include graphic design and typesetting of master forms for your firm's preprinted statements and invoices. A cost-saving alternative is to choose from a variety of stock invoice and statement forms offered by companies who specialize in producing continuous paper for computers. Also, an extra set of the system documentation or manuals may be helpful if more than one person needs them. Duplicate manuals also serve as loss protection. Other costs of the system purchase include special delivery handling, freight charges, special in-transit insurance, and sales taxes.

SYSTEM RECURRING COSTS

This section discusses recurring or on-going costs after the purchase. These include hardware and software maintenance, and operating expenses.

Hardware Maintenance

Because today's small business computers are built with solid-state electronic components, they are far more reliable than equipment built even a few years ago. In addition, computers are designed for easy service. Most of the electronic circuits in any computer are found on one, two, or three printed circuit boards that often can be replaced in a few minutes. In spite of the high reliability of the new computers, unexpected machine failures do occur. Maintenance statistics show that the components most prone to breakdown are disk drives and printers, because they have a higher proportion of moving mechanical parts.

Every computer owner has five basic maintenance and repair options. (Refer to Chapter 9 for more details.) Maintaining high reliability on-site requires either a second complete backup computer; spare, backup peripherals; or a field maintenance contract. The field maintenance can be either full-service (under contract), or a "call as needed" time and materials repair (no contract). Off-site maintenance options include having access to someone else's computer, or carry-in to the dealer or manufacturer for servicing. Only two of these options involve a contractual agreement: on-site field maintenance and off-site repair. In other words, you can have either on-site or off-site repairs under a fixed monthly fee agreement.

Maintenance Contracts

On-site field maintenance is probably the most worry-free arrangement. It stems from the level of service traditionally given to large, mainframe computer systems. Typically, for a minimum of twelve months you pay a fixed monthly charge. The service firm agrees to cover all costs for parts and labor for any servicing. Think of it as repair insurance, since your costs are the same whether the service firm makes four or forty calls to your office. Monthly fees for this level of service are typically 1 to 2 percent of the initial hardware cost. For example, a $10,000 computer system with $8,000 in hardware might carry a 1.5 percent service charge of $120 a month, or an annual cost of $1,440.

You may choose an on-site service contract at the time of purchase or any time after the installation. If you buy this service up-front, most vendors will give fifteen months service for the price of twelve. Here the dealer is tacking on the regular ninety-day warranty granted by the man-ufacturer, except that the manufacturer's warranty does not normally include *on-site* repairs. (Usually, for repairs during warranty you must return your computer to the dealer or the manufacturer.)

On-site maintenance during the warranty period is a definite advan-tage, since most hardware problems, if any, occur during this time. If you decide you want the field service contract *after* the computer is installed, you can expect to pay an equipment inspection fee of $35 to $100. With "used" equipment the service contractor will want to determine that the system is in good working order at the outset of the agreement.

The second type of service contract is much like the field maintenance agreement, with a fixed monthly charge, except that the work is done off-site. The owner must deliver the ailing computer to the repair depot, where the service contractor agrees to make all repairs regardless of actual costs. This arrangement should result in a lower-cost service, and the savings may outweigh the inconvenience of transporting your computer to the repair site. The main disadvantage is that the repair turnaround may be longer than for on-site service.

Almost all other repair work, not under contract, is charged on a time-and-material basis. Labor rates run from $50 to $95 per hour, usually with a one-hour minimum plus the cost of parts.

Using a rate of 1.5 percent of the original hardware cost for our three examples gives a monthly charge for on-site service for System A of $50 per month. System B costs $100 per month, and System C costs $275 per month. Service contracts have the strong advantage of assigning someone else the responsibility for maintaining the continuous operation of your system. The fixed cost contract also allows accurate budgeting for hard-ware maintenance since you won't have to contend with unexpected repair bills.

Maintenance Alternatives

For some people, having a maintenance contract brings a great sense of relief in dealing with complicated technology. For them the annual cost of a service contract is well worth the price in eliminating headaches caused by malfunctioning computers. Others feel the risk involved does not justify the cost of an annual contract, especially when given the alternatives. Sometimes a high level of reliability isn't important, and nearly the same level of service can be achieved at much lower cost. Let's look at two such alternatives.

One choice is to set aside funds in a special maintenance account. You might allocate it at the same rate you would otherwise pay for a maintenance contract. When problems occur, you have funds built up to pay for maintenance. Many users go two or three years with no problems, while others spend only a few hundred dollars per year for maintenance. With this alternative, *you* assume the risk and problems of machine downtime, and you may have to endure periods without the computer while it is being repaired. But if you have access to a local repair service that gives good turnaround, you may do as well compared to field maintenance service, and save a substantial sum by paying only for the repairs you actually need.

Still another alternative is to buy a second complete system that is configured the same as the first. If one system fails, the other is immediately available. You will never be without a working computer, since it is highly unlikely that both systems will fail at the same time. Because they are identical, the programs and data files of one can be transferred easily to the other. The idea of two systems may seem extravagant, yet with declining computer prices duplicate machines are practical and economical because of greater productivity and the savings on field maintenance costs.

For example, if you need a system with two or three work stations from the start, two or three identical stand-alone computers can be less expensive than one multi-user system. And the reliability is much greater. Compare the price of three stand-alone computers to one multi-user computer with three work stations. System C in Figure 11-2, for example, contains three terminals, a twenty-megabyte hard disk, and a letter-quality printer for $18,190. Combining the eight-bit, 64K single user computer, as shown in System A for $2,495, with the same printer shown in System C for $3,195, the price comes to $5,690 for each stand-alone computer.

The three separate computers equal the capability of the multi-user computer in System C, except for the hard disk. However, each of the three computers has its own high-quality printer. The total cost for the three computers is $17,070, which is $1,120 less than the total for System C. With the three computers providing backup for each other, you could easily forego the field maintenance contract on System C, saving $275 per month, or $3,300 per year. Thus, the savings in the hardware cost added to the field maintenance contract for the first year comes to $4,420. The total savings would be reduced by any repair costs on the three systems.

This three-system arrangement is practical for a secretarial service, for example, where the users create data files independently of each other. With an accounting setup, however, each user must share files and other information with other users. A networking system may be an alternative then, since each user has the connections that allow sharing of files between the CPUs. Be aware, however, that the foregoing comparison yields a cost advantage for separate computers up to about three terminals. At four terminals and beyond, a trade-off point is reached at which the cost per work station is generally less for a multi-user computer.

Software Maintenance

Software maintenance can be defined as the general improvement or refinement of computer programs over time. These can be applied to any of the programs used in the computer: application programs, the operating system, or even programming languages.

For example, one type of improvement keeps the programs in step with new requirements in your business. No specific cost figures are possible here, since these changes depend entirely on what you deem necessary. Sometimes you can make these changes without much expense if the facility for making them is already built into the programs. On the other hand, "hard" changes in the program source code require a programmer, whose hourly rates can start at $35. When you are certain you need program modifications, ask your vendor to give you a written estimate of the cost. A good way to save time and money here is to group a number of small changes as though they were one major project.

The other type of software improvement is an update made by software developers to enhance their products. Almost every supplier periodically offers new versions of their application package. These normally do not change the basic functions of the software but simply provide additional features. They may make the package easier to use, or add more capabilities. New versions are usually offered as an option for a nominal charge. For example, when one buys version 3.0 of a software package for $500, a year later the supplier may offer version 3.5 to registered licensees for only $75. These updates, normally found with the most popular application packages, add value to the product.

Operating Costs

The monthly hardware operating costs of microcomputers are almost insignificant compared to large mainframe computers. When a small business computer takes less electrical power than a 250-watt light bulb, the increase in the utility bill is hardly noticeable. The largest on-going hardware expense is probably for supplies. These include floppy diskettes, printer paper and ribbons, and the cost of printing special forms, such as invoices, statements, and payroll forms.

One often overlooked item is the annual insurance premium to cover the system. Like other business insurance, premiums vary with the value or replacement cost of your system, the age and condition of your building, and the fire protection in your area. It may also depend on whether you want to insure the value of the data and the programs stored on your diskettes.

RENT, LEASE, OR BUY?

The question of whether to rent, lease, or buy the equipment is certain to arise. The answer depends on your financial situation and how long you expect to use the system. Whatever you decide, you must know the specifics of financing *before* you order the equipment. To look for financing after you purchase the computer is to court problems or even disaster. For instance, if you obligate yourself to buy and then find that your lender insists on certain conditions to protect his investment, you could find yourself in a mess. This section describes the pros and cons of renting, leasing, and outright purchase, including borrowing the money.

Renting

In most major metropolitan areas you can rent computers much as with cars or televisions. Compared to leasing or buying, renting is probably the most flexible arrangement, since you determine the length of the rental period. It is also the most expensive.

Renting is practical for short-term projects, say less than a year. For example, a building contractor who needs a computer at the construction site for just a few months, or someone whose job is to evaluate software packages on a particular brand of machine are good candidates for renting.

Renting also makes sense when you want to test and evaluate a computer. Suppose you plan to buy several machines for word processing. Renting one machine for several weeks provides you with first-hand experience before committing to a major purchase of a number of machines. Renting is also a good temporary solution for maintaining usage continuity while your equipment is out for repairs. In this case the rental charges should be by the hour or the day until your equipment is returned.

When you rent equipment, the dealer assumes most of the risk in maintaining it. If the equipment malfunctions or fails, the renter can return it for another unit or end the agreement with no further cost or obligation. Compared to leasing or borrowing money for a purchase, a rental agreement is usually the easiest to terminate.

A typical monthly rental charge is 8 to 10 percent of the system's retail cost, sometimes with a minimum charge. For example, a customer who rents equipment for three months can expect to pay up to 30 percent of the original retail price. Sometimes a dealer will offer discounts to encourage longer rentals, such as a three-month rental at 10 percent off, or a six-month rental at 25 percent off.

You should expect to make a deposit on the equipment when renting. Some rental agencies ask for a 10 percent deposit, or one month's rental, refundable upon return. Others may take imprints of credit cards as security deposits. Some rental agreements offer an option to buy, allowing you to apply up to half the rental amount toward the purchase. This amount, however, can be in proportion to the term of the rental agreement. For example, if you decide to buy during the first month of a three-month contract, then the three-month fee can be credited toward the purchase.

Perhaps the two major disadvantages of renting computer equipment are limited selection and software exclusion. The brand names, speeds, and capacities of the equipment available for rent may not be your first choices. Also, renting software packages is not permitted under most software licensing agreements. Unless you already have the software that you plan to use, you will have to add its purchase cost to the rental fee.

Leasing

Leasing is a financial arrangement in which you pay a fixed monthly amount to a leasing company for a specified number of years. The common practice is for the buyer to choose a computer system and then arrange a contract with a leasing company, which then buys the equipment from the dealer. Here the leasing company (the lessor) becomes a third party to the original system purchase. The buyer (the lessee) then pays the leasing company a monthly fee according to the terms of the lease.

One strong advantage of leasing is that it does not require any money down, allowing you to have the computer without depleting your cash reserves. Thus, you can finance almost 100 percent of the total system cost, including the software. The only exception is that some leasing companies ask for partial payment in advance, such as the first and last payments. Only rarely do these first payments exceed 5 percent of the total lease amount.

The term of the lease can be from one to six years, depending on the total amount of the purchase and the buyer's preferred arrangement. But there are "thresholds." Leases up to a total system cost of $5,000 run up to thirty-six months. A system purchase costing between $5,000 and $25,000 may run for sixty months. The monthly fee depends on the cost of the system, prevailing interest rates, and the buyer's creditworthiness.

Leasing is a financing arrangement independent of banks. When you lease you do not draw down your line of credit at the bank, thus preserving your ability to borrow for other purposes. Also, unlike a rental agreement, a typical lease can include the software as well as the computer and its peripherals. Thus, the lease cost can cover an entire system.

Some leases allow for equipment exchanges at the lessee's choice. Also, with some leases you can add to the hardware configuration by modifying the lease, usually at a higher price. Often you can convert a lease to a purchase at any time by paying off the remaining balance.

Financing a lease is more expensive than financing a loan, since the interest rate charged is usually several points above the prime rate. Also, because leasing carries no down payment, the lessor assumes a higher risk than lenders who loan only 80–90 percent of the purchase price. There-fore, the long-term financing cost of leasing is greater than that of borrowing.

Because leasing involves a higher risk for the lessor, a lease can only be arranged when you have an excellent credit rating. Sometimes the lessor may ask you to submit a letter of guarantee from your bank before making any arrangements. The bank in turn may ask for a personal note signed by you for the amount of the guarantee. Or the bank may insist on the right to debit your company's account in the event of default.

Even if you're able to pay off the lease, you should understand the kind of commitment a lease demands. When you lease you do not have as much control as when you own the system. You are obligated to make all the payments regardless of what happens to the computer, or even to your business. Leases tend to be ironclad agreements, and may even call for stiff penalties for cancellation. As time passes, you may find yourself making lease payments on a computer system that is no longer adequate for you. Make sure your lease allows an "out," so that you can return the system to the vendor or leasing company if it is no longer functional.

Since the lessor assumes all the risks of system ownership, he usually requires that you have a service agreement or field maintenance contract. This, of course, adds to your out-of-pocket cost for using the system. Nonetheless, you may have some choice of who provides service and be able to shop around for the most economical agreement.

Look for a lease that provides an option to purchase at the end of its term, usually for 8–12 percent of the system's original price. A lease with this option is called a "full-payout" lease, and gives the advantages of both buying and leasing. With the option to purchase, the user can think of the lease term as building ownership equity. At the end of the lease you have a choice: you can keep the system or go on to something else. The buyer may also have the option of extending the lease beyond the original term at a lower percentage than for purchasing, usually around 5 percent.

One strong advantage of leasing is the extent of income tax deduc-tions. Under a lease, you may deduct the total annual payments, which usually results in a higher deduction than taking depreciation, interest, and other expenses under ownership. Depending on your tax bracket, the tax savings may reduce the actual cost of leasing by 30 to 50 percent. All things considered, this could be a significant savings. In addition to expen-sing the lease payments, you may also be able to take the investment tax credit, which can be arranged through your leasing firm at a slightly higher payment.

These tax advantages occur only under certain conditions. To deduct your lease payments, the lease must qualify under Internal Revenue Service rules (1955 Ruling No. 55-540) by having the following basic characteristics:

1. System ownership must remain with the lessor.

2. The rental rates charged must be competitive and represent payment for the use of the system.

3. The monthly lease payments must be approximately the same throughout the lease.

4. The purchase options must not be predetermined amounts but based on the fair market value at the end of the lease term.

5. The lease term must be less than 80 percent of the system's useful life.

6. The estimated fair market value at the end of the lease must be at least 10 percent of the system's original price.

System Acquisition Options	
Advantages	**Disadvantages**
Renting	
Best for Short Term	Highest Payments
No Financing Required	Software Not Included
Owner Assumes Risk	Requires Deposit
Rent Components As Needed	Minimal Support Provided
Charges May Apply Towards Purchase	Limited Equipment Selection
Leasing	
Finance 100% of Cost	Expensive Financing Costs
Maintain Line of Credit	Means Long Term Commitment
Option to Purchase	Lessor May Require Field Service
Builds Ownership Equity	Contract
Longer Term Than Loan	Stringent Qualification
Tax Benefits—Expense Lease Payments	
Purchase	
Owner Control of System	May Require Down Payment
Lowest Financing Costs	Reduces Cash Reserves
Easier Loan Qualification	Affects Cash Flow
Tax Benefits—Interest, Depreciation,	Affects Future Borrowing
and Investment Credit	Risks of Ownership
	Low Salvage Value

Figure 11-5   System Acquisition Options

If your lease does not meet all of these conditions, the agreement could be deemed a conditional sale rather than a lease. These rules are presented only as a guide, since the tax laws on leases and other deductions change from year to year. Check with your accountant or CPA for the latest information.

Purchase

One of the best reasons for buying your system outright is control of the computer. When you own your system you are free to make any changes you like, including the maintenance arrangement. Buying the system with cash also means no financing costs, and overall costs can be substantially lower than leasing or borrowing. Nor will you have to contend with the paperwork or the waiting period while your credit is checked. Since an outright purchase draws on your cash reserves, however, you may want to figure in the "opportunity cost," or the lost interest income.

Still, it may be best for you to borrow the money for your purchase from a bank or other financial source. This method allows you to keep ownership control while avoiding heavy capital outlays, and qualifying for a loan is usually easier than qualifying for a lease. When you borrow you can expect to make a down payment of up to 30 percent of the purchase price. You can also expect the term of the loan, typically three to five years, to be shorter than the term of a lease. Your monthly loan payments may thus work out to be nearly equal to the payments on a long-term lease. Borrowing not only affects your cash flow, it also affects your line of credit should you need to borrow again from the bank.

Borrowing to purchase has the tax advantages of allowing you to deduct the interest, depreciation, and other expenses, and take the investment tax credit. You can select from several methods of calculating depreciation, depending on the financial effect you want to create. For example, accelerated depreciation, which is allowed only with new computers, has the effect of conserving cash in the first years. If you want an even distribution of cash flow over the life of the computer, use the straight-line method of depreciation. IRS regulations allow depreciating the computer over three to seven years, depending on how it is used. Shorter lives are permitted, for example, where the computer is used in research and development. At the end of its depreciated life the computer may have only nominal salvage value, which is the current market price of the used capital asset.

You may have trouble securing a loan for a computer, since lenders have been slow to take small computers seriously as a business investment. The new business machines are not a traditional item on which banks and other institutions have gathered experience making loans. Bankers also recognize how fast the technology moves in this industry. A computer system used as collateral for a loan can lose its value before the loan is paid off. Because of these conditions, lenders may ask for a high-percentage down payment and a shorter loan term, perhaps two or three years. Due to the uncertain value of computer equipment, lenders may also place greater emphasis on the creditworthiness of the customer. Therefore, the bank may ask you to personally guarantee payment of the business loan or even make it a personal loan instead.

BUY NOW OR LATER?

Someone once said, "The one thing you can be certain of is change." That surely is true of the microcomputer industry. As you search for a system you will see a constant change of products in the market. New products are announced almost every day, while less-than-popular products are all but abandoned by their manufacturers. Sooner or later you will wonder: When is the best time to buy? Should I buy the computer now, or wait for the next advance in technology?

It is impossible to predict the future of electronic technology, except that products will continue to improve. The new technologies combined with higher production levels also mean prices will generally continue to drop, as they did with hand calculators and digital watches. Unlike calculators and watches, however, computers are highly dependent on software, which is labor-intensive. Thus, the continually rising cost of software development and maintenance will somewhat offset declining hardware prices.

You may postpone your computer purchase to wait for a "soon-to-be-released" computer that seems to offer greatly improved performance at a lower cost. This is "technological temptation." It is easy to reason that if you buy the latest computer on the market, then the obsolescence factor will be minimized and the product's working life will be maximized. Beware of the pitfalls in chasing the latest hardware on the market.

For example, one might be tempted to buy a newly arrived sixteen-bit computer rather than an eight-bit computer already established on the market. (See "Should You Buy An 8-Bit or 16-Bit Computer?", Chapter 8.) Consider that applications software is almost non-existent for computers with the newest microprocessor chips. Quite often a time lag exists between the introduction of new computer architecture and the availability of a full complement of application software.

Software developers need months (or even years) to develop packages for the newer computers. Even when a computer manufacturer claims to have application software for his newly-announced machine, it's likely to be only a conversion from an earlier machine's software, and will not necessarily take full advantage of the new machine's capabilities. In other words, eight-bit software converted to a sixteen-bit machine will run with no greater performance than it did on the eight-bit computer. For the best performance the software should be completely rewritten.

Further, computer products often carry higher prices when they are first introduced, because the manufacturer faces higher initial production costs and higher risk until the product has proven itself. Prices go down when the product becomes popular and production costs can be reduced through larger volumes. Also, competitive pressures bring prices down. Therefore, you are likely to pay more for a computer when it's just introduced than after it has been on the market a while. Given all this you may wonder why manufacturers put hardware products on the market with little available software. They do it because they know that among the first to buy will be software developers eager to profit from filling the software needs of a waiting public.

You may avoid these problems by considering only computers that have been on the market for a while, say a year or more. Customer feedback from the early buyers tells the manufacturer what improvements are needed. It's often a better deal to pay a lower price for an established computer that's been tested through actual use.

Also, remember the theme of this book: Software is more important than hardware. Your system performs best with software written to take full advantage of the machine's features. Also, for a *business* computer it does not make sense to buy hardware that runs only a limited selection of software.

When considering a computer for business purposes, give preference to products, both hardware and software, that have been available for at least a few months. A year or more is even better. Sometimes two years pass before outstanding software is available for computers with newly-designed microprocessor chips.

Adopt a wait-and-see attitude. Holding off gives you time to check the product's general acceptance and greatly increases your chances of buying a worthwhile product. Some products that look terrific in the press release do not sell as well as expected. Other products continue to sell well even with some out-of-date features. The market eventually determines the validity of the manufacturer's claims.

In addition to market acceptance, you should also check the computer industry's response to the product. Are smaller companies developing products to "ride the coatails" of the bigger company's product? For example, the IBM Personal Computer accepts a number of expansion boards and peripherals developed and sold by other manufacturers exclusively for it. Buyers of WordStar, a popular word processing package, can choose among a number of supplementary software packages written by independent software companies that work only with WordStar. These include programs for spelling checking, syntax correction, footnoting, indexing and true proportional spacing. In other words, it's a good sign of product acceptance, and better return on your investment, when others in the computer industry create products to be used with it.

In conclusion, buying now is usually a safe bet if the savings and benefits for your situation outweigh the purchase price (see Chapter 10). When the tangible and intangible benefits offset the cost of the system, even though the equipment is less than state-of-the-art, then it's a good investment. If the computer system does the job you want and promises to meet your anticipated requirements for the next few years, the obsolescence factor is not a serious problem.

CHAPTER
12

Written Requirements

By this time you have sorted through the myriad programs in the marketplace and have decided on an application software package. You have found the computer with the features you think will work best for your situation. You have computed the costs, analyzed the investment values, and even determined the expected benefits of the system.

Thus, you may feel ready to pick up the phone and order the system. Don't. Here is where many business people make a mistake. Even if you are confident in your choice of the hardware, software, and services, don't buy *anything* until you have specified the terms under which you are willing to make the purchase. Also, you need to arrange what you have learned into a meaningful statement—in writing—of your requirements. A written statement is essential because it articulates your thinking and helps clarify possible solutions. For these and many other reasons described in this chapter, a written statement, called a Request For Proposal (RFP), is strongly recommended.

Here are the four most common oversights about written requirements:

1. **No Systematic Comparison.**   An objective comparison of systems is difficult but essential. As suggested in this book, when buying a computer you face an overwhelming number of choices in the marketplace. The big decision to buy or not can be made up of hundreds of smaller decisions on costs, features, and capabilities. Without something in writing you will struggle to sort out the strong and weak points of the systems you are attempting to compare. A simple RFP statement eases this step.

2. **Inadequate Buyer Protection.**   Without something in writing, you are vulnerable to legal problems. In the absence of an agreement, federal and state laws may protect the buyer somewhat. However, with the complexities of buying a computer system, legal and otherwise, these laws do not provide nearly enough safeguards. A simple agreement written in plain English can go a long way to help protect you against the failure of hardware, software, or other circumstances surrounding the purchase of the system.

3. **Substituting Presentations.**   To some managers bringing in vendors for individual presentations may seem like a thorough approach. But each vendor will base his presentation on what he perceives as the solution to your business problem, with some fancy guesswork at best. Unless the vendor has spent a lot of time with you and your staff, he can only assess your requirements from a narrow point of view. Thus, a series of vendor "dog and pony shows" is not an objective way to buy a system. A better procedure here is to ask for face-to-face presentations after the RFP has been properly executed.

4. **Delegating the Task.**   Another common mistake is delegating the entire task of producing an RFP to lower levels of management. The RFP does not describe the bits and bytes of the computer, nor is it a set of specifications that only an electronic engineer can understand. It is a high-level document and should be constructed only by top management, especially since it describes a system that supports your firm's accounting operation.

WHAT IS AN RFP?

A formal, written RFP is not something only for corporate buyers the size of General Motors. It is an essential document for anyone who is serious about buying a business computer. Management should be concerned about spelling out the intended uses of the computer, the soundness of the legal contracts, and the associated risks taken in the acquisition process. An RFP facilitates an important need to communicate all this in writing to the vendors.

In simple terms, an RFP is a set of specifications drawn up when preparing to purchase goods and services. It is a written request that describes what is needed, the basic objectives of the system, and the general terms and conditions under which the purchase will be made. It is prepared when you need to select from among several vendors, but it is no less important if you have already chosen one. In other words, the RFP serves nearly all the same purposes even if you have only one vendor in mind.

The RFP generally asks that vendors respond with a proposal, which includes a price quotation. A variation of this in the industry is the Request For Quotation (RFQ), which typically calls for a statement of prices only. For our purpose, only the RFP will be considered, since it's more encompassing and represents more of the total "solution to the problem" than the RFQ. Briefly, the RFP contains these elements:

- A definition of the *hardware* that you believe you need, including capacities, capabilities, and particular features.
- Identification of the *accounting modules* you require, such as accounts receivable and inventory, including a description of the features of the accounting package that are critical factors in the purchase.
- An outline of the various *services* required, such as training, installation, conversion assistance, and field maintenance.
- A statement of the *terms and conditions* of the purchase, which include delivery dates and progress payments for the installation.
- The *conditions of satisfaction*, which generally relate to minimum levels of vendor performance but may also include things like minimum warranty conditions.

An RFP is the blueprint that shows how your system is to be designed and constructed. It is also a management tool by which to solicit proposals from vendors, who in the process qualify themselves as serious candidates to supply your computer. This chapter provides guidelines for preparing your RFP.

WHY A WRITTEN REQUEST?

Although developing an RFP may seem like extra work, the effort serves a number of purposes. Obtaining vendor proposals is the best way to find a system that meets your company's requirements. Recall that your goal is to find a system that is neither over- nor under-configured in hardware and software. Buying a system that doesn't fit is costly and ultimately drains resources that most companies cannot afford. During the RFP process you can judge the suitability of each vendor and his system.

Formalizes Approach

With a set of specifications in hand, computer system shoppers can approach a vendor with some degree of intelligence. Developing an RFP clearly tells the vendor that you have done your homework. This act alone is one of the best ways to gain the vendor's respect.

Putting your specifications in writing, with copies for all vendors, gives each of them identical information. Thus, each vendor is told what to propose by the same data supplied to all other bidders. This consistent information eliminates any biases that might occur in sales calls or presentations. If you specify a particular format for the vendor's response, then each will place answers in the same location on the form. A prescribed format will save time and make it easy to compare each proposed solution. Also, your written RFP gives the vendors time to study the requirements and develop a thoughtful proposal.

With an RFP you also clearly require each vendor to respond to the conditions and requirements as *you* have outlined them. In other words, each vendor must respond to a set of specifications as you perceive to be the solution to your problem. If they have a better idea and want to propose an alternative approach that does not conform to the RFP, they should be allowed to do so, but in a separate document. Here the vendor responds with two proposals instead of one. But the burden should be on them to show that their alternative proposal is better than your original solution.

Requests Written Response

No matter how well prepared your RFP might be, it will undoubtedly leave some questions unanswered in the minds of the prospective bidders. Nonetheless, a properly executed RFP should get you more than 80 percent of the information you need to make a final decision. Since the vendors proposals are in writing, it should also be easy to carefully weigh the pros and cons of each response. In essence, the vendors proposals should provide detailed answers to these three basic questions:

1. Can the vendor configure a combination of hardware and software that will do the job?

2. Can the vendor perform at a level that meets all of your expectations?

3. How much will it cost?

Becomes Contract

Another important reason for using an RFP is that it can become the purchase contract after you select a vendor. With almost everything spelled out in the proposals, it's easy to make it part of the legal agreement between you and the vendor. The RFP should be written in plain English and does not have to contain all the clauses and conditions of a formal legal document. However, it does contain a formal description of the hardware, software, and conditions of the purchase. If you intend to make the vendor's proposal part of the contract, you should say this in the RFP. Making this explicit will help eliminate the non-businesslike, non-serious vendor.

Narrows Choice

One last purpose for developing an RFP is that it becomes an objective way to choose the winning vendor. It is hoped that you will receive more than three proposals, and that all will offer sound, cost-effective solutions. With the vast number of willing bidders in today's market, you can expect to receive proposals that are close to each other in performance and capabilities. However, only rarely are the proposals so close that you might have to decide by tossing a coin.

In almost every case, the differences between the proposed systems are apparent enough that one vendor has more than a slight advantage over the others. Even though the vendors who were not awarded the final contract have spent time and effort in their proposals, they usually accept the RFP method as fair and just. It's a learning process for them as well, and the losing bidders usually use the experience to improve their product or market position.

Finally, the responding proposals almost always present an opportunity to learn more about the products and services available in the marketplace. You may even learn something that will cause you to alter and improve your buying objectives. In any case, you will benefit from the education gained. It is also likely that the time you spend putting together the RFP would otherwise be spent working informally with the individual vendors.

WHAT AN RFP CONTAINS

An RFP has no standard format. It can be a simple one-page letter, or it can be a one-hundred-page highly-detailed publication. The actual content of your RFP depends on what you want to achieve, how complex your situation is, how much you have studied your operation, and how far you have gone toward arriving at a realistic solution. Creating the RFP is an individual matter, but it should be constructed well enough to tell your story to the bidding vendors. Do it in a manner and style most comfortable to you. The list below outlines the basic items that go into most RFPs. These are only suggestions. Other categories of information may occur to you, or you may want to omit some shown here.

   I. Purpose and Objectives

  II. Background Information

 III. How To Submit Proposal

 IV. System Hardware

  V. Application Software

 VI. Vendor Services

 VII. System Costs

VIII. Terms and Conditions

 IX. Vendor Background

Unless you already have a particular vendor in mind, you should plan on attracting proposals from three to five vendors. Fewer than three vendors may not provide a good enough basis for comparison, and more than five may needlessly complicate matters. You should anticipate some dropouts, but limit the number of vendors to whom you send the RFP so that your resulting responses are in this range.

You should be selective in the original list of vendors from whom to solicit proposals. If you mass mail the RFPs, vendors won't pay serious attention to them. Also, when you send out an RFP, remember that you are asking someone to do more than just a few hours of work. To adequately respond, the vendors will have to draw on a number of resources, all of which require time, effort, and money. Therefore, to protect your standing in the business community, it's not wise to do this unless you are sincere in following through with your intent to purchase a computer.

Proposal Item Descriptions

This section of the chapter describes each of the nine categories listed above, with a sample RFP following. For your convenience, the roman numerals in the following headings are keyed to the outline items shown in Figure 12-1.

The cover letter, which is the first part of your RFP, introduces your story to the vendor, and it can easily contain the first three items on the above list. It can be a summary of your purpose in obtaining a computer, state your company background or the general environment of your application, and explain how to properly respond to the RFP. These are explained in the next three sections.

I. Purpose and Objectives

The cover letter can briefly state what functions you want to computerize. For example, "Our company wishes to obtain a multi-user computer for general engineering estimates and related problem solving, and for office accounting, including inventory control, payroll, and general word processing use." This brief statement of what you want the computer to do helps summarize your overall objectives.

The cover letter should also state the schedule you want for the purchase and installation of the computer. It is better to state a date of installation completion rather than to leave it open. Vendors look for a schedule, and are usually aware of the importance of the timing, particularly if, for example, it corresponds to a growth stage for your company or it's the beginning of the fiscal year. Be prepared to find, however, that delivery conditions in the industry may require you to remain flexible on your completion date.

If you think it will help your cause, you might also say how you expect to benefit from the computer system. For example, you may intend to eliminate costly outside services or save a target amount on your inventory costs. Stating these objectives in the cover letter tells the vendor what you want to accomplish.

II. Background Information

The cover letter should include some pertinent background information on your company. You should state your product or service and indicate the size of your firm. For example, "ABC, Inc. manufactures magnetic tape recording heads used in equipment sold to television and broadcast stations throughout the country. Our company is about three years old, employs about thirty-five full-time people and has annual sales of $6 million." This information helps the vendor estimate the size of computer you need and how well their software can be adapted to your operation.

You should also include a brief statement of how you currently do the application you wish to computerize. For instance, you should say whether everything is done manually, or if you use an outside computer service, or even an in-house computer that you want to replace or upgrade. You may want to include present sample forms or facsimile reports with the RFP. If you have been using an outside service, you might include copies of their reports, the costs for this service, and the amount of disk or tape storage you have been using with your processing. This information helps the vendor determine the reporting details and the disk storage estimates.

You should state whether you have exceptional considerations in your computer installation, such as special timing circumstances or peak processing loads. For most companies, the heaviest usage is at month-end closing, when balances have to be updated, the general ledger has to be posted, and the statements or invoices have to be prepared, followed by the opening of the next month. Nonetheless, some organizations have seasonal loads, like fruit packing companies and income tax preparers. Commercial produce markets, for example, bill on a daily basis, all of

Request for Proposal Outline/Checklist

I. *Purpose and Objectives*

   A. Functions to be Computerized
   B. Purchase/Installation Schedule

II. *Background Information*

   A. Present Methods
   B. Previous Computer Experience

III. *How to Submit Proposal*

   A. Due Date, Time, Place
   B. Contact Person
   C. Proposal Questions

IV. *System Hardware*

   A. Central Processing Unit (CPU)
     1. ☐ Single User ☐ Multi-User: Number of CRTs_____
     2. ☐ Expandable Slots ☐ Non-Expandable
     3. Dual Processor ☐ No ☐ Yes
     4. Microchip Architecture:
     5. ☐ 8-Bit ☐ 16-Bit ☐ 32-Bit
     6. Main Memory Size:
       ☐ 64K ☐ 128K ☐ 256K ☐512K ☐1024K
     7. Operating System Software:
       ☐ CP/M-80 ☐ MS-DOS ☐CP/M-86 ☐ MP/M-86
       ☐ Concurrent CP/M-86 ☐ UNIX ☐ CP/M Net
   B. Mass Storage Devices:
     1. Total Storage Required:
       ☐ 400K ☐ 500K ☐ 800K ☐ 1MB ☐2MB
       ☐ 5 MB ☐ 10MB ☐ 20MB ☐ 40MB ☐ 60MB
     2. Size of Floppy Disk Drive:
       ☐ 3½'' ☐ 5¼'' ☐ 8''
     3. Hard Disk Drives: _____MB
       ☐ Fixed ☐ Removable Disk ☐ Tape Cartridge
   C. Work Stations (Terminals):
     1. Screen Size ☐ 7'' ☐ 9'' ☐ 12'' ☐ 13'' ☐ 14''
     2. Screen Resolution
       ☐ Standard Resolution (80 columns × 24 Lines)
       ☐ High Resolution (_____ Rows × _____ Lines)
     3. ☐ Upper/Lower Case ☐ Upper Case Only
     4. ☐ Multi/Color Display
     5. ☐ Single-Color Display
       Display Color: ☐ White ☐ Green ☐ Amber
     6. Type Keyboards:
       ☐ Detachable ☐ Non-Detachable
       ☐ Standard Keys ☐ Special Function Keys
   D. Printers:
     1. ☐ Dot Matrix ☐ Full Character
     2. Carriage Width: ☐ 8'' Paper (80 Cols.)
                   ☐ 14'' Paper (132 cols.)
     3. Print Speeds: _____ cps or _____ lpm
   E. Data Communications:
     1. Modems: ☐ 300 Baud ☐ 1200 Baud ☐ 2400 Baud.

2. Communications Software.
3. Networking

V. *Application Software*

A. Accounting Modules
    1. General Ledger
    2. Accounts Receivable
    3. Accounts payable
    4. Order Entry/Inventory
    5. Payroll
    6. Purchase Order
    7. Job Cost
    8. Fixed Assets
B. Other Application Software
    1. Word Processing
    2. Electronic Spreadsheets
    3. Data Base Management
C. Vendor's Alternative Recommendations

VI. *Vendor Services*

A. Systems Analysis/Design
B. System Hardware Integration
C. Training
D. Installation
E. Conversion Assistance
F. Field Maintenance

VII. *System Costs*

A. One-Time Purchase
    1. Hardware
    2. Software
    3. Services
    4. Other Costs
B. Recurring Costs
    1. Hardware Maintenance
    2. Software Maintenance
    3. Operating Costs

VIII. *Terms and Conditions*

A. Conditions of Purchase
B. Financing Methods
C. Contracts:
    1. Software License
    2. Maintenance Agreement
D. System Acceptance Tests
E. Warranties

IX. *Vendor Background*

A. Selling Vendor
    1. Size of Firm
    2. Financial Stability
    3. References
B. Hardware Manufacturer
C. Software Supplier

Figure 12-1   RFP Outline/Checklist

which is done by noon. This situation could require extended hours for the field maintenance contract. Special installation requirements might mean installing a remote terminal in the executive's home, or equipping each of the branch offices across the country with its own computer and communications to the home office.

The background information could also include whether you want to start with current data in the computer system or if you want to store data going back several years for historical purposes. Doctors, lawyers, and insurance companies usually have these kinds of requirements. Obviously, this affects the disk storage requirements and the effort of the data conversion during the installation.

You should certainly include whether you or your staff have any prior computer experience. Word processing or personal computer experience often helps in understanding the operating concepts of the computer. Knowing your experience level will help the vendor estimate how much training you may need. Overall, the background information greatly helps the vendor by providing a general overview on the environment in which he is asked to install and support the computer system.

III. How To Submit Proposal

The last subject to include in your cover letter states the rules on how the vendor should respond with his proposal. Since you are likely to be dealing with a number of vendors, make sure the conditions for returning the proposals are clear and fair to everyone.

You certainly want to specify the due date and the place, which is normally your business address. You will find that a response time of two to four weeks after your RFP mailing is usually acceptable to most vendors. You should specify the time of day, such as noon or 5 P.M., or you may have to legally accept RFPs any time up to midnight of the due date. You might want to state that if the proposals are sent by common carrier, such as the U.S. Postal Service or United Parcel Service (UPS), they must be postmarked by the due date or they will be rejected.

Also, you will want to specify a person to contact for vendor questions. It's best if this is one person for all concerned, so he or she can provide equal information to all the bidders. You will also want to say how these questions are to be handled. An open policy, for example, allows any number of telephone calls or even personal interviews by the vendors. Each vendor can take advantage of this to the extent desired.

A closed policy allows no vendor communication until after all proposals are received. But you may choose to have a bidders' conference to clarify points of the RFP. If you do this, you should state the date, time, and place for the conference. In addition, you should announce the ground rules, especially that the conference is not for sales presentations but is a forum for asking specific questions about the RFP. The main advantage of the bidders' conference is that it makes all the information equally available to all vendors at the same time.

Two other key dates to include in your RFP are a due date for notification of the vendor's intention to bid, and the date you intend to decide on a vendor. The notification date can be a week or ten days after you send the RFP. By then you will know the response to expect. A dropout rate of about 40 percent is common, but it can be anywhere from 20 to 100 percent. If far fewer bidders respond than you expected, you may need to alter your RFP and attempt the process again.

Shortly after the RFPs are mailed, you can expect a phone call from at least one vendor asking, "Who are my competitors?" While revealing the competitors to vendors is a matter of personal choice, you may find it has some advantages. Vendors with experience in the industry already know how well they compare with the others on your list. If one vendor feels strongly about his product offering and is confident of winning, they may be motivated to do a better job and make the bid more competitive. On the other hand, if a vendor feels weak and figures the chances are slim, they may decline to offer a bid. This self-imposed selection process, akin to Darwin's survival of the fittest, can save you time when you compare proposals.

IV. System Hardware

Your system requirements are, of course, the heart of your RFP. It details all the hardware components and the software for accounting and other applications. The outline provided in Figure 12-1 can serve as a checklist to help prepare your RFP. It is simply a guide and you need include only those items that apply to your situation.

In specifying the hardware components, you do not have to fully describe each component. You need only identify the main components and their basic attributes. For example, you might say, "We need a computer system with floppy disk storage of at least two million characters." Or, if you are not certain of the storage required, you might say something like, "The mass storage device, preferably a floppy disk–based system, must be sufficient to support the applications described in this RFP, yet must be expandable enough to accommodate our future growth."

Be certain that you specify something for each of the four basic components described earlier in this book. They are: the central processing unit, disk drives, terminals or work stations, and the printer. In preparing this section of the RFP, avoid vague statements such as, "The central processing unit must be sufficient to operate all the system's devices in a responsive manner." This is like saying, "All the water in the river must run downstream." Where possible, be specific in your requirements. For example, the statement above could be restated as, "System response times on the terminals averaging more than five seconds when major applications are executed are unacceptable." This specific requirement gives the vendor useful information to work with.

If it's important to your application, specify the speeds at which the various components operate. The speed of the central processor, for example, determines how fast it can execute a number of instructions per second. The term normally used to express this is called megahertz, which means a million cycles of electrical current per second. The abbreviation for this is "MHz." Microcomputers commonly operate at speeds of four, six, eight, ten, and twelve megahertz. The higher the number, the faster the computer's processing speed. Four to eight MHz is acceptable for single user systems, while eight to twelve MHz is better for multi-user systems. Printer speeds are rated as "cps" or "lpm," which mean the number of characters printed per second or the number of lines printed per minute. Floppy disk drives have no particular speed rating, except that recording in double density has a faster access time than single density.

During your investigations you have probably learned of hardware features that you think might be nice to have but are uncertain as to their real value. For your RFP you can separate and identify the "must have" features from the "nice to have" features. The "must have" features reflect your essential requirements; those which you absolutely cannot do without, and whose absence from any proposal is cause for rejection.

If the "nice to have" features cost the same or only slightly more, then it's probably best to get them in your original purchase. For example, many terminals are available with green or amber screens at no additional cost. Or a printer with twice your specified printing speed for only $200 more may be worth the difference. You may find it best to specify a component performance level within a range or to a set of outside limits. For instance, instead of asking for a printer that runs at forty characters per second, you may ask for printer speed between twenty-five and fifty characters per second. This approach allows leeway for the vendors to propose an optimal performing configuration or alternatives.

Although your specifications of the hardware and software often dictate the operating system, you may want to indicate its minimum capabilities. For example, some operating systems are better at providing data security than others. Other operating systems enable the user to run more than one job simultaneously on a single user computer. Concurrent CP/M by Digital Research is such a multi-tasking operating system. If you specify a multi-user system with an accounting package, ask for an operating system with file-lockout capability (see "Operating Systems," Chapter 8).

You should not purchase any system without projecting your future requirements; that is, what you may need two to five years from now. For purchase considerations, ask each vendor the maximum amount of main memory, the maximum amount of disk storage (floppy or hard disk), and in the case of the multi-user system, the maximum number of terminals the computer will support. Even if you do not intend to expand the system to these limits, it helps to know about them, and it could be a deciding factor if you receive two proposals nearly equal in all other respects. To sacrifice this option could also cost a great deal more money in the future when you must convert to a completely different system.

You should also explore the potential upgrade path, a later step in which you keep some or all of the peripherals but exchange the central processing unit for one larger and faster. If your future operation depends on these factors, you should ask your vendors how compatible your software will be with the more advanced system. The brochures call this "software upward compatible." It is highly desirable (if not mandatory) to have all your application software operate the same on a larger system, provided it still fulfills your needs.

V. Application Software

This section of your RFP describes the application software, the most important part of your computer system. Restate the basic modules you want, such as accounts receivable or inventory control. Also elaborate on the functions to be computerized that you mentioned in the cover letter. For instance, you may need to show more detailed information on the customer statements, such as the date of the order, items back-ordered, current payments or partial payments, and sales order numbers. Or, for inventory control, you may need an inventory package that handles work-in-process and bill of materials processing with at least four indented levels.

You do not need to describe every feature of the accounting packages, but the RFP serves you better if you highlight those features critical to your operation. These should be stated as the must-have features, or those special provisions in the accounting package that are essential to your business operation (see Chapter 6). You should also request a complete set of sample reports from your vendors. You may want to include copies of your own manual reports, which further define what you want. You should review the documentation of the software package before you decide to buy, and you may request this in your RFP. Quite often vendors will charge extra, as much as $50 per module, for accounting package documentation. Try requesting that the manuals be loaned to you for a specified period at no charge.

The vendor can provide a more accurate proposal if he knows the volumes or the typical number of transactions your business handles in a given accounting period. The vendor can translate these volume figures into file sizes, which then determine the amount of disk storage you need. Another reason for providing this information is to show the vendor the

Accounting Transaction Volumes			
		Current Volumes	
Module / Transaction		**Avg.** **Peak**	**Future Volumes**

General Ledger
  Number of Accounts
  Previous Year Accounts
  Budget Accounts
  Number of Journal Entries per Month			

Accounts Receivable
  Number of Customers
  Number of Invoices per Month
  Number of Credit Memos, Debit Memos
  Number of Cash Receipts per Month
  Number of Open Invoices			

Accounts Payable
  Number of Vendors
  Number of Open Invoices
  Number of Payments per Month			

Inventory
  Number of Line Items
  Inventory Receipts per Month
  Issues and Adjustments per Month
  Number of Sales Orders per Month
  Number of Line Items per Sales Order
  Number of Line Items Shipped			

Payroll
  Number of Employees
  Number of Timecard Entries
  Number of Payroll Deductions			

Figure 12-2   Accounting Transaction Volumes

size of your business so he can avoid offering an accounting package with limits too restrictive for your needs. Figure 12-2 is a worksheet to help develop transaction volumes for your RFP.

The vendor will have an easier time assessing your storage if you express your transaction volumes in three different ways, as suggested in the worksheet. First, for current activity, the vendor needs to know the average and peak transaction volumes. Since transaction volumes fluctuate during an accounting cycle, the disk storage must accommodate the "high-water" level. Second, unless you assume no company growth, you should also include how much you expect these volumes to increase over the next few years. State your transaction levels for both your present size and your growth projected over three to five years.

Some accounting packages are designed so that one module will not operate unless certain others are present, even if you do not plan to use them. For example, a package may require the accounts receivable and general ledger modules even if you only want to use the inventory control module. While the RFP specifies your requirements, you should ask the vendors what non-specified items you must buy in order to make the system operable as you have described.

Your RFP should state any other application software you need, such as word processing or electronic spreadsheets, especially if you plan to start using them upon installation. Mention any future accounting modules you plan to implement, but show that you intend to purchase them later. In this section you should also state if you plan to do any programming, or need a data base management system or communications software.

While your search for a computer system has probably led you down a path of your choosing, and while the RFP is one of your last steps, you should allow the vendors to respond with a modified or different approach to your problem. Your RFP should state something to the effect that you are open to vendors' recommendations of alternate solutions. Quite often, for example, a new version of an accounting package just about to enter the marketplace can offer improvements for the same or less money. This strategy works only if the waiting period does not provide undue hardships. Be clear with vendors, however, that they should first respond to the RFP as you have stated, and that any recommended alternatives should appear in a completely separate proposal.

VI. Vendor Services

Include in your RFP any of the following services you think you will need:

Systems Analysis.   Systems analysis means conducting a small study to find the most appropriate hardware and software solution to your company's operation. It is sometimes called a feasibility study. These studies should actually be done before the preparation of the RFP, but you may want to be assured that your vendor has the competent staff to provide this service for the future.

Training and Installation.   You certainly want your vendor to provide these basic services. Your RFP should request that the vendor detail the major steps in the installation and the approximate time to completion. Training details should be shown, such as who does the instructing, the main topics, and the hours allowed. (Aspects of the training are described in Chapter 16, and the installation is described in Chapter 17.)

Conversion Assistance.   You should ask for the vendor's advice on converting the accounting data to the computer (see Chapter 17). The vendor should outline this process and estimate the time and costs of this involvement.

Systems Modifications.   If you decide the software package needs to be modified, be certain that your vendor is authorized and competent to do it. The scope of the modifications needs to be specific enough in the RFP so the vendor can have his programmers give an accurate cost estimate. The vendor should state the approximate hours, the charges, and whether or not he can do the modifications before your hardware is installed.

Field Maintenance.   Here you should specify the extent and the performance level you want. Extended hours, for example, go beyond the regular work week and can include evenings, weekends, and holidays. The level of performance is the response time, which means how quickly the vendor is obligated to respond to your call. (See Chapters 9 and 10 for field maintenance details.)

VII. System Costs

The responding vendors should, of course, tell you what the system will cost. You should request that they itemize, or "unbundle," the cost figures as outlined in Figure 12-1. You should also request that they prepare a one-page summary of the one-time costs, showing the component figures and the overall total. In the absence of a special RFP format this one-page summary makes it easy to compare proposals. The other costs in the one-time purchase category may include such items as shipping, freight, taxes, and other incidentals to get the equipment to your site.

In the recurring costs, software maintenance may include annual fees for software updates or new versions from the supplier. Other costs may include supplies such as diskettes, paper, and printer ribbons. This category may also include occasional costs for the use of a backup machine. If you plan to lease your equipment, ask your vendor to estimate the monthly leasing costs. All of these cost factors are discussed in Chapter 11.

VIII. Terms and Conditions

The terms and conditions of your RFP are the minimum requirements or the special circumstances under which you are willing to purchase a small business computer. Reveal these conditions in your RFP so the vendor can understand and respond to them in his proposal. The terms and conditions can cover all the activities of the purchase from beginning to end. If you want the equipment delivered at midnight or the cabinets painted blue, say so in this section.

The terms can be whatever you choose. For example, they can cover anything from the way the proposals are submitted to the sub-clause of a two-year warranty. If you don't specify any terms and conditions for the purchase, you leave yourself open to the vendor's terms and conditions. These three statements are almost always found in a well-prepared RFP:

1. NON-DISCLOSURE. Specify that the contents of the RFP are not to be discussed or shown to anyone outside the vendor's firm. It is not uncommon for a vendor to do business with your competition. You may even ask the vendor to sign a non-disclosure agreement.

2. ASSUMPTION OF COSTS. A statement that any costs, direct or otherwise, in the preparation of the proposal are assumed completely by the proposing vendor.

3. DISCLAIMER OF CONTRACT. An explicit clause that the RFP is not a contract and that you have no obligation to accept, in whole or in part, any of the bids presented.

In this section you should state whether you plan to purchase or lease the equipment. If you plan to purchase outright, most vendors will accept a purchase order from an established company with the proper references. For a small business or an individual, vendors typically ask for a 10 to 20 percent deposit. The vendor needs to know if you plan to lease or borrow the money since this may involve a third party for financing. In this case, payments to the vendor depend on cooperation with someone else unless the vendor carries the papers themselves.

In soliciting proposals, you should ask for sample contracts. You want to review them before you accept the proposal. Sometimes for competitive reasons vendors hold back these legal documents until they are certain you are ready to sign. Reviewing a blank contract may answer many of your questions about the legal ramifications of the purchase and installation. Some representative questions to consider, with legal advice, are:

1. How much installation responsibility does the vendor assume?

2. Are the acceptance test criteria part of the legal contract?

3. What provisions exist for either party to cancel the contract?

4. If a software product is discontinued, can the customer obtain its source code?

5. Does the vendor or the manufacturer permit "foreign" attachments to the hardware or software?

You should stipulate that you expect the vendor's proposal to become part of the final agreement. Tell the vendors what part of the written specifications are to be incorporated into the legal contracts. It is also good to know what the buyer's options are (legal and otherwise) in case the vendor defaults at any stage of delivery, testing, training, acceptance, or on-going operation.

Typically the acceptance test is that the computer system performs according to its manufactured specifications. The new computer should do no less than function as described in its documentation. For example, the reports generated by the computer after it is installed should match the report samples in the manuals. The vendor need only show that the system operates properly and that the accounting package does what the software supplier designed it to do. The accounting package's documentation, therefore, is usually the standard for the acceptance test criteria, unless you have requested special program modifications.

Your RFP should also stipulate that payment for the computer system will be made in a series of mutually agreed upon progress payments rather than one lump sum. You should state that mutually agreeable checkpoints for the installation process will be written into the agreement. In no case should you be obligated to accept hardware or software in advance of seeing satisfactory performance.

Most hardware manufacturers in today's market offer a standard ninety-day parts and labor warranty. In unusual cases, such as an extreme operating environment for the hardware, or if your system will be placed in an isolated location some distance from the service center, you may want to state a requirement for higher-level warranty. At the very least you should ask for standard written warranties on both the hardware and software.

IX. Vendor Background

Request information on the vendor's background so you know who you are doing business with as well as what you are buying. Ask for credit and bank references. This information is commonly requested in an RFP, since it can make the difference in your decision to buy or not to buy. Some of the key factors are the size of the firm and the scope of its business, its financial stability, and whether or not the vendor is willing to provide references. Other factors include the age of the business and the size of its customer base, although some vendors are reluctant to give specifics here for competitive reasons.

You may also want to ask for background information on both the hardware and software suppliers, although information provided on the hardware manufacturer may be nothing more than an annual report. It is probably more relevant to know the background of the software supplier. As a rule, software suppliers are smaller than hardware manufacturers and are privately-held companies. Stability in a software firm is more important than its size. You should look for some evidence that the software supplier can survive the long haul in a fast moving, competitive marketplace.

SAMPLE REQUEST FOR PROPOSAL

The following is a sample Request for Proposal from Sampson Electric Company, including a cover letter, hardware and software requirements, and other items as described in this chapter.

Sampson Electric Company 300 Voltage Way Sunnyvale CA 95559

(415) 286-8088

January 23, 1985

Mr. John C. Goodenough
Goodenough Data Systems, Inc.
3921 Hamilton Ave.
Palo Alto, CA 94310

Dear Mr. Goodenough:

Sampson Electric Company wishes to obtain a small business computer for accounting purposes. You are invited to submit a written proposal for a turnkey system, including all hardware, software, and related services, by February 24, 1985. We are looking to have the system installed by April 16 of this year.

Sampson Electric is a small company with annual sales of $4.5 million and twenty-eight full-time employees. We manufacture solenoids and electronic controls for industrial grade audio and video tape recorders.

We are interested in obtaining a microcomputer to handle our accounts receivable and inventory, which are currently done on a manual basis. This will be our first in-house computer, but we are currently processing the payroll through a local bank. We also do some proposals and contract bidding, and are interested in a word processing system.

If you are interested in responding with a proposal, please notify me by telephone by February 1, 1985. We ask that you provide two copies of your proposal no later than 3 P.M. Friday, February 24, 1985. If you have any questions or you need any further information, please contact our controller, Mr. George Adaman, at this office.

We look forward to hearing from you.

Sincerely yours,

Robert O. Catchall, President

Sampson Electric Company

Request For Proposal

Our company seeks to computerize accounts receivable and inventory control systems to achieve speed and efficiency in day-to-day operations, as well as greater control over cash receipts and customer billings.

Target date for hardware installation is April 16, with the computer and its software to become operational by May 1, 1985, at our office in Sunnyvale, California.

Our accounting functions are presently handled by a long-established manual system using four full-time staff persons, two part-time clerk/interns from a local Jobs for Youth program, all under the direction of one supervisor. The company has no previous in-house computer system experience. For the past three years, payroll has been processed off-site by our commercial bank.

Proposals should be submitted to our office, 300 Voltage Way, Sunnyvale, CA 95559, not later than 3 P.M., February 24, 1985. Contact person is Mr. George Adaman, Controller, for any questions you may have on the RPF. We are receptive to personal visits to our office, but we ask that you keep them to a minimum.

COMPUTER REQUIREMENTS

The computer should be configured as a sixteen-bit, single user system but be expandable to at least four work stations future growth. There are no fixed requirements for memory size, devices, and operating system, except that the minimum should

be 64K for the main memory and 750K bytes for the disk
drives. The system should be sufficient to handle the
applications described below. Cost of the hard disk, if available,
should be quoted separately.

Present requirement is for one work station, in which the screen
should be eighty columns wide by twenty-four lines down, upper and
lower case letters, and a twelve-inch-diagonal-measurement display
with an easy-to-read color (green preferred). Keyboard should
be detachable, with a ten-key numeric pad, and the layout
should be easily learned by experienced typists.

Printer must be a full-character type in the thirty to sixty cps
speed range, highly reliable, and suitable for proposals and
customer correspondence. Carriage must be wide enough to
accommodate standard financial spreadsheets used for
inventory reports.

SOFTWARE REQUIREMENTS

Application software must include accounts receivable
and inventory modules. Accounting software must provide for
full receivables analysis, including aging of accounts and
flagging of delinquencies. Sampson presently has 400
customers, with 250 of them being billed each month on the
average. The active billing is expected to increase to 500 by
1986 under a new marketing program. The general ledger and
accounts payable are to be added at a later date.

Inventory software must accommodate finished goods and
work-in-process composed of thirty separate components from eighteen
different suppliers. The inventory currently has 400 line
items, but this will increase to 800 by 1986. Software must
also include, or be compatible with, word processing software
for correspondence and contract bidding. All software must be
easily learned by employees with only high-school education.

INSTALLATION AND TERMS

Installation must be scheduled with a minimum of disruption
of our regular business routine. Proposals must
provide costs and schedules for training four full-time employees
plus one supervisor in operating the system. Vendor should
also assist in the transition from manual to computer system.

The costs of field maintenance and repair shall be shown
two ways: one for on-site calls during the regular work week,

and the other for off—site repairs, providing equipment loaners
or rentals are available.

Our objective is to purchase the lowest—cost system that
meets or exceeds our minimum specifications. Total system
purchase price not to exceed $12,000. Annual service and
supply costs not to exceed $2,000. Please itemize costs for
hardware, software, installation, training, and maintenance
separately.

Purchase transaction shall be an outright cash sale, with
acceptance of system contingent on an agreement that the
system meets all specified and agreed—upon requirements.
Payment shall be on a negotiated "milestone" schedule. Vendor
shall warranty that system meets manufacturer's specifications
and will be repaired or replaced at purchaser's option.

Vendor shall not disclose any of contents of this RFP to
anyone outside the vendor's firm. This RFP is not a contract
to buy, and Sampson Electric has no obligation to accept any of
the bids presented. Vendor shall assume all costs and
liabilities in the preparation of his proposal.

Evaluating Proposals

By this time, you have diligently constructed your RFP and sent it out to a half dozen or more prospective vendors. You have, perhaps, given the vendors four weeks to prepare their proposals and respond. The time passes, with several phone calls and a few visits with some of the vendor candidates. You discuss your situation, answer their questions, and for the most part they seem content, with a few minor objections to the process. Then finally the vendor proposals begin to come in. Some of the proposals appear quite impressive, since they come in fancy binders with four-color brochures and carefully arranged equipment photographs.

MAKE A CHART

You may be pleased at the response, but you may also feel overwhelmed at the task of deciding which proposal is best for you. It seems that the reading and analyzing will take hours or days. One approach is to break down the process so that each segment can be judged independently. Look first at the software capabilities for each, then the hardware, the costs, and so on. Looking at each part and comparing one proposal against another should make this task easier. Select the best proposal and vendor by evaluating information according to the following main categories:

1. Software features and capabilities

2. Hardware features and capabilities

3. System ease of use

4. Vendor services and support

5. Cost of the system

6. Future expandability of hardware

7. Vendor reputation

Other information may also be considered, such as market acceptance of the product, or the general reputations of the hardware and software suppliers. To make judging the proposals easier, you may want to construct a chart like the one shown in Figure 13-1. This chart shows the main categories listed above, but you may subdivide any of these or add others that are important to you. If a vendor proposes an alternative system, then it should be a separate set of entries on the chart, as if it were from another vendor.

The chart both provides easy reference to individual items from each vendor, and also summarizes all the proposals, which helps you compare solutions to your problem. Despite the proposals, impressive appearance, you may find that in some of them a number of key questions go virtually unanswered. The chart quickly shows what information is missing and what follow-up you must do with the vendors.

A method for scoring vendors' proposals may help you remain objective during this process. Some reviewers develop a scoring system consisting of 100 total points, assigning an equal number of points to each section. Others develop a weighting scheme, giving proportionally higher scores to the more important elements. For example, certain accounting functions may be more important to you than others. Perhaps computerizing accounts receivable will mean more to your business than accounts payable or payroll. Or a system whose hardware is expandable may mean more to you than than a lower initial system cost.

Vendor/Proposal Comparison Chart			
	Vendor A	*Vendor B*	*Vendor C*
Software Features and Capabilities			
Hardware Features and Capabilites			
System Ease of Use			
Vendor Services and Support			
Purchase Costs: 　Hardware 　Software 　Services			
Recurring Costs: 　Hardware 　Software			
Future Hardware Expandability			
Vendor Reputation			

Figure 13-1　Vendor/Proposal Comparison Chart

You will have to develop the scoring scheme that best suits your interests. One approach is to devise a system that determines how well vendors responded to what you stated in the RFP. In other words: How close did they come to your specifications? Another way is to develop a scoring system that evaluates the contents of the proposals combined with a sales presentation from the finalists. Again, you will have to determine what scoring or evaluating system is best for you.

Other Factors

While the proposals contain the key information for your decision, they are not the *only* factors for you to consider. Other matters of equal importance, although more difficult to quantify, include:

1. General acceptance of the products in the marketplace.

2. How fair is the purchase and service contract between the two parties?

3. The true financial stability of the vendor.

4. The quality of the instruction and technical assistance from the vendor.

5. The resulting level of cooperation and communication between you and the vendor.

At this point you probably have eliminated all but a very few of the vendors. You may find that as you narrow the choice, your first impressions of the proposals may have changed. The one or two proposals that at first inspired a positive impression may now rank only third or fourth on your list. Another proposal, which did not make a good first impression, may now look more attractive to you.

After your review, the next step is to check vendor references, even if one proposal clearly appears superior to the others. Even if a vendor has taken care to select his best references, he cannot control what his customers will say to you. Nor can he "prompt" or prepare them with answers to all the possible questions you may ask. You can expect that customers will be more candid in their conversation than the vendor would sometimes like them to be. Most small businessmen tend to be open and honest in discussions of their successes or failures, compared to those customers found in the larger, *Fortune* 500 companies. If you hear a few negative comments, don't make that immediate grounds for rejection. Find out the basis of the problem. Practically every businessperson with any amount of experience has gone through incidents he would now handle differently. You should ask the vendors' customers questions such as:

◪ How did delivery compare to what was promised?
◪ How well did the vendor keep things on schedule?
◪ Were there any major unexpected costs?
◪ Were there any significant problems during the installation that could be attributed to the vendor?

Taking the references a step further, you can contact some of the vendor's customers whose names were *not* given to you. Through user groups and other sources, customers are often aware of others who have bought from the same vendor. Thus, you can find out the "non-referenced" customers by asking those whose names were given to you. Don't expect the vendor to have a perfect score here. But all in all you should look for comments that weigh on the positive side.

Negotiating Price

At some point you will enter into serious discussions with one or more of your chosen vendors about contract terms and system prices. During these negotiations you will learn just how far each vendor is prepared to go on prices, warranties, and other commitments. How much vendors are willing to negotiate price, for example, usually depends on how badly they want the business. Some companies will not negotiate price at all, while others seem willing to bend to your every request. Use caution here: those with too much flexibility may be going through some period of business instability. If you push too hard on the price you may contribute to a downfall. The ideal vendor will be eager to reach an agreement but still maintain some sense of what the limits are as well.

When you're settling the terms of the sale you have to consider the effects over the long haul. Even if the vendor is strong, your keen ability to negotiate could put them in a box from which the only escape is to use shortcuts in service and support after the sale. Even a solid company becomes weary of servicing a client whose business brought in only marginal profits. Remember the "No Free Lunch" theory. Consequently, your bargaining savvy may only serve to weaken after-sale support.

BENEFITS OF AN RFP

Now that you have reviewed the making of a Request for Proposal in the previous chapter, and the evaluation process in this chapter, probably you have acquired some appreciation for the RFP's place in your computer acquisition. Here are some additional reasons for doing so.

Methods Reviewed

The process of creating your RFP involves more than just informing vendors of your intention to buy. The exercise is worthwhile even if you are not serious about getting a computer. One reason is that it prompts a review of the company's current systems and procedures. This investigation may bring to surface situations in which work is performed differently than once established. Sometimes the effort reveals functions that should not be computerized, as well as improvements that can be made with the computer in mind. Some of these can even be implemented before the computer arrives, and others can be accomplished at little or no extra cost.

Requirements Defined

Developing an RFP before bringing a computer into the business should stimulate management to examine and clarify long-term objectives. You have to look at where the business is, and where it should be headed. You also have to visualize how the computer is going to help meet these long-term goals. This process compels you to set aside day-to-day concerns temporarily and think about the future. The RFP is not the company president's wish list, but rather a statement of realistic, clear goals. Planning is an important part of management responsibility, and an RFP effort aids the overall planning process.

Management Control

Another major benefit of writing an RFP is it puts management in control of the buying and installation process. You determine how you will obtain the computer, which greatly reduces the risks of leaving these major decisions up to the vendor. Without an RFP you subject yourself to vendors' sales pitches and the ideas of people who don't know your business nearly as well as you do. An RFP tells them what you need, instead of them telling you, and keeps you in control.

Saves Time

Another clear benefit of developing an RFP is that it saves you and your staff time by not having each vendor make an independent study of your business. Without the RFP approach each vendor must spend substantial time and money to conduct his own investigation. This includes tours of your facility and redundant interviews with your key people. Even if you allow this method, vendors cannot afford to make as thorough a study of your requirements as you can (unless you compensate the vendor as you would a consultant). They can only skim the surface and quickly judge what will work in hopes of getting the contract from you. With the RFP method the only time you need to spend with vendors is answering specific questions.

Vendor Relationships

The RFP makes dealing with the vendors easier. A sufficiently detailed RFP tells the vendor specifically what the buyer wants. Without it, selling becomes a guessing game in which the buyer may not get what he needs. Most vendors have greater confidence in what they propose when they work with hard facts rather than vague generalities. If you provide them with solid information they are much more likely to propose a successful solution.

More importantly, a fact-based solution can mean lower costs, since the vendor has less cause to hedge against the unknown. Without accurate information from the RFP, most vendors will inflate prices to cover unknown contingencies. When you multiply the realistic cost-effective solutions among a number of vendors, you greatly increase your chances for finding the ideal computer system.

Documents New System

The RFP is not as short-lived or temporary a document as you might think. The main purpose for the RFP is to provide communication to the vendors, but the RFP can give valuable information to others as well. For example, if financing is required, the lender may need a copy for reference. Your staff may also benefit from copies to refer to throughout the installation. Planning for a computer involves many decisions, which few people will remember long afterwards unless they are available in writing. The RFP can also be used as a reference in training new staff members. In addition, the RFP can contain the details of any programming modifications you may require, which will help the staff understand how it differs from the original packaged software.

USING A CONSULTANT

At some point you may feel that you could use some help in the buying process. An outside consultant can be a good resource for this kind of assistance. A consultant can help articulate your needs and accelerate your buying program. He or she can help you understand the ins and outs of applying a computer to a business, and provide sound principles from a computer professional's point of view. A consultant should not be a substitute for management in the purchasing process. It would be a mistake to call in a consultant and simply turn over the whole project—it's imperative that management remain involved. Consultants can often provide a fresh perspective based on his experience with other companies, quickly pinpointing problem areas in your operation and providing solutions that they know have worked before.

Consultants can be assigned the task of analyzing your operation, determining your computer requirements, writing the RFP, and assisting in the selection of the final vendor. Consultants can also provide valuable assistance in contract preparations and negotiations, and in all phases of the computer installation (see the last two chapters of this book).

In choosing a consultant, look for one with experience in working with businesses similar to yours. A consultant experienced largely with construction firms, for example, will probably not be of much use if you are computerizing a wholesale distributorship. You should also look for a consultant with microcomputer experience, as opposed to one who has worked only with large mainframes or minicomputers. Also, find someone you feel comfortable working with, someone whose manner and style fit with your operation.

CHAPTER
14

Where to Buy

Before the 1980s, computers were advertised mainly by a few large manufacturers using direct mail and trade publications. No one at IBM or Control Data Corporation, for example, would have considered using mass media, such as newspaper, television, or radio, to generate consumer interest in their products.

Early in the 1980s, radio stations began spot advertising small computers for home and business. Newspapers and television stations also began running ads for small computers for consumer markets. Today, manufacturers and their suppliers routinely advertise their products in

the mass media. While such advertising has definitely raised public awareness of small computers, it also has added to the confusion in the marketplace. The consumer faces a bewildering choice of products from an
equally bewildering array of manufacturers. For manager's considering a
business computer, these complexities are a real concern. If they know
little about *what* to buy, they may know even less about where to buy or
who to buy from.

Consider the case of the owner of a small but prospering nursery
business located on the outskirts of a large city. The owner, George, doesn't
know much about computers, but he knows other businessmen who bought
a famous-name computer and who are doing well with their purchase. He
thinks if this brand works for them, it should work for him. So he goes
to the closest computer store and buys the same computer as his neighbors.

Unfortunately, George bought only half of what he really needed. Adding a computer to his business did not go well because he made the basic
error of buying from a retailer who was not well acquainted with business
applications. Also, he found less after-sale support than he needed because
the computer dealer he chose was a hardware "merchandiser," someone
who sells computers the way retailers sell hand calculators and clock
radios.

Deciding where to buy your computer is as important as deciding
which computer to buy. Just as no single computer is best for every business, no single place to buy is best for every customer. In a word, you
select a vendor with the same caution you use in selecting the computer
system. This chapter explains the different types of vendors and shows
you how to pick the best one to do business with.

DISTRIBUTION CHANNELS

The highly diversified U.S. computer industry distributes its products in
a variety of ways. The list of vendors below shows sixteen channels of
distribution for computer products. You can buy these electronic devices
in more kinds of places than you can stereos and television sets. Worse
for the consumer, all these vendors bombard the marketplace with biased
information, which makes the buying decision more difficult.

The list is divided into two groups to show that Group I is more likely
to satisfy the business customer. Why? One reason is that these firms
depend on the sale of hardware and software for their main source of
revenue. They are thus motivated to protect their reputation and income
by taking good care of their customers. They are in the business not just
to sell hardware but to provide honest, day-to-day solutions to business
problems. Firms in this group general'y provide the best follow-on sup-

port, which is a key factor in your decision. (Recall that the business user buys after-sale support, not just equipment.)

The first category on the list comprises the large, name-brand manufacturers; the handful of companies that have been around long enough to be well entrenched in the marketplace: Burroughs, Data General, Digital Equipment Corporation (DEC), Hewlett-Packard, IBM, NCR, Texas Instruments, Wang, and Xerox, to name a few.

Second are smaller manufacturers that are also considered traditional sources. These companies were established before microcomputers were invented, and include firms like Cado, Quantel, Basic Four, Prime, and Four Phase. The next two on the list are original equipment manufacturers (OEMs) and software/systems houses. These are typically small independent companies who operate on a local or regional basis.

The last of Group I, retail computer stores, include franchises like Computerland and Byte Shops; company-owned stores like DEC, IBM, Texas Instruments, and Xerox; wholly-owned chains such as Businessland, Radio Shack Computer Centers, and Sears Business System Centers; and the vast number of independent retailers throughout the country.

Channels of Computer Product Distribution

Group I
Large, Name-Brand Manufacturers
Other Established Manufacturers
Original Equipment Manufacturers (OEMs)
Software/Systems Houses
Retail Computer Stores/Dealers

Group II
Service Bureaus
Timesharing Firms
Office Equipment Dealers
Industrial Equipment Distributors
Manufacturers' Representatives
Data Processing Consultants
Electronic Appliance Stores
Retail Chains and Franchises
Department Stores
Discount Catalog Houses
Mail Order Houses

The first two types of vendors in Group II have for years offered the use of their own large computers on a pay-as-you-go basis. Service bureaus and timesharing firms include established names such as Automatic Data Processing (ADP), Computer Sciences Corporation (CSC), the Service Bureau Company (a division of Control Data Corporation), Tymshare, and Xerox

Computer Services. The others in this group are companies that provide sales and services on a local or regional basis, and are found under the same headings in your telephone directory.

Again, what distinguishes those listed in Group II is that selling and supporting small business computers is *not* the mainstream of their business. Group II firms often sell computers of the same shape and color as those in Group I, but revenues from these sales are only a small portion of their total sales. They may have less incentive, or may not be organized, to fully support your computer system. They simply may not give a hoot about your problems after the sale. Unless you are an expert in computers, you will need this support. If your geographic location limits your choice of vendors to those in Group II, check the after-sale experience of others before you buy.

What other general differences will you find between these two groups? Almost all vendors advertise their products and services (if only in the yellow pages), making a variety of claims, from honest to deceptively exaggerated, about how their products can be used in business. Some offer a true business system, which may meet your needs, while others offer a home-type computer not at all suited to a business environment. The last five vendor types in Group II are mass consumer–oriented and may be good places to buy home computers, but generally do not sell the software and services needed by most businesses. These include: electronic appliance stores that sell televisions and stereos; retail chains similar to department stores; large department stores; discount catalog houses; and mail order houses. While mail order prices are tempting, first-time buyers should avoid these outlets.

Still others may offer a true business system at a low price, but without the essential service and support. This variety of offerings and prices makes it difficult for a first-time computer buyer. Two questions will clarify your approach and narrow the choice. These are the main considerations in your search for a legitimate vendor: Is the vendor offering a true business computer as described in this book? Does the vendor *support his sale* with the necessary services of installation, training, and maintenance?

FULL-SERVICE VENDORS

Let's look more closely at the characteristics of vendors listed in Group I, the manufacturers, OEMs, systems houses, and retailers. Compared to those in Group II, these can be characterized as full-service vendors.

No clearly established definitions exist for the way vendors operate. The different types of vendors are defined only for the purpose of this book, and to help distinguish one kind of operation from another. For

Full Service Vendor Comparison			
	OEM	*Systems House*	*Dealer/ Retailer*
Market Orientation	Caters to one specific industry	Expertise in number of selected industries	Broad market; walk-in trade
Hardware Products	One large, name-brand mfgr; may add other brand peripherals	Usually does not sell hardware	Number of brands to choose from
Software Products	One package for particular market segment	May sell DBMS, operating systems, and utilities	Sells DBMS languages, operating systems, and applications
Software Sources	OEM value added developed package	Writes custom software to suit specific needs	Off-the-shelf packages from various suppliers
System Demonstration	In-house development system	None; uses customer's purchased system	Walk in for showroom demonstration
Services Provided:			
Analyze User Needs	Yes	Yes	Limited
Software Changes	Yes	Yes	Third Party
On-site Installation	Yes	Yes	Yes
On-Site Training	Yes	Yes	Seminars
On-going Support	Yes	Yes	Limited
Equipment Maintenance	No; contract with hardware manufacturer	No; contract with hardware manufacturer	Carry in for service
Contracts	Contracts with OEM except hardware maintenance is pass through	Software only	Suppliers standard software license agreement
System Cost	Mid-Range	Highest	Lowest

Figure 14-1   Full-Service Vendor Comparison

example, not everyone in the industry agrees on what an OEM is, or what a systems house does, or what a retailer sells. Some vendors combine functions of others, making it difficult to place them in the categories described here. Thus you may find several functions within one organization. Still others may have more narrow roles than those defined here. All in Group I, however, are considered full-service vendors, which makes them best suited to the needs of the business customer. Briefly, "full-service" means they have the resources to cater to all your interests, from your first decision step through the life of your computer system. This term is more fully explained later in this chapter.

Manufacturers

Of the vendors in Group I, the manufacturers have the best name-brand recognition. Originally these included only a handful of companies, such as IBM, Control Data Corporation, Honeywell, Burroughs, and Univac, who made large and very expensive mainframe-type computers. Some of these big companies have followed the trends and added the new, small computers to their product line. Typically, their products, training, documentation, and support are the best. Most of these manufacturers market directly to end-users through their own sales representatives, but high sales costs force them to focus their activities on other large *Fortune* 500 companies rather than small companies or prospering individuals.

The manufacturing group includes those who have built the mid-sized machine called a "minicomputer." Some of the traditional minicomputer manufacturers are Digital Equipment Corporation (DEC), Hewlett-Packard, IBM, Data General, and General Automation. This group also includes such office equipment manufacturers as Xerox, Wang, and Victor, who are selling "office of the future" computers. Small business computers are a logical extension of their traditional product line.

The change in technology during the mid-1970s, which produced the microcomputer, has led to still a third breed of computer manufacturer. These companies, although not as well established as the others, have grown rapidly in the past few years and are now sizeable manufacturers in their own right. The list includes Alpha Micro Systems, Altos Computer Systems, Apple Computer, Commodore Computer, Cromemco, Northstar Computer, and Vector Graphic. Some of these manufacturers started by producing home and personal computers, but their second generation products compare well with other business computers. With state-of-the-art technology and admirable product capabilities these companies compete well against the large, established manufacturers.

All these manufacturers produce hardware and provide operating systems and equipment instruction manuals. They usually do not supply application programs, such as accounting packages, nor do they offer the follow-on support that businessmen need. In fact, since their main role is manufacturing, most of them do not *want* to deal with the final consumer. They prefer to leave this function to the OEMs, systems houses, and retail dealers. If you should send your RFP to a manufacturer, for example, they will probably forward it to a support vendor for follow-up. Manufacturers who do sell hardware directly to the consumer provide a list of qualified or approved third parties to complete the system and implement the application programs.

Because most manufacturers do not provide on-going support to the business user, the remaining vendors on the list in Group I are the best choices. They are: the OEMs, systems houses, and retailers. Look first among these three. While they differ somewhat, their service character-istics as a group make them preferable. For example, they normally pro-vide full-service training, installation, and follow-on support. Because they are local, they are readily accessible in time of need. They typically want to establish a long-term relationship with you and your business. Also, these vendors are usually independently owned, which makes them flex-ible in setting policy to suit your needs.

Original Equipment Manufacturers (OEMs)

The term "OEM" stands for Original Equipment Manufacturer, which today is something of a misnomer. The phrase was coined years ago when small manufacturers assembled components made by others and then sold them under their own names. For example, OEMs would buy power sup-plies from one company, printed circuit boards from another, and cabinets from still another. After assembling these components, they offered the finished goods for sale as their own product. Today some of the largest computer manufacturers still order "nearly" finished goods from smaller subcontractors to complete their final products, and thus act somewhat like OEMs.

Today many OEMs are small, independently-owned companies serv-ing only a local or regional area. They typically develop expertise catering only to one specific industry, such as medicine, insurance, or wholesale distribution. Many OEMs operate by buying complete, finished products direct from a computer manufacturer (leaving the brand name intact) and adding their own software packages to make a complete system. Or they sometimes buy a central processing unit from one manufacturer, printer or disk drives from another, and merge them into a complete system. Here the OEM can mix and match various components to suit the buyer. Since these systems are ready to use when delivered, they are sometimes called "turnkey systems," since you just turn the key.

The OEM usually has a staff of programmers with experience in devel-oping application software for a particular market or industry. Combining the software with the hardware creates a "value-added" product. Since manufacturers do not usually offer application software, the OEM serves a necessary function in the distribution of computer products to the final user. Because the OEM develops the software, he has full rights to sell it and is free to modify it to suit the buyer's needs. The OEM tends to specialize in one industry, and his experience enables him to readily understand the characteristics of your business and meet your requirements.

The OEM buys hardware from the manufacturer at a discount, usually at a lower price than if you bought it directly. In addition, since he has developed a specialized package and sells it to many buyers, the OEM charges less for software than if you had the same job done by a custom programmer. These economies of scale enable the OEM to offer attractive prices for a total computer system. The price of a complete OEM system, though, falls somewhere between prices charged by system houses and retail dealers.

When you buy from an OEM, your contract is with the OEM, not the manufacturer. This includes the agreement to purchase and install the system, as well as any financial or legal obligations for the software package. Since the OEM normally does not have a repair staff to maintain the hardware, he simply passes the maintenance contract through from the hardware manufacturer to the buyer. The OEM is responsible, though, for all other aspects of your system.

Systems Houses

For our purpose, the phrases "systems house" and "software house" mean the same. What sets a systems house apart from the other vendors is that the systems house creates custom software while the others offer pre-programmed packages. The systems house does not sell off-the-shelf application programs, except for generalized software such as data base systems, operating systems, and utility programs. Nor does the systems house usually sell hardware directly to the end-user, although he may work with you in choosing a particular system. Instead, you buy through one of the other vendors described in this chapter.

The systems house is prepared to analyze your particular needs, install the programs on your computer, and provide on-site training and support. Like the OEM, the systems house maintains a staff of programmers who can work on a project for you. After you have decided to purchase a particular computer, the staff writes special computer programs for your business, once your needs have been defined. You should contract for customized software from a systems house only when you have highly specialized requirements that no available package can satisfy.

However, a systems house may have expertise in a number of selected industries. Also, the systems house is more flexible than the OEM on the brands of computers it will work with, provided your chosen computer can be programmed in a language they know.

Buyers who use the services of a systems house typically have a three-party contract with the hardware vendor and the systems house. A fourth party may be involved for financing. Thus, you may do business with three or four different entities, since the systems house contracts only to develop the software. Because you are paying to have your own software created, you retain full ownership rights in the programs. Contracting with the systems house is the highest-cost choice in a group that includes the OEM and the computer dealer, but if your requirements are so specialized that there are no alternatives, the systems house is your answer.

Retailers

By definition, retailer and dealer mean the same kind of vendor. The retailer has a business with a showroom and depends primarily on walk-in trade for his business. Retail dealers, who first appeared about 1976, are like specialty shops located in shopping centers and other commercial areas. They sell to local "neighborhood" markets and are of two types: those who independently select and sell products from various manufacturers, and those who sell only their own brand, such as Radio Shack, DEC, IBM, and Xerox. This second type of store is usually a franchise when not owned by the manufacturer.

While retailers originally sold to computer hobbyists, many have changed their products and showroom decor to appeal to the business-person. Retailers can give you on-the-spot demonstrations; and, like the OEM and systems house, the computer dealer often provides a complete solution. Also, in a large, well-stocked retail store you can select from a number of different brands of hardware combined with off-the-shelf packages to suit your needs. The dealer typically carries packaged software for applications such as word processing, electronic spreadsheets, data base management, and general accounting. He also offers packages or "tools" to develop software, such as programming languages, editors, and systems utilities.

Since the retailer carries a number of brands of computers, unlike the other vendors, he may be more objective in serving your interest. But even with a choice, can you trust the retailer to be objective? For various reasons, computer store people favor one brand of computer over another. You may suspect that the profit is greater for the machine they tend to promote. Bear in mind, however, that a dealer committed to his customers will promote one brand if it is proven to be reliable, has the essential features, comes from a good manufacturer, and is priced competitively.

The computer dealer sells to a broad market and doesn't specialize like the OEM or the systems house. While the dealer does some "hand holding," you can expect less help from him than the other two types of vendors. If you choose a retailer, you should be better prepared before buying the computer, and you should plan to be more self-sufficient after the sale. While the retailer is a new channel of distribution, many stores have changed their method of operation since the mid-1970s. Some of them function like OEMs and systems houses and offer the same advantages. The dealer, however, has come to be a legitimate channel of distribution since he offers a low-overhead approach to bringing small business computers to the consumer.

SELECTING A VENDOR

Locating Vendors

Almost all active vendors advertise in the yellow pages, which can be a good place to start looking for full-service vendors. You can expand your search, however, by asking your accountant, banker, lawyer, acquaintances, or others in the same business. Perhaps one of the best and quickest ways is to ask a local data processing consultant. Don't overlook annual computer fairs, trade shows, and conferences as possible sources for vendor leads. The West Coast Computer Faire, the National Computer Conference (NCC), and COMDEX are among the biggest such shows in the country. Checking the ads and feature articles on computer products in the trade periodicals, such as *Business Computer Systems* and *Interface Age*, can also lead to naming local vendors.

Now that we have identified the various places to buy and their similarities and differences, plus learned where to look, how do you go about choosing the best one for your purpose? Let's look at the characteristics of the ideal vendor.

What Every Vendor Should Know

Every vendor should know the hardware well enough to custom configure a system for the buyer's purpose. This includes knowing all the options and peripherals available for each kind of computer. In addition, they should provide you with a choice of peripherals, such as disk drives, printers, terminals, and so on, and should know how to integrate them well enough to make *all* the features work properly. The vendor's knowledge should allow them to assemble the various components without depending heavily on anyone outside the firm.

Vendors should know software well enough to be able to demonstrate any aspect of the package, answer your questions about it, properly install it on your system, and help you learn to operate it in your business. They should also be equipped to make modifications or changes to the programs as you might require, although a retailer might call on a third party for these kinds of services.

The real test of vendors' knowledge of the hardware and software is simple: They should know enough about the system to help you quickly troubleshoot any problems. Vendors should have enough experience so that they don't have to spend hours or days picking through manuals for the answers to simple questions.

Finally, vendors should know enough about business to understand how the computer fits into your organization and how it will help accomplish your goals. They should know enough about accounting practices, for example, to be able to follow (at least in concept) the entry of sales orders, journal entries, purchase orders, inventory items, and so on, through to the month's end closing. They should understand how different accounting functions, such as accounts receivable, accounts payable, and general ledger, work together. And they should be able to relate the differences between a manual system and a computerized system. The test here is that vendors should understand enough of the detail level to pinpoint and quickly resolve problems at the operational level. At the same time they should also take a management point of view so that practical solutions are proposed that meet your objectives.

What Every Vendor Should Offer

The ideal vendor offers three things. First, the vendor should be local, within easy driving distance of your office. Look for a vendor who can readily make "house calls." On-site, in-person calls are necessary for consultation, training, and maintenance, especially when problems cannot be resolved over the telephone. Your supplier should be able to assist with just about anything that occurs during the use of your computer. This support effort can include many activities, such as:

- Obtaining "systems design" help, which means detailed advice on the best way to set up a new application for the computer.
- Tutoring new operators on how to use the computer and its application software packages.
- Getting answers to questions not explained in the manuals and documentation.
- Installing newly added software packages or accounting modules.
- Obtaining new versions or "updates" of operating systems, programming languages, and application software packages.
- Connecting new printers, disk drives, monitors, and other peripherals to the installed computer.
- Rendering timely assistance when your computer doesn't do what you think it should, or when you encounter new situations.
- Running diagnostics to isolate problems.

Second, the vendor should have full responsibility for your installation. When running a computer, it's often much easier and more efficient to deal with one firm than several. Avoid multiple vendors where possible. This eliminates finger-pointing and buck-passing problems. It might also give you more influence with the vendor you've chosen.

Third, your vendor should be able to provide all the services you might ever need. The full-service vendor is an extension of the single source concept. Full-service means providing *everything*, from systems analysis, to installation, to consummable supplies such as paper, printer ribbons, and diskettes. Also, if you're considering a retail dealer, find out if it has a repair department, if so, is it an authorized service center for the equipment you're buying? If it is not authorized, it may have to send your computer back (or send for parts) to the manufacturer, even though it can do other repairs. Authorized dealers have technicians who receive factory training and have spare parts in stock.

Five Questions You Should Ask

How can you quickly assess whether or not you are pursuing a worthwhile vendor? Listed below are five key qualifying questions you should ask any potential vendor before you commit to a purchase.

1. **Why did you select this particular system for me?** This question is most appropriate in the case of a dealer who has a choice of systems to sell. With an OEM, you should ask how they arrived at the recommended configuration, and how it compares with other systems on the market. Find out what the salesperson's criteria were and whether you think they fit your business needs. Was the reasoning sound? Would anyone else have come up with the same answer? The system proposed should reflect an understanding of your current needs as well as any future needs. In other words, is the proposed system adequate for your immediate requirements and also expandable for the future? Also ask if the vendor guarantees that the system will meet the specifications contained in the documentation. This may show how confident the vendor is in offering the system. Again, the answer here should reflect the ideal solution to your data processing needs as an independent consultant might determine for you.

2. **How many systems like this have you sold?** This question shows the experience and track record of the vendor. Be very careful if you discover you are one of the first to be offered this system. Normally, after a few installations, the vendor will have worked out all the kinks, which should make it easier for you. Find out if the previously sold systems were to companies in situations similar in size and scope to yours. The vendor's sales record means little if the sales were only to mom-and-pop-type operations and you have a medium-sized corporation. You should ask when the first system was sold, and how many have been sold over the last year. You might also follow up with: How recent was the last sale? Do you still support the product? Look for a track record with other firms similar to yours to have some assurance the vendor is qualified.

3. **Who will do the training and installation?** Look for more than one of the vendor's staff to be involved with your installation. This lowers your risk in depending on only one person who knows the ins and outs of your system and your operation. You should ask about their qualifica-

tions and experience, which aid in quickly solving problems. You should find out if the salesperson remains involved after the sale, or if the account is turned over to the support people as he or she disappears. You are better served when the salesperson stays involved, since he or she was the first to understand your problem, and can call on the appropriate resources when you need them. You should also find out the ratio of support staff to salespeople. If there is only one technical person for five salespeople, obviously his or her time is spread among many different customers, which dilutes support for your business.

4. **Do you have any references for the proposed system?**   Can the vendor provide names, addresses, and telephone numbers of people who have bought similar systems? The references should be in your geographic area. If the answer is "No," it's important to find out why. Sometimes excellent products have just arrived in the marketplace and can offer a higher performance for less money. You can check these by looking for any published reviews or evaluations, and determine the general reputation of the company making the new product.

If the answer is "Yes," get at least two or three customer references from the vendor. Make an effort to check them out. Call and ask if they feel satisfied with the vendor and the computer installation. Ask if the vendor delivered as promised. Find out, if you can, how well the vendor met commitments, the general level of performance, and if there were any particular problems. Find out if any major changes were made in the proposed system, or if any unexpected costs surfaced. A negative answer does not mean you automatically reject the vendor. Find out why. Sometimes customers cannot pay their bill or do not meet their commitments.

Also, user groups are a good source for evaluating a particular system or software package. User groups are typically non-profit organizations that focus on a particular product and meet to exchange information among members. User groups tend to form after a product is established on the market and has maintained some level of success. Some of these groups charge for membership, have regular meetings, and publish newsletters. They are also sometimes instrumental in improving a product by channeling feedback to the manufacturer. Since user groups are not organized to sell anything, they may be a good source for objective information.

5. **How long have you been in business?**   Recalling that you should be looking to establish a long-term relationship with your vendor, this question gives you some idea of that probability. A better question might be, "How long do you expect to be in business?" but no one can give you an accurate answer.

The longevity of your vendor is important simply because it's troublesome to change vendors in midstream should the original one go out of business. Look for circumstances to indicate that the vendor will be around for a few more years, although there is risk even with the largest firms. A few years ago, three well known *Fortune* 500 companies; General Electric, RCA, and Xerox, were in the business of manufacturing large, million-dollar computers. In the last decade all three have decided to get out of the business and have stopped producing computers (although Xerox currently makes small computers.)

With this question you should find out the general size of the vendor, whether they have multiple locations, how many employees they have, and so on. If it is a new firm, determine how they are financed and what else they have in their favor. You should also get background information on the hardware and software suppliers, since the same question applies. How long have they been in business? Keep in mind that the micro industry didn't exist before the mid-1970s, and that the "quality" of the supplier is as important as the number of years in business.

COMPUTER REPAIR SERVICES

Sometimes you may need to buy a computer from a dealer who does not have his own service department, or has an inadequate facility. Where can you go for service outside the dealer? Or what if your dealer goes out of business? One source is the manufacturer, who will often make repairs directly for customers. The manufacturer should offer the best in trained technicians and spare parts availability. This kind of repair outlet is most practical when it is close to your location, and your processing unit, terminal, and disk drives are of the same brand. Manufacturers, of course, repair only their own products. If you have mixed-brand components, you may have to isolate the problem unit yourself and arrange to take it to the appropriate repair facility.

Another possible source is the dozen or so nationwide service chains, which include such notables as General Electric, RCA, Sorbus, and TRW. These companies are independent from the manufacturers and offer only repair service. The service chains generally have a good reputation for their work, offer factory-trained technicians, and can be relied on for spare part inventories. These large firms are equipped to handle most popular brand-name computers and peripherals. One advantage in working with the large independents is their willingness to work on systems with mixed-brand components.

Still another possible repair facility is a local independent service firm or another computer dealer. You may need to buy your computer at one place and get it serviced at another, sometimes competing dealer. Due to the cost of keeping a trained staff and adequate spare parts, local dealers are usually strong in one or two brands, but weak in others. Go by their reputation and talk with some of their customers for references. In checking these, some questions to ask are:

National Computer Service Companies

Bell & Howell Company
6800 McCormick Road
Chicago, Ill. 60645

Bunker Ramo Information Systems
35 Nutmeg Drive
Trumbull Industrial Park
Trumbull, Conn. 06609

Computer Systems Support Corp.
9112 Gaither Road
Gaithersburg, Md. 20877

Control Data Corporation
Engineering Services Division
5720 Smetana Drive
Minnetonka, Minn. 55343

Decision Data Computer Corp.
400 Horsham Road
Horsham, Pa. 19044

General Electric Company
Instrumentation and Computer
   Service Department
1 River Road
Schenectady, N.Y. 12345

Indeserv
P.O. Box 923
531 King Street
Littleton, Mass. 01460

International Association of
Service Companies
7975 W. 63rd Street
Shawnee Mission, Kan. 66202

Kalbro Computer Repairs
Division of Kalbro Corp.
101 Foster Road
Moorestown, N.J. 08057

RCA Service Company
Division of RCA Corp.
Route 38, Bldg. 204-2
Cherry Hill, N.J. 08358

Sorbus Service Division
Management Assistance Inc.
50 E. Swedesford Road
Frazer, Pa. 19355

TRW, Inc.
Customer Service Division
70 New Dutch Lane
Fairfield, N.J. 07006

Western Union Telegraph Co.
Field Service Division
7 Arrow Road
Upper Saddle River, N.J. 07458

Figure 14-2 National Computer Service Companies

- How are the technicians trained?
- Are spare parts kept on hand for repairs?
- Are the service rates published?
- Is there a minimum charge?
- What is the policy on repair estimates?
- What is the normal turnaround time on repairs?
- Is an equivalent loan unit available, or can equipment be rented during repairs?

THE BOTTOM LINE

To summarize this chapter, you are most likely to receive satisfaction from a vendor whose main activity is selling and supporting business computer installations. This vendor is most likely to be an OEM, a systems house, or a retailer, who should have a good working knowledge of hardware and software and an understanding of how computers are used in business. Also, they should be in your geographic area and should provide all the services you need.

Perhaps the most important underlying factor in your choice of a vendor is their commitment. How can you judge commitment? Probably the best indicator is their track record—what they've done in the past. If you're looking at a new firm, look for a vendor with experienced people who will take the time to discuss your situation and provide a reasonable solution. If you are buying a system for accounting, look for a vendor who is willing to accept payment in stages during the computer installation. (Accounting, compared to other applications, is usually customized for the buyer and is often subject to sequential steps of completion and acceptance.) You should be leery of a vendor who demands payment in full on the day of installation. Another sign of the vendor's commitment is a willingness to negotiate agreements rather than force you to sign a standard contract form.

What about those advertised bargains? It's every manager's responsibility to save money where he or she can. In the microcomputing industry, particularly at the retail level, discounting is common. Generally, follow the old adage: "You get what you pay for." If you're looking for a home computer, and you know what you want, it's worth the effort to shop for a good price. When you're buying a system for your business, however, price is only one of the major deciding factors. You may be shrewd enough to wangle a discount out of your vendor, but you may suffer when you and another buyer, who paid full price, both knock on his door at the same time for help. Obviously, the one who paid full price will get his attention first.

While hardware and software features are important, so is the quality of your system and your relationship with the vendor. Try to be objective, but don't completely put aside your gut level feeling for the vendor you think you can work with best. The benefits you receive from a vendor who is responsible and competent will save you money in the long run and more than offset the short-term advantage of a so-called bargain-priced system.

CHAPTER
15

Contracts

The contract is usually the last item considered when buying a computer system. When the inquiring customer decides to purchase a system, he immediately becomes a buyer asked to sign a contract. This chapter shows the legal aspects of computerizing your business as buyer and seller come to agreement. The chapter also makes the following assumptions: one, the contract is for a purchase, not a lease; two, the purchase includes hardware, software, and hardware maintenance; and three, the purchase is covered by a written contract.

The chapter is divided into sections discussing the following main topics:

Format—The organization of the printed contract.

General Provisions—Clauses that deal with the legal interpretation of the agreement.

Uniform Commercial Code—A set of commercial laws regulating business in most of the United States.

Subject Matter—Contract clauses that relate to the purchase and installation of the computer.

Maintenance—Provisions regarding the hardware maintenance.

Software—Contract clauses for the special treatment of application software.

The discussion covers both those elements found in all contracts and those peculiar to the individual contract. For example, a maintenance contract has unique provisions or clauses plus general provisions found in all contracts. When a section or a provision applies to more than one type of contract, the text indicates it.

The chapter discusses only the major provisions and their substance, purpose, and possible effect—the specific wording of contracts is used only for illustration. The purpose is to present in general terms the possible legal effect or interpretation of a contract element, rather than the specifics of contract law.

Black's Law Dictionary, a standard legal reference book, defines a contract as, "The writing which contains the agreement of the parties, with the terms and conditions, and which serves as proof of the obligation."

The definition has two distinct elements: agreement and writing. Underlying an agreement is the theoretical concept of freedom of contract, which assumes the parties have bargained until they achieved a "meeting of the minds" on the contract terms and conditions. The writing, although not mandatory, since contracts may be oral, embodies the negotiations between the parties and guides their conduct in performing their obligations. The legal system leaves to the parties, with some limitations, the right to determine their obligations, that is, who is to perform what, where, and when. So much for legal theory. The reality of business practice is often another matter.

In real life, the standard contract is not the product of bargaining efforts. Instead, the buyer usually faces signing a contract drafted to protect the vendor, leaving the buyer to face most of the risks. Most vendors use a standard contract which, in addition to limiting their risks, attempts to achieve uniformity and avoid the costs of making a special contract with each buyer.

Also, the standard contract does not reflect "a meeting of the minds."

The buyer usually discovers a wide gap between what he or she expects and what the contract provides, usually because of the salesperson's presentation and the buyer's own ignorance. Nonetheless, our legal system generally views such contracts as enforceable, and the purchaser's ignorance or failure to bargain is not an acceptable excuse.

Further, the vendor may ask you to sign not one contract for the entire system but up to three separate contracts: one covering the system purchase (hardware and software), another for the software license, and still another for hardware maintenance.

When the vendor offers a standard, preprinted contract you should not give up your right to bargain with him. You are responsible for making the agreement serve your needs and desires. To prepare for this you should ask the vendor for a copy of the proposed contract early in your buying investigation.

FORMAT

While vendors use a variety of formats for a standard contract, the ideal contract should be readable and easy to understand. It should have a title page, a table of contents, and a descriptive heading for each provision. Also, the text should be written in plain English rather than legalese. The paragraphs that relieve the vendor of responsibility should be set off in bold type, larger type, or a different color ink.

The typical standard contract may also use separate paragraphs for the subject of the contract and the contract itself. Often this division is not readily apparent. Also, clarity may suffer due to paragraph composition, the use of archaic words, or overloading a paragraph with several provisions. Purchase order contracts are often the worst in this regard, with the contract "hidden" on the back of a multiple part form.

GENERAL PROVISIONS

A series of provisions relating to the contract itself usually appears under the heading "General Provisions" or may appear at the end. Most of these provisions deal with the legal interpretation of the agreement. The following discussion covers provisions of two kinds: those relating to the meaning and substance of the agreement, and those concerning procedural aspects of interpretation.

Complete Agreement

This provision is also called an integration or merger clause. It means that the writing is the only proof of the buyer's and seller's obligations. The purpose is to eliminate any extraneous material from the contract, whether oral or written. When the parties negotiate various terms, they want the final wording to reflect the results of the negotiations. However, this provision has the effect of excluding statements and promises that are inconsistent with the printed contract. Therefore, many of the purchaser's expectations, stemming from contact with the salesperson, may go unrealized.

The merger clause may read something like this: "The customer acknowledges that he has read this agreement, understands it, and agrees to be bound by its terms and conditions. Further, the customer agrees that it is the complete and exclusive statement of the agreement between the parties, which supercedes all proposals or prior agreements, oral or written, and all other communications between the parties relating to the subject matter of this agreement."

No Modification

This clause prevents oral changes to the agreement once the contract is signed. It is similar to the complete agreement provision except that it covers the period after the purchase. It protects the vendor against subsequent unauthorized promises or statements to a possibly unhappy buyer.

Incorporation by Reference

This clause includes material from outside the contract without adding the actual wording to the current text. For example, you and the vendor may want to include in one contract certain provisions from another contract between you.

Another way to achieve the same result is to attach the desired material, such as the vendor's proposal. The problem with attachment is knowing who attached it and when. An alternative is to insert a provision that identifies the desired material and incorporates the appropriate language.

The best course is to include any supplementary material in the agreement by reference, especially documents of interest to the purchaser, such as a request for proposal, system specifications, or sample reports.

Recitals

These provisions at the top of the contract, often beginning with the archaic "whereas", can have significant legal effect. For example, on a vendor-supplied form the recital language can act as a disclaimer. It may say the purchaser is responsible for selecting and using the system and for the results of its use. The recitals clause often shows the intent of the parties which, in the event of a dispute, will help a court or arbitrator interpret the contract.

No Assignment

This clause prohibits the purchaser from substituting another purchaser by "assigning" the agreement to him or her. The idea behind assignment is that a contract consists of rights and obligations of each party, which may be transferred to another. Assignment occurs when either of the contracting parties transfers its right to receive a performance, or its duty to make a performance, to another, non-contracting party.

Again, real-life commerce is different from legal theory. The vendor may in effect assign the right to receive money despite this clause. For example, a vendor may transfer to a bank the right to receive payment. If the vendor later goes out of business, the purchaser remains legally obligated to pay the bank.

Severability

A provision is often inserted to prevent a contract from being declared unenforceable because one or more of its parts is illegal, invalid, or unenforceable. These parts are severed from the contract, and the remainder is enforced.

No Waivers

When dealing with disputes about performance under a contract, the courts look at what the parties do rather than what the contract says. For example, if the buyer fails to perform a duty under the contract and the seller ignores the non-performance, a court may decide no breach of contract has occurred. A "no waiver" clause prevents this acceptance of non-performance by requiring that both parties ignore any waiver of performance that would be a breach unless the waiver is in writing.

Force Majeure

This provision excuses the vendor for non-performance due to forces beyond its control. These include such natural causes as fire and flood, but also cover failings of the vendor and its suppliers. Language can also be inserted to provide an escape clause for the buyer if the vendor delays beyond a specified time limit.

Non-Performance Procedures

The above clauses ensure that the contract exactly meets the definition of a contract. The next series of paragraphs concerns procedures if either party fails to perform as agreed.

Attorney's Fees. This clause provides that the losing party in any contract dispute pays the other party's litigation expenses. If this provision is absent, the general rule is each party pays its own expenses.

Arbitration. An arbitration clause allows the parties to use a relatively inexpensive way to resolve disputes. Two general approaches are common. The parties may spell out all the details of arbitration, such as the number of arbitrators and what is to be arbitrated. Or they may agree to use a commercial arbitration organization, such as the American Arbitration Association, which provides all the necessary rules and procedures.

Arbitration gives an alternative to expensive and time-consuming litigation. To effectively prevent litigation, though, the clause must be properly worded or you may find yourself arbitrating and then litigating the same issues. Also, arbitration may be self-executing, so that one party's refusal to arbitrate will not prevent it, but whether it's self-executing depends on state law.

Governing Law. When the seller and buyer reside in different states, this provision says which state's law will be used in the event of disputes. The governing law does not dictate the state in which a lawsuit can be filed, which is the jurisdiction, it shows the courts the parties' choice of law. For example, a contract might provide that the laws of New York apply, but California courts may have jurisdiction to hear the case and apply New York law. Courts are not required to follow that choice, but they usually do.

Limitation on Actions. To promote early resolution of contract disputes, state laws limit the time period in which the complaining party may sue. Although this time period is usually fixed at three years, the parties may agree to a different amount of time. Vendors typically insert a fairly short time, perhaps one year, which may have the effect of denying the buyer's legal recourse.

Defaults/Termination. When the contract extends over a long period, as a field maintenance agreement does, a provision may be inserted to resolve issues of non-performance or terminate the contract. Generally, the contract should give the defaulting party an opportunity to correct any default. This provision should reflect the parties' desire to resolve any potential dispute affecting the value of the contract.

Notices. In many business dealings, situations arise that require one party to notify the other. For example, the vendor may require that the purchaser give notice in a specific manner (such as "return receipt requested") within a certain time. This provision aims to ensure that the vendor receives the notice and that the purchaser acts promptly. Failure to give notice as required may be taken as no notice. This provision should be worded so that both parties must give notice in the same way.

The above discussion should help you become aware of the general content of contracts. Although many of these provisions are non-negotiable, you must know what they are and their effect on the legal relationship with your vendor.

UNIFORM COMMERCIAL CODE

The Uniform Commercial Code (UCC) is a body of law applicable to the world of commercial trade and industry. The UCC attempts to provide a series of uniform statutes regulating business throughout the United States. In practice, however, the entire commercial code has not been adopted by every state. Also, state courts do not necessarily interpret or construe the language in the same way. Although sameness is lacking, similarity is not. In most situations, the courts decide issues consistently.

The UCC affects ordinary contracts in that it "favors an agreement," meaning that if the parties fail to include certain terms, the UCC provides them. For example, if the contract fails to state the place of delivery, the UCC assumes it is the seller's place of business. The UCC may also correct omissions of price, performance time, quantity, delivery, and payment.

When one of the parties fails to perform as agreed, the UCC provides self-help remedies for the seller or buyer. For example, the purchaser may return a non-conforming product to the vendor. Litigation remedies allow either party to compel the performance as promised or to obtain an award of money for damages, which serves to compensate for any monetary loss caused by the other party's non-performance. (A court-enforced performance is unusual.) In addition to recovery of the purchase price, an award may be for loss of profits (consequential damages) and reasonable expenditures incurred because of the non-performance (incidental damages). At best, damage awards restore the buyer's financial condition to what it was on the date the contract was made.

The commercial code also provides certain warranties (promises or statements of fact) as to the quality and character of the product. "Merchantability" means the product is as good as other similar products on the market. A computer that never functions properly after installation breaches this warranty. "Fitness for a particular purpose" means the product will perform its stated function. For example, if a computer system purchased for inventory control fails at that task, it is not fit for that purpose.

Finally, the UCC applies to goods not services. Software publishers and sellers tend to argue that software is a service, but the buyer and seller can agree to make the UCC applicable to the software. Without some provision making the UCC applicable, though, it may not cover software purchases and maintenance contracts. Overall, the UCC does not impair your freedom of contract. As a buyer, though, you should watch for contract language that may negate your rights under the UCC.

SUBJECT MATTER

The following provisions relate to the subject matter of the contract: the computer system. The typical vendor's standard contract omits many of these clauses, but they should be included. They tend to be missing because the buyer has not had the opportunity to negotiate a contract that fairly distributes all the risks. Instead, the buyer relies on the vendor's reputation and integrity, which may not be the best approach.

The following discussion concerns buying both hardware and software, except where a distinction is needed. The first section covers a typical purchase agreement, while the second deals specifically with computer-related issues.

Typical Provisions

Security.   Until the vendor receives full payment, it retains a security interest in the merchandise. This provision serves to minimize the risk of losing both the system and the payment should the buyer fail to pay, due to bankruptcy, for example.

Shipment/Delivery.   These details are usually covered in the typical clause and need no further explanation. Notice, though, that the language may permit the vendor to set back the shipping date. Establish a realistic shipping date, since a delayed delivery could cause you undue hardship.

The typical vendor contract lacks any concern for the purchaser's risk or burden due to delay in delivery or partial shipment. You may ease this burden by inserting language giving the vendor an incentive to perform, such as a penalty or contract termination.

Risk of Loss or Damage.   Closely connected to shipment and delivery is the problem of who bears the risk of damage to the equipment once the system leaves the vendor's place of business, including any damages in transit. This risk is usually covered by insurance, but it should be clear who is to obtain the coverage and for what contingencies. In most cases, the contract contains a mercantile term (for example, "F.O.B. the seller's place of business") that allocates the risk. Where the contract fails to provide this, the UCC determines the appropriate risk.

Definitions.   Since the vendor is familiar with the technical terms associated with the subject matter, he has little incentive to insert definitions in the contract. Including them, however, makes it clear and more understandable, thereby preventing later disputes over interpretations.

Description.   All vendor contracts have space for product descriptions, but usually not enough space to include the details needed to prevent contract disputes. Both buyer and seller are protected if the contract includes such details as description of the computer system, features, capabilities, and configurations. Append the vendor's proposal to the contract if it contains such descriptions. (See also "General Provisions, Incorporation by Reference" earlier in this chapter.)

Computer System Purchase

The following items are unique to the computer system purchase once it has been delivered.

Installation. Typically, the contract obliges the vendor to install the system according to the vendor's or manufacturer's specifications, while the purchaser must provide a suitable environment. Notice that this means the purchaser must learn what is required to prepare the computer site (see Chapter 16).

Whatever the contract language, it should give you the installation details: the requirements, the procedures, and the definition of a completed installation should all be obvious. In many contracts, an installation is complete when the system is in "good working order," which is determined by the vendor, but there are certain ambiguities. The contract should specifically address the installation of any application software, and leave no doubt who is responsible for the system or its components.

Acceptance. The contract almost never addresses the matter of purchaser acceptance. An installation clause alone may not assure you of a reliable and functional system. The contract should state that the vendor's obligation is not fulfilled until you have a system that performs according to its documented specifications. Also, you should define acceptance and provide performance incentives to the vendor. For example, you might insist that the system meet a minimum standard of reliability. You may also want to make the final payment contingent on meeting these criteria.

Warranty. In making any agreement, the parties allocate various risks. One of the most important risks is the after-purchase responsibility for system performance. Usually the vendor will not warrant the entire system.

For hardware, vendors usually warrant that during the warranty period they will ". . . provide, at no additional charge to the customer, service to keep the machines in, or restore the machines to, good working order." Also, because certain additional warranties may be implied by law, vendors carefully limit or disclaim this added responsibility. For example, the above warranty is often followed by language such as: "THE FOREGOING WARRANTY IS IN LIEU OF ALL OTHER WARRANTIES EXPRESS OR IMPLIED, INCLUDING, BUT NOT LIMITED TO, THE IMPLIED WARRANTIES OF MERCHANTABILITY AND FITNESS FOR A PARTICULAR PURPOSE."

A warranty for packaged software is not common. Also, the UCC-implied warranties may not apply to software because of the legal controversy as to whether software is goods or services. Most vendors avoid this risk by expressly disclaiming all pertinent warranties with the following wording: "CUSTOMER AGREES TO ACCEPT THE PRODUCT AS IS."

Even though the contract provides a limited hardware warranty, the vendor should be willing to negotiate effective warranties for the system, or at least offer alternatives such as a hardware service and a software support contract. To achieve full value of the warranty, the starting date should not overlap other related time periods. For example, the warranty period should begin only after customer acceptance and the maintenance contract should begin only after the warranty period ends.

Limitation of Liability/Remedies.   Vendors attempt to limit their liability for non-performance with contract language such as: "Vendor's entire liability and customer's exclusive remedy shall be as follows: . . . ," and "In no event will vendor be liable for any damages . . . or other consequential damages. . . ."

Generally, the essence of vendor liability is that as long as the hardware can be repaired, the vendor may make the repair as he chooses. This is often declared to be "purchaser's exclusive remedy." If the hardware cannot be repaired, the vendor is liable only for a fixed amount of money. The limit is either stated in advance or determined by a fixed formula. Generally, the amount does not exceed the purchase price.

Although vendor's limited obligation for any non-performance is a difficult area for bargaining, you should at least consider expanding your remedies to include replacement of the entire system.

Progress Payments.   A typical payment clause requires full payment either before or upon delivery. While this requirement is appropriate for consumer products, a business computer is not a "plug-and-go" item. A test period is necessary before one knows it operates properly.

Under the usual payment provision, the vendor receives the full purchase price whether the system works or not. The ideal provision, however, makes full payment conditional on complete performance by the vendor. For example, you may ask that full payment be made only when you accept the system (see "Acceptance," earlier in this chapter) and partial payment be made as the vendor reaches certain milestones.

Withholding payment gives you some leverage in improving the vendor's performance. This form of financial incentive is especially appropriate for custom software development, during which significant time passes between the beginning and the end of the project.

Indemnities.   The contract should require the vendor to defend you in any legal action claiming that the system (hardware or software) violates a third party's proprietary rights, such as patents, copyrights, or trade secrets. This provision should also protect you against any copyright action prohibiting use of the software. Moreover, the vendor should assume sole responsibility for the defense, including paying costs, damages, and attorney's fees.

Price Protection.   Many contracts allow the vendor to increase the price before shipment. Discovering this possibility requires careful reading of the contract. The best protection against a price increase is specific language preventing it. When available, price protection generally covers a limited period before shipment. This period may be tied to the shipment date, which is changeable at the vendor's option. A price increase outside the protected period may give you the option to terminate the agreement if you give written notice within a short period, usually fifteen days. Usually, the buyer receives the benefit of any price decrease before delivery.

Ideally, price protection freezes the price on the day the contract is signed. Price protection for other system items, such as hardware maintenance and software support, is also worth pursuing.

Education/Training.   Purchase contracts do not usually provide for customer education or system training, but are usually treated in a separate contract. Some minimal training is necessary for any computer system, although what the vendor routinely supplies may not satisfy your needs or expectations. The contract should state exactly what training or education is included. At the minimum, the contract should cover initial training and describe the method of training.

Documentation.   User manuals and documentation are often included with the system purchase. These are important, because a third party may provide maintenance or support. The contract should state the quantity and nature of the manuals and other materials.

Many of the foregoing provisions do not appear in the vendor's standard contract. Even when included, they are narrowly phrased to give the vendor maximum protection in a dispute. Some clauses are difficult to draft and most vendors resist rewriting their standard contract. Yet, awareness of these issues gives you some room to negotiate a stronger position.

MAINTENANCE

The following provisions concern hardware, although similar provisions can be used for a software support contract. They may be found in the main system purchase contract or in a separate contract.

Term

Term refers to how long the contract is in effect. The initial term is generally one year, with automatic renewal. This feature effectively creates an indefinite term, but you should be able to terminate the agreement at any time on relatively short notice.

Determine the starting date relative to other contract provisions of the system purchase. For example, the maintenance term should not overlap the warranty or acceptance period. This is especially important when there are separate contracts for service and purchase.

Termination

Usually, either party may terminate the contract after some period of notice. While this period is generally longer for the vendor, it should be long enough for you to find alternative services. For example, one major vendor gives the customer twelve months' notice but requires one month's notice from the customer.

Equipment

A sound contract accurately describes what is to be serviced by listing the equipment, serial numbers, and locations. You are required to give the vendor's personnel complete access to the system. Restrictions on moving the equipment and changing the present system configuration help the vendor control his costs for performing the contract.

Service/Support Categories

The contract may specify the type of service while omitting such crucial details as service definition, service quality, and service response time. The type of service includes whether it is done at your location (on-site) or at the vendor's place of business (carry-in). If carry-in, you must transport the equipment to and from the vendor's location at your own risk.

Maintenance service is usually called corrective or preventive. Maintenance performed at your location may be either type, while service at the vendor's location is only corrective. Many contracts do not define what corrective or preventive maintenance entails. For most small business systems, however, you can do most, if not all, preventive maintenance.

With on-site service, the contract should state two conditions of the vendor's response to your request for service: one is, during what hours the work is done; such as, the regular work week excluding holidays. The vendor may also agree to answer a service request during second or third shifts, weekends and holidays. The other time factor is, how quickly a service technician must arrive at the computer site, which is called "response time." The contract should also state what actions you may take if the vendor fails to respond as agreed.

Another item absent from most agreements is the quality of the service, meaning the time to repair and the time between failures. You can be assured of high quality when the contract requires the equipment to be maintained at a specified standard of reliability. The contract also should state the training and experience of the service personnel, especially when the contract is with a third-party maintenance organization. Since service personnel may have access to confidential business data, a non-disclosure provision may be necessary.

Excluded Service

Similar to an insurance policy, a service contract does not cover all necessary service situations. Usually, the exclusions are reasonable: fire, water damage, power failure (including fluctuations in power), and tampering by unauthorized personnel. Some of these risks are best covered by insurance. A particularly important exclusion is "false" service calls due to programming or operator errors. In practice, vendors perform excluded services, but at an extra charge. Therefore, a list of excluded services is important in order to help determine the unplanned cost of the service contract.

Charges

Whether maintenance is a separate agreement or part of the system purchase agreement, the fee is usually a percentage of the system price. Payment may be a one-time annual charge or a fixed monthly charge during the maintenance period. Although the typical contract commits the vendor to provide maintenance for a fixed rate, it usually allows him to raise the charges when it is renewed.

Your chief concern should be what is usually missing from the contract: a definition of the potential cost of service. You may not know in advance the real cost of service because the contract lacks a full description of all service-related charges. Thus, such items as replacement parts, travel expenses, and excluded services should all be stated in the contract. Inserting the proper language in the contract may enable you to get the service you need at a fair price.

SOFTWARE

Software development is labor intensive and therefore expensive. It is probably the largest single cost in any computer system, large or small. Developers of packaged software try to protect their investment under copyright or trade secret laws. They do this by restricting a software purchase so that it is not a sale where you take title to the programs. Instead, you "buy" a license to use the software for an indefinite period. Software license provisions may be a separate contract or included as part of the main purchase agreement.

License

Under the license, you are called a user or licensee, and the vendor is the licensor. Because the vendor seeks to prevent unauthorized use or distribution of the software, the license is purposely restrictive. The language is generally as follows: ". . . a non-transferable and non-exclusive right to use. . . ." This means you may not transfer the software to another, and you are not the only licensee.

Second, the license may dictate the specific machine on which the software must be used. Thus, a separate license may be necessary for each system. When one owner has several machines, some software suppliers may make a multiple license agreement. Further, the license may limit the number of program backup copies, which are necessary because the original master copy may be lost or destroyed.

Third, the license may require non-disclosure of confidential information, such as a trade secret. The typical prohibition says: "The licensee agrees not to provide, disclose or otherwise make available . . . to any person. . . ."

Contracts generally say nothing about how to prevent disclosure. To be safe, you should treat the software as if it were your own trade secret. Two important considerations are control of and access to the software. Theoretically, if you fail to prevent disclosure you could lose your license to use the software and be forced to pay compensation to the licensor.

The term of the license may be either indefinite or definite with an automatic renewal feature. Whichever it is, either party may terminate the license. The licensor should terminate only if you fail to adhere to the provisions of the license. This termination should require a notice of the alleged failure and an opportunity, except for flagrant violations, for you to adhere to the license provisions.

Finally, the vendor is usually not the producer of the software, but has an agreement to distribute or sublicense the software. Some assurance is needed of the vendor's right to sublicense.

UCC Applicability

As previously mentioned, the Uniform Commercial Code applies to goods or hardware though a few courts have held that it applies to a complete system, meaning both hardware and software. To assure you some recourse in case of disputes, you and the vendor should agree to consider the software as goods for purposes of the contract.

Title Transfer

If you have in fact bought the software (custom programs), the contract should state that the title has transferred. Also, a Warranty of Title provision will ensure that the vendor has the right to transfer the title.

Software Changes

Because software is complex, designers often find ways to improve it, called modifications, enhancements, or upgrades. Future changes may not be necessary for you, but you may want the licensor to be obligated to provide them. In addition, the terms "modifications," "enhancements," and "upgrades" should be clearly defined, since they are only similar, not identical. Modifications are changes to correct program errors, while enhancements and upgrades are additions made to improve the product.

In the usual clause, the vendor is committed only to "advise" you of any change. Since the software warranty is usually "as is," the vendor has no other obligation. You should receive design changes, especially those improving the quality of the software, as they become available. The contract or license should also clarify who pays for and installs the changes.

Source Code Access

Usually, business users do not have the software in source code form, which is like having the secret key to the program's structure. If every user had access to the source code, the software producer would have no protection for his trade secrets. On the other hand, source code is vital to you if you want to modify the program, assuming the license permits it. Also, access is important in the event the vendor goes out of business.

Either because of the software producer's policy or the sheer expense of providing it, source code access is not a negotiable item for the user of a small business system, (except in the case of custom software). The software producer is not likely to risk losing control over the investment by permitting almost anyone access to the source code. When dealing with a vendor who is not the original developer, however, be certain it is authorized and has access to the source code in order to support your installation. A way to protect yourself should the developer go out of business is to arrange for the vendor to keep a copy of the source code in escrow.

Software Development

A software development contract involves vendor services including reviewing or studying the task to be computerized, programming and testing, and implementation. This contract is usually a concern only after you have bought a system. When only custom software will do, keep certain cautions in mind.

Ownership is crucial. The title and source code of custom software should transfer to you. The price of development should reflect the fact that the developer will make money on later, similar projects with other customers. While the buyer typically has full ownership rights in the programs it paid to have developed, the developer benefits from the learning experience paid for by the client. Thus, you should bargain for a lower price if your software developer has plans to sell the same or similar programs to others.

The contract should run according to mutually agreed stages of completion. Also, you should make proportional payments at various development milestones. Title transfer, progress reports, and software installation should also occur at stated intervals.

You must be in command at all times. The vendor should be required to warrant the original development and software performance. Because the vendor may have access to your sensitive business information, it also must be required to maintain confidentiality. You can ensure vendor compliance by designating acceptance criteria, as well as by withholding progress payments or ending the contract for non-performance.

Finally, software support is crucial. Regardless of what documentation is supplied, the developer must be committed to your future support.

SUMMARY

For numerous reasons, the vendor's standard contract may not fully protect all your interests. Contract deficiencies may not surface, or matter, until a dispute arises over the vendor's performance. Then you may want to complain of the contract's unfairness. Fair or not, the contract is likely to be enforceable because our legal system obliges the business person to know what the contract contains. Your signature on the contract implies that you have read it, that you understand all of it, and that you agree to abide by its terms and conditions.

The law also assumes that you contracted freely, that is, that you either negotiated the terms and conditions or agreed to abandon the right to negotiate. Thus, you and the vendor may agree to whatever you choose, however inequitable it may appear to others. You can hope for little sympathy or legal recourse if you later find the vendor not performing as expected because of your ignorance of the contract's provisions. However, as a disappointed buyer you may have legal recourse, beyond contract law, if for example the vendor has lied or withheld important facts.

While the standard vendor contract may be difficult to read and understand, ignorance is no defense. The law also assumes the contract includes the complete agreement. Your failure to seek legal recourse quickly may result in no recourse.

In conclusion, the standard advice regarding contracts applies: let the buyer beware, get a copy of the proposed contract, seek competent legal advice, and do not sign until you are satisfied the contract is acceptable.

CHAPTER
16

Installation Preparation

If you have faithfully followed the advice and guidelines in the first part of this book, you have spent considerable time in selecting hardware, software, and a vendor. With that effort now behind you, perhaps you are tempted to take an "everything should now fall into place" approach. Hold on. Installing a computer in your business is more than just installing hardware and software.

It's on the eve of the installation that the real work begins. You cannot simply sit in your easy chair, follow the experts' advice, and expect everything to turn out all right. You must continue to oversee the computer project and, with your vendor, establish detailed procedures to organize the many steps to complete the installation. You must also organize yourself well enough to stay on top of the computer implementation, and make sure the project does not get out of hand.

This chapter later describes the three main areas of the preparation process, which are:

1. Preparing your organization

2. Training the office staff

3. Preparing the computer site

When installing a computer, most companies follow the sequence above. However, these activities always overlap with each other and circumstances may demand that you proceed differently. Chapter 17 explains the steps and considerations of the physical installation.

Your should expect and prepare for some changes in your business during and after the installation process. It helps to decide in advance, if possible, what can and cannot change. You should also expect this process to yield new ideas that will help you improve your way of doing business. For example, many of the informal and impromptu methods of a manual system may no longer work for you under automation. The "scratch-pad" occurrences of a manual system are not built into an automated application. You will find that the computer dictates how some things must be done. At first these differences may bring frustrations, but over the long haul the new ways will offer improvements.

As has been mentioned, your ultimate success in computerizing the business depends on your relationship with the vendor. The ideal relationship is marked by teamwork. Each party shares the same objective: a successful installation. You should also share a detailed plan to meet this objective. You should take the lead in executing your plan, set the pace, and follow through. Failure to provide this leadership may cause costly mistakes and sometimes lead to problems that are difficult to recover from. For example, one company mistakenly thought the *vendor* had ordered the new preprinted invoice forms for the computer. With no invoice forms available, the company faced an expensive six-week delay in billing. Take the position that this is your project. Your vendor is there to help you, but since it's your system, you call the shots. If the vendor is not doing its part in completing all the steps and meeting the schedule, you will know right away and can take corrective action.

Your system purchase contract may in some ways define the areas of responsibility for you and the vendor. The contract will state what the vendor supplies in hardware and software, along with a tentative delivery schedule. Generally, the vendor is responsible for:

1. Delivering hardware and software

2. On-site component assembly

3. Hardware and software tests

4. Installing the accounting package

5. Initial accounting package tests

The vendor also does the staff training and helps supervise the conversion of the accounting data to the computer. The vendor further provides technical support and consultation throughout the installation project. On the other hand, the customer generally must:

1. Gather, edit, and prepare the data to be entered into the computer

2. Order necessary items such as preprinted forms

3. Prepare the physical site for the computer

4. Schedule the staff for training

5. Enter the information for data files into the computer

6. Test the system both with sample data and live data

ORGANIZATIONAL PREPARATION

The best possible planning and detailed preparation are keys to a successful installation. Properly installing the computer is crucial to creating a powerful information utility for your business. This integration process requires carefully thought out step-by-step procedures.

When a computer fails in business, lack of planning is most often the cause. Specifically, the most common faults are the failure of management to set sound, realistic objectives, and to train staff adequately. Allow time for the staff to adjust to a new way of doing things. They are certain to make errors while they learn and will need time to recover. Keep the schedule flexible. Your plans should include alternative procedures (the infamous "Plan B") in case of mishaps or delays. The fail-safe procedure allows the staff to revert to another method to get their work out at any point in the installation process. If done carefully, your contingency planning will give you peace of mind in knowing that the business will run smoothly no matter what. (When it comes to computers, Murphy wasn't an optimist—he was a dreamer. A variation on Murphy's Law is: What may have been a small problem to correct before an application goes into production always becomes a big problem to correct after the system is installed.)

Therefore, if the installation process is not handled properly, the unchecked power of the computer can quickly compound your problems. For example, suppose you discover the computer-generated billing statements are inaccurate. Rather than creating cash flow problems through delayed receivables, you may be smarter to fall back on manual statement preparation long enough for the computerized application to be corrected and returned to production.

The message bears repeating: Management must devote enough time and energy to the installation of the computer to make sure no problems become monumental.

The final two chapters of the this book assume: one, that you are converting from a manual system to a computerized system; and two, that you are installing an accounting package rather than developing your own custom software. If you are converting from using an outside service bureau or a timesharing service, the section "Accounting Data Conversion" (in Chapter 17) does not directly apply. If you are developing your own custom accounting package, the steps in the system installation section (also in Chapter 17) will require more time and extensive testing as the programs are developed.

The following section outlines the basics of preparing your staff for the computer installation with the focus on qualifying and readying those who will be using the system.

The Office Staff

Computer systems work best when combined with a well-organized, trustworthy, and competent staff. Never underestimate the importance of a good relationship between the computer and the people in your organization. Lacking this important human ingredient, there is little on which to build a smooth-running, dependable system. Your staff should be involved long before the machinery starts arriving, and a big part of your effort includes preparing the office staff for the "new member."

Your main job is to create an open, positive environment to allow the staff to support this computer adventure. Management must make clear these three points:

1. To install and use a computer has become necessary for the business. Things could get worse otherwise.

2. We expect the computer to do what it is proposed to do, that is, to work properly and improve the organization.

3. Those involved with the computer will benefit from the experience. Things will be done differently, and there may be some discomfort, but those who use the computer will develop some new skills.

It's human nature to resist change. For the most part, you can expect your staff to have some reservations about it. No better effort can be made in laying the groundwork than for management to recognize and deal with feelings and attitudes about the computer. One of management's main responsibilities is to help each person feel comfortable with the process and involve the employees as much as possible. Just as you were sold on the idea of getting the computer, you in turn may have to do some old-fashioned selling to your staff. You will have to show them how they will benefit, and convince each person that he or she will be able to handle the change.

Actually, selling the computer idea may not be that difficult. You may find that your people are ahead of management in their computer awareness. The desire for relief from the drudgery of simple but time consuming tasks may "percolate up" from the staff. This is especially true when many young employees have taken computer classes in school and are eager to apply the new technologies to their jobs.

Show Objectives.   In addition, you should stress that the computer is not intended to eliminate some of the office staff. Show that the computer is a new and important tool that will make each employee's job easier. Handling the fear of a possible layoff is especially critical if you have someone who is, in effect, carrying your business around in their head. It's up to you as the manager to demonstrate from their point of view the main objectives of computerization, which are:

1. **To reduce tedious jobs.**   Although the business may be profitable, computers are often installed *after* the point at which the staff is overworked. A computer system can allow the office workers to produce the same amount or more in a shorter time.

2. **To allow faster growth.**   Many small companies can grow faster than normal with a computer. A growth rate of 30–60 percent per year with computerized accounting is not uncommon. People tend to stay with a company when jobs are made easier, and increased growth improves the chances of promotion from within.

3. **To develop new job skills.**   Part of the excitement with a new, to-be-installed computer is that employees anticipate a chance to sit down and use it. For many this means not only a change of pace and a chance to use sophisticated technology, but also a chance to learn a new, valuable job skill.

One aspect that helps create a positive attitude about the computer is that you will not have to bring in a specialist, such as an operator or a programmer to run the system. Make it clear that each person involved will have the opportunity to learn how to use the computer, and the company will draw on help from the outside only as needed.

The Team Approach.   As discussed earlier, the best chances of a successful installation come from organizing your staff around the team approach. Ideally, the team consists of one or two people from the vendor (one of whom is identified as the project leader), a member of the company's management staff, and at least one person from each of the functional areas that will use the new system. This team should be identified in advance of the system implementation, and good communication among its members should be encouraged through regular meetings. All team members should clearly understand what goals are to be accomplished, how, and with what resources. The team members should also agree on an installation schedule. The schedule should include all phases of the implementation, such as site preparation, hardware/software set-up, testing, entering the accounting data, checking the parallel runs, and the final cutover to the new system.

Unless your business is quite small, do not expect one person to install an accounting system on a computer. You stand a better chance of success when the system is installed by a group of people who all understand their part in the process and share the responsibility for its completion.

When you first thought of obtaining a computer, you probably had in mind some of the people who would be operating the system. If you are unsure who may be most adept at learning and using the computer, pick the person you believe has the strongest *interest*. Do not automatically use age and background as main criteria. People who do best in using the computer as a new experience are typically those who are open to change and who are better at working through day-to-day problems. They like to share enthusiasm for something new and have an element of confidence about what they do.

Before the computer arrives, assign a system manager or a key operator to maintain the system. This is the chief custodian of the computer. This assignment means that someone is responsible for keeping the machine operational for all other users. It entails such things as maintaining the data files on the diskettes, which includes backing them up on schedule. This person is also the primary contact with the vendor, which means calling for servicing when necessary, or when operational problems occur. The system manager may order supplies for the computer, such as paper, ribbons, and diskettes. He or she may also train new employees as they come onto the staff.

Keep the Staff Posted.   Keep the staff posted on what's going on. Provide them with all the details to help them understand how all the pieces go together. Regular meetings are usually essential here. Also, each individual's progress needs to be communicated to management to prevent little problems from growing into big problems. You need to know the cause before developing a solution for each problem. Proper feedback from the staff can alert you to the unexpected, which often occurs since system specifications and implementation planning cannot cover every detail and every possibility. Only you, working with your team, can fill in the blanks. In short, you have to stay active and involved by managing the project.

Schedule Activities. You may find it useful to produce a chart that shows the scheduling of all the installation activities. A Gantt chart works well and a sample is shown in Figure 16-1. This type of chart gives a quick visual reference to what is supposed to happen and approximately when. Consider also using other, more detailed charts (or sub-charts) that break down each of the activities on the master chart.

Installation Activities Schedule										

Activity	_____ Week Number _____									
	1	2	3	4	5	6	7	8	9	10
Organizational Preparation										
Staff Assignments	XXXX									
Software Modifications	XXXXXXXXXX									
Staff Training		XX		XX						
Computer Site Prepared	XXXXX									
Items Installed:										
Electrical Power Line	XX									
Telephones			XX							
Furniture		XX								
Supplies	X									
Physical Installation										
Hardware Assembled, Tested		XX								
Accounting Package Installed		XXX								
Preliminary Package Tests			XX							
Accounting Conversion										
Account Codes Established	XXXXXXX									
Enter Master File Data:										
General Ledger		XXXXX								
Accounts Receivable				XXXXX						
Accounts Payable										
Inventory Description					XXXXXX					
Payroll										
Enter Transaction Data:										
General Ledger					XXX					
Accounts Receivable							XXX			
Accounts Payable										
Inventory						XXX				
Payroll										
Test System With Live Data								XXX		
Final Acceptance Test									XX	
Cutover Date										X

Figure 16-1 Installation Activities Schedule

Software Modifications

Another element in the preparation for a computer is the planning of any required software modifications. These are the must-have program changes to make your system operational right from the first days. Usually the vendor is responsible for completing these modifications, which can begin well in advance of the equipment delivery. Typically, the vendor can start working on the changes just after you've ordered the system, and if they are not extensive, have them tested and ready when the computer is installed. This shortens the waiting time until the computer can produce for you.

Once the computer is installed, though, defer any further software modifications until some time after the computer is operating smoothly. (Recall the advice to wait until after the first three months for any software changes.) This avoids the compounding of problems in testing and debugging software modifications while bringing up a new system.

Accounting Information

Obviously, before any accounting information is printed or displayed on the video screen, it must first be entered into the computer. This requires several steps of selecting, editing, and preparing the data from your manual files. This step offers a good opportunity for most companies to purge and clean up the data before it's fed into the computer. These preliminary steps can begin any time before the system is installed. While they seem like extra work, these steps help build a solid base of detail information for your future operation. Once the manual information is prepared to be entered, the consistency and accuracy of the computer makes it easy to maintain. (See the section on "Accounting Data Conversion" in the next chapter for more specifics.)

Converting Can Be Stressful

During the phasing in of the computer, keep in mind that your organization will be undergoing changes in almost every aspect. While computerization is justified as a change for the better, changes can be stressful. Your staff will be learning to contend with a new system while trying to keep the business running as usual. Your operators will be learning how to enter, manipulate, and report the information with the same ease as in the manual system. In the short run, and especially during the conversion, workloads are actually increased. Most companies cannot afford, nor find it practical, to hire part-time or temporary staff during this conversion period. For a while your staff will be maintaining two different systems, that is, continuing the old one until the new one proves to be workable and accurate. Maintaining two systems for the short run can be a burden. You need to be aware of this potentially stressful period and to make allowances to prevent employee morale from falling.

STAFF TRAINING

Learning how to operate the computer is the crux of the installation process. It is the primary means to the successful running of your computer. Not every possible problem in the operation of the computer will present itself during these early stages, nor even perhaps for the following few months. Thus, in the training of the staff it is equally important for them to learn when something is wrong or doesn't look right as well as when something is correct and looks as it should. This might be called "defensive training," so that the operator does not become complacent in operating the computer.

Running a computer, especially with an accounting package, requires continual monitoring, almost like running a nuclear power plant. A properly trained staff, knowing how to make the computer do what it should and how to find and correct errors, is good insurance in avoiding problems that might be expensive or time consuming to recover from.

The Barriers

Bringing a computer into the business often frightens some employees. Management should be alert to the various psychological barriers that may be found in staff awaiting a computer installation. Probably the most common form of resistance is the fear of change. Even with all the benefits of the computer system firmly established in everyone's mind, a computer still represents change in the way things are done; a change from established, familiar procedures to new and different ways. The staff may also fear that management will change its expectations of employee performance.

Fear of job loss is also common. It is best to announce early and clearly that you do not intend to eliminate staff members (providing, of course, those *are* your intentions). It is in everyone's interest to show that the computer is meant to help make everyone's job easier, rather than lead to layoffs. Handling these kinds of negative reactions is especially critical if one or more of your staff is carrying the unwritten inner workings of your business around in his or her hip pocket.

Employees may also fear not being able to cope with the computer. From the viewpoint of the uninitiated, computers are seen as complex and sophisticated machines. Some people even think (incorrectly) that if they did not do well in math in school they will not do well with the new computer. Fortunately, many of these fears disappear when the training starts and the office staff replace their doubts and ignorance with knowledge and experience. As they learn more precisely what is expected of them, and what they can accomplish, they generally welcome the computer.

In addition to the training, other steps will minimize these fears. The staff can learn by doing as they enter the master file information. Having the staff enter the master files offers good hands-on experience with meaningful data. Since this information can easily be checked and rechecked after entering it into the computer, it is a low-risk, introductory operation. (Entering the master files is explained further in the next chapter.)

If after all of this you still encounter cases of computerphobia, a frivolous application such as computer games almost always works. Programmers, in their idle moments, have devised games for just about every computer in the world. At the very least there are games like Adventure, Blackjack, Lunar Landing, Keno, and others that take full advantage of the computer's video screen. Sometimes games are the first thing a newly-installed computer is used for. All you need to do is to show your staff how to start the game and then leave them alone. Games demonstrate to people that computers can be fun and that they cannot ruin the hardware by pushing the wrong button. If you give them an opportunity to play the games on their lunch hour and coffee breaks, you will find that the most resistant people will drop their computer defenses without even thinking about it. If this kind of usage becomes an obsession, however, you may have to buy a separate game computer for the lunchroom.

Management and Staff Training

For several reasons, management should receive the same formal training as the office staff. First, management can better understand the conditions in which operators use the computer, and perhaps smooth the operation by removing some of the bottlenecks in the flow of data to and from the computer. Second, employees will have fewer complaints if the manager shows a willingness to do what is asked of them. Third, workers gain confidence when management is aware of what's involved in using the computer day-to-day.

In one company, the manager was the first to install and use the computer for particular purposes. Gradually, each of the office members came to use the computer for his or her own tasks. In this case, the office staff received no training from the vendor. The manager was the first to learn how to use the computer, and then was able to show each of them how to relate it to their particular function in the office. Although this system was used primarily for word processing and electronic spreadsheet calculations, rather than accounting, it proved to be one of the most effective ways to overcome the sturdiest resistance to using the "new-fangled gadget."

What Training Includes

Training in how to use a computer can be both generalized and specific. It goes beyond what buttons to push on the computer and its peripherals. The initial training is the responsibility of the vendor, but is best accomplished with the full cooperation of management and the office staff. The following should be included in the training and can serve as a checklist in working with your vendor.

Basic Concepts. The introduction or overview should include basic concepts, such as identifying the various components of the system, and how data is entered, stored and retrieved through the video screen and the printer. It should also include an overview of the accounting package, how it relates to the business, and the general flow of information to and from the computer. In other words, this part identifies the overall environment in which the computer is expected to function.

Hardware Operation. This is probably the simplest part of the training, since it shows how to turn on the computer, how to insert the diskettes, and how to load programs into memory. It also teaches the purpose of the control keys on the keyboard, the central processing unit, and the printer. This step includes how to load paper in the printer and clear paper jams, but probably the most important part is the care and handling of the diskettes. (See "Care of Diskettes," Chapter 9.) The hardware training should also include the most frequently used commands and utilities found in the operating system.

Accounting Software Procedures. The accounting software procedures include all the steps that constitute the general flow of work during the accounting period. Sales and cash receipts have to be entered before customer balances are affected. Inventory transactions have to be entered to determine quantities on hand in order to set production schedules. Detailed journal entries have to be made before final posting to the general ledger in order to close the month-end. All these are accounting activities that require definite procedures or steps in a particular sequence. These accounting procedures make up the necessary events in using the computer system as it functions within your business. The general outline of these steps is normally found in accounting manuals, but it may be necessary to expand or modify them to suit your needs.

Data Entry and Update. Data entry is not a short course in touch typing, but determining what accounting programs have to be called into memory to enter the data. This part of the training includes how to use the special control keys and functions on the keyboard, and the proper way to correct and recover from operator mistakes. Updating is calling the information back to the video screen from a previous session and either correcting information from earlier transactions or adding new information. Entering and updating the data constitutes the most frequent use of the computer. Since it is best accomplished by hands-on experience, it is usually the easiest part to learn.

Error and Exception Handling.   Training on how to handle *all* types of errors that may occur cannot be done during installation, since all types cannot be known. Initially, only the more frequently occurring conditions, based on the vendor's experience, can be part of the training. Handling errors depends on how well the software is designed in allowing recovery from them, and how well the documentation explains them. Training in how to handle exceptions also depends on software design, and on those differences between the mechanics of the accounting package and how you operate your business. It is important to spend some time learning the rudiments of these procedures. Later the vendor should be available (at least by telephone) to answer questions.

Data Backup Procedures.   Data backup means making an identical copy of the data disk used to record the day's activities, as described in Chapter 9. It takes only a few minutes of the operator's time and is normally done at the end of the day after all transaction activity has stopped. Your vendor should have procedures established for backing up the diskettes.

How to Use the Manuals.   Using the manuals may seem like an elementary part of the training process, but the more sophisticated accounting packages may have the documentation spread over several binders. The vendor should take at least a few minutes to show you how the material is organized and how to find what you want.

Training Methods

One of the most effective methods of training your staff is on the job, in your own office. This kind of training is best because it uses your computer configuration and your company's data, which are most relevant to you and your employees. On-site training also allows the vendor to focus on your particular installation and answer specific questions from your staff, as well as modify or amend the training as the need arises.

Computer manufacturers, software suppliers and dealers are constantly looking for new ways to make training more effective while reducing the cost. Listed below are some of the methods of training now used, which may be more to your liking depending on the nature of your installation. Some of these methods are tried-and-true and some represent new technologies. If you find on-site training the best to start with, you still may want to consider another method for on-going training as your business expands or as key personnel change.

Vendor Seminars.   Vendor seminars may be much like those the vendor provides on-site, except they are held at their location. The cost of training may be lowered, however, by teaching a group of customers at one time. Some people feel they can concentrate better away from their office environment, and the format allows getting immediate answers to specific questions. Group seminars may also offer some advantage in learning of the experiences of other attendees in similar situations.

Computer-Assisted Instruction. Computer-Assisted Instruction (CAI) is much like a self-paced study guide, except that the learning experience occurs on the computer itself. A special set of computer programs is used to help tutor the operator in a particular application. Some of these CAI programs are very sophisticated and are programmed to accelerate or double back to review material, depending on the student's progress at the keyboard. One of the purposes served here is giving the operator actual computer time while learning. However, if the computer is a single user system it cannot be used for anything else while running the training programs. These programs also may be quite expensive.

Manuals, Tutorials, and Guides. Suppliers of the better software packages have taken great pains to provide documentation that is easy to use and assists in the learning process. Some manuals include tutorials, which are series of lesson plans including examples of how to use the computer and the software package. Sometimes the software diskettes include data files to practice with, coinciding with the examples found in the tutorial manuals. The main advantages of a tutorial are that it is generally available for the price of a book and that learning is paced to the individual. The reference guides are cards that summarize all the commands of the software package and serve as handy reminders when using the system.

Video Cassettes and Discs. Video cassettes and video discs are better suited for small groups of students, or for those who find it difficult to learn from a manual. Of course, video equipment is needed, but a good video presentation can be worth more than several pages of manual explanations. In its simplest form, the program gives the operator a sight and sound explanation. He or she then puts the video on "pause" and tries to duplicate the same thing on the computer. The more sophisticated video training programs are integrated with the computer and can automatically alternate between the television monitor and the computer terminal. Here the computer is programmed to display the appropriate material when the operator needs to review certain portions of the lessons. These methods can be very effective, and some consider them to be the next best thing to an instructor.

Staff Feedback. Be sure your staff reports to you on the quality of their training. If the material is not presented clearly enough, you should find out why and correct the situation with your vendor. You will need to determine whether the training is too technical, doesn't cover the right subjects, or if psychological barriers are inhibiting the process. Getting your computer installation off to a good start is synonymous with adequate training.

COMPUTER SITE PREPARATION

The new generation of small business computers do not need a special environment, such as an air-conditioned room. In addition, microcomputers are much easier to place in an office than their predecessors were, since the physical space needed for the components takes about as much room as a desk or a filing cabinet. These computers and their peripherals also can be plugged into ordinary electrical outlets, thus avoiding the installation of higher voltage circuits. Despite these advances, you must consider a number of items in preparing for the physical installation of your computer.

Computer supplies should be ordered in advance of system delivery in order to keep the installation on schedule. For example, you may have to order preprinted forms for the computer's printed output. These might include statements, invoices, and checks for accounts payable and payroll. The accounting package often dictates the spacing and layout of these forms.

Special insurance may also be needed to protect against such risks as fire, theft, and various forms of property damage. Some special policies now cover the software, including data and programs stored on the diskettes. Other risks include data loss through short circuits or power surges, corrosion or rust from normal air conditioning, and the losses incurred due to interruption of normal business operations. If you already have insurance, check to make sure it includes the computer hardware and software.

You may also need to order a separate power line for the computer, special telephones, and computer furniture. These last three items are explained in more detail later in this section.

Environmental Requirements

Let's look at the physical environment in which the computer is expected to operate. An acceptable room temperature for the human operator is also acceptable for most computer systems. The best room temperature for microcomputers is between sixty and eighty degrees Fahrenheit. When the temperature rises much above eighty degrees, the computer should be shut down. Always avoid placing the computer in an area of direct sunlight, which may also affect the diskettes and tapes, even when they are not in use in the machine. Many microcomputers have built-in cooling fans to minimize heat build-up. Remember that some of the larger micros actually generate heat and over a day's time can raise the temperature of a small room by several degrees.

Static electricity is probably the least suspect but most common of environmental threats to a small computer system. Many computers are sensitive to even small electrical charges (overlooked by humans), especially in a dry environment. Just a few steps across a heated, dry room can generate a static discharge of 5–35,000 volts. To protect against this disruption, your computer and its peripherals need three-pronged, electrically grounded plugs. The main contributors to static electricity are nylon rugs, insulating shoe soles, low relative humidity, and cool North winds. The three main defenses against static electricity are:

◪ Keep the relative humidity at 50 percent or above
◪ Avoid standard nylon carpeting
◪ Use anti-static mats and sprays

Keep in mind that an anti-static spray is not a permanent cure-all for persistent static electricity problems. If used frequently, it eventually finds its way into the inside of the computer system and can literally gum up the works.

In comparison with many other devices, small business computers are highly durable machines that can hold up very well under continuous day-to-day operation. What surprises most people is that an estimated 80 percent of all computer failures (instances when the computer needs technical repair) are caused by some misuse or abuse by the operator. The frustrating thing about computers, though, is that the effects of mistreatment may not show as a malfunction until days or even weeks later.

For instance, an accidental thumbprint on a diskette may not become a problem until that spot has accumulated dust or dirt which then makes it unreadable. Therefore, when a number of people use the computer, it's wise to establish some precautions to follow. For example, no smoking, drinking, eating, or excessive dust should be allowed around the computer site. Minimizing dust may mean changing the filters on the air conditioning unit on a regular basis, or even simple things like closing outside windows, particularly in an industrial area. It may also mean restricting janitorial services in the area, since their cleaning methods may threaten the health of the computer.

Power Requirements

Almost all microcomputers and their peripheral devices are designed to run on standard line voltages found in office buildings and residences (110–117 volt AC, 15–20 amp line). Providing access to regular voltage need not be a major concern.

The *quality* of that power line is a consideration, however. To run smoothly and process data accurately your computer must have steady, non-fluctuating current. Many electronic appliances, such as television sets, desk calculators, and video recorders, are not as sensitive to power line fluctuations, so these variations go unnoticed. The nature of disk operations and main memory makes computers a special case. Power line fluctuations are called "transients" or "line noise." When excessive they can negatively affect the operation of the computer and even cause damage.

You can take two steps to improve the computer's electrical supply. First, put the computer on a separate power line (independent circuit) from the main power source of the building (the circuit breaker box). This means an independent line with no other electrical devices on it. A separate line minimizes the effect of various loads otherwise placed on the circuit, such as unavoidable changes when electrical motors from heating and cooling units turn on. Second, the computer should be grounded with a three-pronged outlet rather than a two-pronged one. Be sure that the computer and all its peripherals have the same grounded polarity. An easy way to accomplish this is to plug all the devices into the same wall outlet. If you need more than two outlets, a multiple-outlet power strip works well.

If a separate, grounded line does not solve your voltage problems, you can have an electrical contractor attach a device that monitors and records the fluctuations in the line. If these tests show wide, persisting fluctuations, special devices, called surge protectors, can be added to stabilize the current. A surge protector, also called an AC line conditioner, is an electrical device that plugs into a wall outlet. It's a small "black box" with standard outlets that you plug the computer into. These devices only prevent the sudden increases in electric current, called "spikes," from reaching the computer, and are not a solution to power line dips. Check with your computer dealer or an electrical contractor to locate a suitable line conditioner.

Physical Layout

The location of the computer site in your office and the physical layout of the components can make a big difference in fostering positive attitudes when your workers use the system. Computers have ways of inducing their users to spend long hours in front of the keyboard and video screen. Every measure should be taken to reduce fatigue during these extended sessions. Such things as adequate light, comfortable seating, pleasant room conditions, and sufficient work space are essential, just as in any productive office.

Component Layout.   Physical arrangement of components is important: Rather than spacing them out along a desk or table top, use an L-shaped layout. This puts all the components within easy reach of the operator and creates a cockpit effect. Some computers have all components except the printer built into one enclosure, which requires locating only two separate cabinets. The most important aspect of the physical location is to make sure the keyboard is the optimal height above the floor, which is usually twenty-six to twenty-eight inches.

Other systems have the computer, disk drives, video screen, and keyboard in separate enclosures. In this case the computer cabinet must be located closer to the disk drives than the other units, because the high-speed data transfers between the computer and the disk drives require short cables. The other peripherals, such as the CRT and the printer, can be located at a farther distance. Again, the operator should have an easy reach from the keyboard to the disk drives and to the controls on the printer. Keep in mind that the operator may frequently have to change the diskettes in the drive units and watch the printer during its operation, especially for paper outages or an occasional jam.

One often overlooked condition in the planning of the computer site is the amount of glare or background light reflected on the video screen. Reducing this glare minimizes eyestrain and fatigue. Avoid placing the video screen opposite a large outside window or door; use an inside wall.

Noise Levels.   Take some care to hold down the noise generated by the computer. Aside from the built-in cooling fans, the largest noise generators are printers and hard disks. The noise from printer hammers impacting paper to make an impression is an inherent characteristic of the printer. Separate offices or partitioned enclosures will help minimize the disturbance. If necessary, loud printers can be housed in special acoustic enclosures, which have built-in noise absorbing materials. Access doors that open like automobile hoods and other aperatures permit the normal manual operation of the printer while it is inside the enclosure.

Hard disk drives tend to be noisy because the disk inside spins at about 3,600 rpm, which to some people can sound like a jet engine. This is particularly true of hard disks with removable cartridges. Fortunately, the Winchester-type technology virtually eliminates this problem because these are relatively small drive units located in special hermetically sealed units.

Telephones.   A telephone at the computer site is a convenience for the operator, but is essential if the computer is configured to talk to the outside world via a modem and telephone lines. If computer communications are to be installed, use two telephones—one dedicated to data communications, and the other a regular dial-up line for the operator to talk to vendors and service people.

A regular telephone is also handy during diagnostics and maintenance of the machine. Your operators can be executing programs on the computer while receiving instructions from the service technician over the phone. A second phone is essential when your vendor is equipped to troubleshoot your system by dialing up your computer through a terminal from his location. With this arrangement, he is able to operate and diagnose your system just as though his terminal was one of your own. For the operator's convenience keep a list of the important computer-related phone numbers near the equipment.

CAUTION: Because of the quirks of magnetic fields and vibrations, the telephone should never be placed on a floppy or hard disk drive. A ringing phone can do damage to these units. This hazard is best controlled by making the telephone cord short enough so that it cannot be placed on top of the disk drive units.

Furniture.   Today's small business computers work quite well on ordinary office furniture, such as desks, tables and counter tops. Special computer furniture is available, though, which is aesthetically pleasing, provides a convenient arrangement of the components, and permits desk-top space for working materials. Some manufacturers make computer furniture specially designed and fitted for particular brands of computers and configurations. These pieces provide shelves, for example, that are large enough to hold the components below the working surface and yet give easy access to the controls and disk drive units. This allows more working area. The computer site should contain shelving for storing disk-ettes, manuals, and other materials so that the immediate working area remains uncluttered. Ordinary filing cabinets or desk drawers are safe for storing diskettes in their protective boxes.

Whether you should put the printer on a separate printer stand or the desk top depends on the type of printer. Small, low-speed, dot matrix printers can be placed on the same desk or counter as the computer with no vibration interference. However, high-speed dot matrix printers and full-character printers are best installed on a separate pedestal or printer stand. These heavier, faster printers normally generate vibrations that could affect sensitive disk heads while they operate.

One reason for putting the printer on one leg of the L-shaped arrangement is to allow the operator easy access to the backside of the printer, where the continuous forms or fanfold paper settles. You must allow space for the paper to stack after it winds through the printer. Some printers and printer stands allow a bottom-feed operation, in which a special cut-out is provided in both the printer and the stand to allow the paper to feed directly from below. This arrangement offers fewer problems with paper jams and takes less space at the back of the printer.

If you place your computer components on shelves or in special enclo-sures, be sure to allow plenty of clearance for the cooling fans to circulate air. In some computers the components are in separate cabinets, each enclosure may have a cooling fan. A minimum of three inches clearance is usually all that you need, but check the manufacturer's recommendations.

Even the simplest installations will have cables and power cords dan-gling from the backs of the components. Special computer furniture and desks have the advantage of providing space for these connectors. In any case, take some care to route the cables so they are out of the way. Avoid placing cables alongside electric power lines, other office appliances, or powerful transformers. Also, cables should not be routed close to fluorescent fixtures, and they certainly should not be left on the floor to be stepped on. Ask your vendor to label the cable connections as he installs them. Even though cables may look alike and have standard connectors, their internal wiring may be different and therefore will not work properly if hooked up to another peripheral.

Media Storage. Diskettes or any other magnetic media used to store programs and data should be kept in their respective containers when not in use. Store diskettes vertically and preferably in closed metal cabinets to avoid problems with extraneous magnetic fields. Blank diskettes, backup diskettes, and working diskettes should each be stored in a separate location to avoid mistakes by grabbing the wrong disk. Backup diskettes are best stored in a locked cabinet or vault which is fireproof and waterproof.

Remote Terminals. If you have a multi-user computer with remote terminals, they can be placed almost anywhere in the building up to a distance of about fifty feet from the central processing unit. Data communications, as described earlier, can be used for longer distances. Remember, though, that when someone wants to access the computer from a remote terminal, the computer will have to be turned on and the proper diskettes loaded in the drives. A hard disk offers the convenience of any remote user having access to the particular files without having to change diskettes, as you would in a floppy disk system.

Smoke Detectors. Small business computers do not pose any extraordinary fire hazard compared to other home and office electrical appliances. Operators and users of the equipment should be aware of particular hazards, however, such as the obstruction of ventilation outlets on the cabinets and the dropping of metal objects like paper clips inside the enclosure, causing a short circuit. Also, a printer paper jam left unattended for an extended time can cause the printer to dangerously overheat. Thus, a smoke detector installed at the computer site can give an early warning and prevent extensive damage. If a fire occurs, it is often easier to replace the equipment than to replace the information on the diskettes, which typically involves many hours of labor.

PREPARATION CHECKLIST

An installation preparation checklist is shown that contains the key points of this chapter. Spaces are provided to indicate the personnel assigned to these tasks and a start and completion date for each item. You may want to expand on this list to best suit your own installation process.

Installation and Preparation Checklist			
	Personnel Assigned	**Start Date**	**Finish Date**
Organizational Preparation			
Computer Operators Identified			
Vendor Contacts Introduced			
Operator Responsibility Assigned			
Installation Activities Scheduled			
Data Conversion Requirements			
Software Modifications			
Staff Training Scheduled			
Maintenance Agreement Completed			
Computer Site Preparation			
Designate Physical Space			
Items Ordered:			
Insurance			
Pre-Printed Forms			
Electrical Power Line			
Telephones			
Furniture			
Media Storage			
Smoke Detectors			
Surge Protector			
Supplies:			
Standard Computer Paper			
Printer Ribbons			
Printwheels			
Blank Diskettes			
Computer Site Rules			

Figure 16-2   Installation Preparation Checklist

CHAPTER

17

System Installation

Now that you have prepared your organization, started the staff training, and set up the computer site as suggested in Chapter 16, you are ready for the final steps of your computer installation. This chapter focuses on three remaining areas: the physical installation of the hardware and software, converting the accounting data from the manual documents to the computer, and the final cutover to the computer, using either the parallel or the phase-in methods. Notice the emphasis on constantly testing the new system. According to an old Arabic saying, one should, "Trust in

Heaven, but tie up your camel." Modified for the world of computers, you should, "Trust in Heaven, but test everything else."

HARDWARE INSTALLATION

System installation is the physical setting up of the computer and its software. It requires many small steps from the time the cartons arrive until everything is ready to use. Even before the system is delivered to your business, the vendor typically does a dress rehearsal of setting up and testing the hardware. This off-site test helps ensure that your system is as it should be when it's delivered.

The vendor begins by making sure the order is received complete, including items like hardware options and hook-up cables. During unpacking the vendor inspects for any shipping damages, and also verifies that the latest engineering changes in the hardware, and the current versions of the software packages, have been included.

Next, the vendor sets up the hardware, much as he would in your location, and performs some initial bench tests to make sure it is working properly. During this phase the vendor sets numerous "dip" switches, each about the size of the tip of a ballpoint pen, which are found inside the cabinets of the various components. These switches commonly establish the rate of electronic transmission speed between the computer and its accessories. Setting these switches is technical in nature, but provides some flexibility in customizing the final hardware configuration.

The bench test includes completing the cable connections between the peripheral devices. Computer manufacturers use several different types of connectors having as many as twenty-five, thirty-six, or fifty tiny wire connections running end to end. To make matters more complex, computer manufacturers have not agreed on which wires are to be used for what purposes. In other words, there are no standards, which means your vendor may have to change the use of these wires, commonly called "pin assignments," depending on what device you use. These hook-up considerations are especially important if you want different brands of computer and printer.

Next the vendor installs the operating system, which is the software package that makes the computer work. Operating systems have such trade names such as CP/M, MS-DOS, and UNIX. The operating system is normally supplied by the hardware manufacturer, but often it has to be configured to your particular computer. This may involve reprogramming portions (or adding sub-routines) of the operating system to make the printer, disk drives, and other peripherals work with the main computer unit.

Then the vendor integrates the particular packages of application software, you have ordered. This may include the software for word processing, electronic spreadsheets, or the accounting package. Typically, a one-time step here "tells" the applications software what kind of hardware it has to work with. Usually a special program, called the install program, is supplied with each of the application packages to facilitate this step.

After the vendor completes these steps at his shop, he disassembles the components, repacks them in their original cartons, and readies them for delivery to your business.

So the day finally arrives when the vendor puts your computer into a van and delivers it to your office, where you have prepared the computer site for the arrival. The vendor continues with the installation by setting up and reassembling all the components. Again everything is tested, much as in the shop, to insure that nothing was affected during shipment. Next the vendor prepares the user diskettes. These are also called "working copies" and are the diskettes your staff uses regularly. The working copies are often altered versions of the original diskettes, called masters, which are stored in a safe place and used only to make newer working copies.

SOFTWARE INSTALLATION

Next, the vendor initializes the accounting package. Although this does not normally include any programming, it has the effect of tailoring the accounting package to the way you want the computer to help run your business. The more sophisticated software packages will contain numerous choices as to how you want the accounting to function. These options are built into the package and are normally set only once, when the software is installed. Some examples are:

- Do you want inventory costing by the LIFO, FIFO, or average cost method?
- Are accounts receivable aged by invoice or due date?
- Are salesmen paid commissions? If so, how are they calculated?
- Are finance charges to be applied on the invoices?
- How are sales taxes to be computed?

The vendor will set these variables by answering questions posed on the video screen by a special initializing program that comes with the package. This may be done with the information you have already supplied to your vendor. If everything is working properly at this point, then the focus shifts to the testing procedures.

Once the accounting package is initialized, the system is tested by entering some sample data. Now you may want to enter enough data to run through all the basic procedures of the accounting package. This enables you to simulate a complete accounting cycle in your business. The idea is to compress the time of a regular accounting period into a few hours to learn what kind of problems might occur and how the system handles them.

During the installation, any difficulties your staff has in following instructions, in the manuals or elsewhere, will become apparent. Better to force problems to surface now, since your staff has devoted only minimal time to the data entry. Testing of the hardware and software continue as they are being installed.

Installation Tests

While the main purpose of the installation, thus far, is to test the software and become familiar with the accounting package, this is a good opportunity to test the system for error handling. Your objective here is to check the system's integrity when entering the data. Some of the conditions to be tested include:

◪ Entering alphabetic data in numeric-only data fields
◪ Trying to post in a month that's closed
◪ Entering illegal codes such as unassigned general ledger account codes or inventory part numbers
◪ Conflicting conditions, like entering an account code for one customer with a sales order number of another customer

You can also do other types of tests. For example, the data may be correct but the procedure involved may be illogical, such as trying to generate an invoice before a sales order has been created; or trying to deplete an inventory item before the balance on hand has been entered; or attempting to run payroll before the time card data has been keyed in.

Overall, you and your staff should explore the system extensively. Now may be your best opportunity to further test and learn about the system without jeopardizing the live data you will use later.

To help your operators gain confidence in using the system, have them proceed through the activities of an entire accounting period. These include opening the files for the current month, entering realistic examples of the data, generating checklists and other required monthly reports, and then conducting a month-end closing. The data entered should be as representative as possible of all the types of transactions you normally encounter.

For example, sample data can be constructed to test the sales order function, which might include the following:

A sales order from a wholesale account

A sales order from a retail account

An order for taxable and non-taxable customers

An order for products to be back-ordered

Orders for cash payment, credit cards, or accounts

Orders with partial shipments and partial payments

An order for a discontinued product

You might even want to make acid-test kinds of transactions. For instance, you might try an order exceeding a customer's credit limit, accompanied by a partial payment and requiring a back-order. Again, testing the system this way with no-risk data helps the operators become comfortable by learning what to expect. It also helps you as manager to identify problems and resolve them with fixes before they become critical.

During these tests, make sure your operators follow the directions as they appear in the user manuals. See how well they can be followed, and how well the documentation can stand on its own. Your staff should judge the ease of finding answers to questions in the manuals and give you feedback on their readability. Also check the manuals for completeness. The best manuals identify the different programs and data files and how they are used; tell how to edit, update, and correct previous entries; and indicate when the various reports are run and what they should look like. The better the documentation and the more self-sufficient your organization becomes, the more time you save by getting answers that you would otherwise have to ask your vendor.

To sum up, by this time you and your staff must be intimately involved in the installation. Keep in mind that these tests are artificial to some extent and do not totally duplicate a true operating environment. However, your giving final acceptance to the system may depend on the results of these tests. If you have difficulty, ask your vendor to help. It's a good idea to ask questions, especially of the "What if this happens?" variety to find flaws or weaknesses in the design of the system or its documentation. For future reference, make notes on what the vendor does and how. The vendor's demonstrations can be useful and a good opportunity to spot gross misunderstandings early in the installation process. These tests are your rehearsal for what follows, that is, entering the accounting data and actually running the system.

ACCOUNTING DATA CONVERSION

Regardless of the computer you buy, your accounting data must be converted from its present form into a machine-readable format. Whatever accounting modules you use, you will have to key in the required information, such as balances to be carried forward, or inventory part numbers and descriptions, before you can fully use the computer. Moving your data into the computer is like "priming the pump." The data conversion process entails gathering, editing, entering, and verifying the accounting information from your ledgers and other documents into the computer. Even with simple, straightforward accounting procedures, you need a conversion of some kind.

Some companies with a simple billing application can lift the pertinent information straight from the monthly statements or invoices. Other companies may require assembling pieces of data from various sources. For example, starting up a payroll application may require getting the employee's background from the personnel files and the wage and deduction amounts from the payroll journal ledger. Still other companies may require creating completely new information, such as account codes, customer codes, or inventory part numbers that may not have existed in a manual system.

Often when a company installs a new system, the necessary information for the computer comes from a combination of sources. It is unlikely that the existing system and the computer will use the same data formats. Some prior manipulation will have to be done. It is equally unlikely that all the data used in a manual accounting system can be used by the computer. A manual system almost always involves special situations and exceptions that cannot be handled by the computer without special programming. For example, computers usually process accounts in strict ascending numeric order. If a few customers receive special billing date treatment, then account codes must be assigned to permit these special dates to be handled in a numeric sequence.

Purge and Clean Up Data

Generally, the one-time step of converting data offers management an opportunity to purge documents and clean up the data before it is entered. Take full advantage of this step to assure an accurate financial data base. Remove outdated or "dead" accounts, update files to obtain the most current information, and check for completeness. You should also review the account codes, such as the chart of accounts, and restructure them or assign new ones if necessary. The computer can generate checklists to ease the cleanup and editing process. During data entry the computer can also help verify its accuracy, but don't expect the machine to automatically correct garbage data. In other words, if you try to automate a mess, you will only have an automated mess. Only solid, clean information will get your computerization off to a healthy start.

Establish Account Codes

During a regular monthly accounting period, various transactions are entered into the computer at random. Customer order information, inventory item changes, and journal entries go into the computer as they occur. Reference numbers (or code numbers) for the transactions enable the computer to properly store them in their proper place on the diskettes. This is how the computer processes the transaction activity and matches it with the other data stored in the computer, and also how it quickly and easily sorts transactions into a particular sequence for reporting. The lowest code numbers appear at the beginning of the report, while higher numbers are at the end. The accounting package usually determines this sorting sequence, and in most cases it's a strict ascending numerical order.

The numerical nature of the computer requires that all elements of all types of transactions be assigned numeric codes. Such items as the chart of accounts, customers, inventory items, vendors, and employees all must be labeled by number. In a manual system, customer numbers are typically not created, because records are kept in a tub file with alphabetical-by-last-name access. For the computer, however, you must plan for and assign customer code numbers. Your software package indicates how many digits are reserved for this number. Usually packages reserve five spaces, which allows up to 99,999 customers. You will normally have complete discretion in assigning these numbers and it is a simple matter to maintain the alphabetical sequence while under numerical control.

For example, suppose you have 500 customers and the last names run the full range of the alphabet. Instead of assigning them numbers from 1 through 500, as you might be inclined to do, you can assign the numbers 10 through 5,000, separating each name on your list by nine digits. Thus, the first two names on the list would be numbered 10 and 20, leaving numbers 11 through 19 open for new customers as they come along. All other names would also be nine spaces apart. This data processing trick allows you to add new names to an alphabetical list without having to delete existing customer numbers or reassign new ones each time.

In the general ledger chart of accounts, the numbering system can be used to create a different effect. Suppose your accounting package allows seven digits for the chart of account codes. Here the account number can have a prefix and a suffix to achieve different levels of reporting, and the code number format is often hyphenated for readability, as in "12-345-67." For example, the first two digits or the prefix can be the major classification, such as assets and liabilities. The next three digits can be the main account number, which allows up to 999 different accounts within each prefix. The last two digits or the suffix can be a sub-account number. This allows for summaries or detailed reports by departments, profit centers, or branch offices, whichever you need. Some accounting packages provide the utmost in flexibility and allow to you make up any desired numbering or formatting scheme.

By carefully planning the assignment of code numbers, you can achieve many different goals. Your vendor and the documentation should help provide guidelines in setting up these code numbers.

Entering the Data

Master Files. In establishing files, data to be entered into the computer may be labeled in one of two categories: static and dynamic. Static data is that which changes little in the course of business, such as customer names and addresses. Dynamic data (or transaction information), by contrast, changes constantly. Static data files are called master files when they are stored in the computer. Unlike in a manual system, master files are stored and treated separately from transaction files. Because static files are less subject to change than the dynamic, they are generally entered first into the computer. They can be keyed in and edited long before it's necessary to do the same with the dynamic files. This accomplishes two purposes. First, it provides a foundation or a data base for which to enter the transaction data later. Second, it enables the staff to learn to use the computer without the risks and time constraints of entering the dynamic files. Converting the master files generally includes the following information:

1. General Ledger
   Account codes and account descriptions
   Year-to-date amounts or historical data
   Previous-year and current-year budget information

2. Accounts Receivable
   Customer codes
   Customer names, addresses, phone numbers
   Other customer background, such as credit limit, terms, and tax status

3. Accounts Payable
   Vendor code numbers
   Vendor names and addresses
   Other background, such as terms and shipping method

4. Inventory
   Part numbers and descriptions
   Part location codes
   Cost or pricing information
   Vendor code numbers

5. Payroll
   Employee numbers
   Employee names, addresses, pay rates and deduction classifications

Transaction Files. Dynamic data consists of the daily transactions that frequently change balances over the accounting period, like inventory quantities-on-hand. Since this information can quickly go out of date, it is normally entered just before the cutover to the computer. Transaction activity includes such information as account balances, open items detail, new orders, and payroll timecards. Obtaining good results in using the system after installation depends on the accuracy of the transaction data. This fact and the timely manner in which transactions files must be entered demand some control or means of checking to ensure accuracy.

For instance, the total accounts receivable outstanding should be the same in the new system as it was in the old just before the conversion. One way to achieve this is to separate the entries into small groups or batches in which totals for each have been calculated with an office adding machine. If, after entering, the totals from the adding machine tapes differ from the computer, the problem can usually be isolated to one particular batch. This system of balancing separate batches can determine when transactions have been omitted or when one or more amounts have been entered erroneously. The data entered to create the transaction files generally includes the following:

1. General Ledger
   Current account balances
   Current detailed journal entries

2. Accounts Receivable
   Invoice line items, quantities, and amounts
   Customer balances being carried forward
   Back-order items

3. Accounts Payable
   Vendor account balances payable
   Back-order items

4. Inventory
   On-hand product balances
   Current issues and receipts

5. Payroll
   Year-to-date earnings
   Year-to-date deductions
   Number of hours worked to date

For all the accounting information to be entered into the computer, some provision must be made to do the editing and make corrections. For example, the system should provide a way of creating printed reports showing all the data entered in the files. It's easy to scan the printout for incorrect or missing information. This printing can sometimes be done with the standard reports built into the accounting package. Or special edit checklist programs may be provided for this purpose. Either way, the operator should make a habit of running off the checklist frequently, say at the end of each computer session. This computer "feedback" assures accuracy during the installation process and also helps the operator gain confidence in using the system.

Outside Service Conversion

If you have been using an outside service bureau for any of your accounting functions, you may be able to save considerable time by retrieving your company's data in machine-readable form. Some service firms have refused to assist in these conversions with the weak hope that you will not discontinue their services. Some will even say you have no right to it, since they own the programs. That may be true, but the programs and the data are almost always maintained separately in the computer. You only need to assert your right that you do indeed own the data of your own business.

The service bureau may ask for a legitimate fee, however, for the time and materials needed to transfer your data into an acceptable format. The popular media of the large-scale computers, such as half-inch open reel magnetic tape or punched cards, are unacceptable simply because microcomputers do not have the peripheral equipment to read them. You can, however, accomplish the data transfer in two practical ways. First, you can ask the service firm to copy your data files onto an 8-inch diskette, providing of course they have an 8-inch disk drive attached to their computer. You may have to accept the data in the single sided, single density format, which is the only floppy disk format standard in the industry. If you have a floppy disk size other than the 8-inch, your vendor may have to convert the files a second time for your system.

Second, you can ask that the data be transferred over a telephone line using computer telecommunications, which bypasses the disk formatting problem. With this method your data travels from the mass storage device of the service bureau's computer to your disk drives via the main memory of each computer. This method requires that you have a telephone modem and communications software for your computer. In any case, your vendor should be willing to help by contacting the service firm directly to resolve any formatting problems. If none of these alternatives is workable, as a last resort you can key in the necessary information from the hard copy reports from the service firm.

CONVERTING TO THE COMPUTER

Converting to the computer marks the beginning of the final phase of computerizing your operation. This is the last major step of the installation process, when the new system is put to the final test. Maintaining control of your business, while continuing to test the new computer, requires that you overlap phasing-in the new system with letting go of the manual system. The actual time required for this transition depends on your situation. One to three months is common for most companies.

Going live with the computer should start with one of the accounting cycles, or the beginning of the month. Some companies deliberately plan the purchase and installation of their computer to coincide with their new fiscal year. In either case, begin operating your new application on the first day of a new accounting period.

Some business people might think one day you stop using the old system and the next day you start using the computer. This "cold turkey" method is risky, since you have nothing against which to compare the accuracy and performance of the new system. This method might be appropriate only for a very small business, such as a one-person operation.

Two other methods more commonly used and more appropriate for larger organizations are the "parallel" and the "phased-in" methods. The parallel method uses both the old and new systems side by side. This allows you to directly compare one against the other. With the phased-in method you separate each accounting function into its component parts and convert the parts to the computer one at a time. When one part works well on the new system, you convert the next. Let's look at the merits of these two methods.

Parallel Method

Running live parallel is one of the best ways to determine whether the new system meets its specifications, or whether changes must be made to bring it up to standard. As mentioned, running parallel means to operate the old and the new systems concurrently using the same data. Because of this direct comparison, it is the lowest-risk method and it readily highlights any flaws in the new computer. If you discover serious deficiencies that require shutting down the new computer, little harm has been done to the regular flow of work and the business can continue in a normal manner. This is a fail-safe method, which allows you to revert to the previous system at any point without jeopardizing the business. It may be far better to fall back on manual procedures long enough for the computerized system to be corrected and put back into production rather than attempt to patch the mistakes of the computer while maintaining both systems simultaneously.

How long should you run the two systems in parallel? No set formula applies, since the answer depends on the complexity of your business. Some companies achieve their goals in a few weeks of running parallel, others take as long as six months or more. Confidence is an important factor: You can stop running parallel when you are confident that the new system performs adequately.

Ideally, you may want to test every conceivable transaction with your new computer, but obviously not all kinds will be encountered in the first few days, nor will all the possible exceptions show up. For example, a customer's credit limit will not show a warning until orders have accumulated to the limit amount. Or if the detailed transactions are carried forward for quarterly reporting, then data storage capacities will not be tested with only one month's running. The time and expense involved also make testing every conceivable condition impractical. One strategy is to plan one month of parallel operation, followed by a second month only if minor problems occur, with the total cutover to the new system in the third month. Generally, a good rule is to run parallel as long as you have remaining doubts about the new system, or as long as it is practical and beneficial to do so.

Some systems cannot run in parallel mode. If the old and the new differ widely, they may not be comparable point for point. For example, procedures designed into the new system may constitute a departure from the way things were done before. A manager may choose to make such dramatic improvements when bringing in a computer that little basis for comparison remains. Reconciling two substantially different methods may require an extraordinary amount of work to backtrack and crosscheck the results of one system against the other. In these cases, the phase-in method may be more appropriate.

One reason to weigh carefully the impact of running parallel operations is that it literally doubles the amount of work. The staff must process each change and transaction twice, plus taking extra time to compare and reconcile the two systems. On top of this they are learning to contend with the new computer. These demanding experiences may appear to contradict the claim that the computer will help them save time and effort. You should anticipate their frustration and make allowances for the time, patience, and financial resources needed to bear with this period. Also, some companies may not have sufficient resources to operate in both modes for extended periods. For these and other reasons, the phase-in method may be the better choice.

Phase-In Method

The phase-in method consists of dividing the accounting functions into separate, identifiable components. In accounts receivable, for example, you divide the total number of customers into groups, such as those whose last names range from A through H, I through Q, and R through Z. To start, only the A–H group is entered into the computer, while the other customers, names I–Z, remain on the manual system. When the records of the first group of customers are running as they should, then the second and later groups can be implemented. This method minimizes the double workload of the parallel mode, where all customers are brought onto the computer at one time.

The phase-in method can be used for any of the basic accounting functions. In inventory, for instance, selected products or categories of products can be entered into the computer one group at a time. In accounts payable, a variation of the phase-in method can be used. All the old balances could be paid manually, while only new purchases are entered into the computer system. Here a cut-off date marks the boundary between the old and new method. Whichever accounting function is used, the dividing and identification of these groups or categories should be simple for the office staff to remember.

While the phase-in method requires some extra effort from the staff, it may be the simplest and easiest way to start the new system. Overall, the implementation period here may be longer than the parallel method, but the main advantage is that it minimizes the double workload. Also, if problems occur, smaller portions of data are easier to correct, thereby conserving time and human energy. A conservative approach uses a combination of the two methods. You can implement divided portions of an accounting function while maintaining the manual system until the computerized system has proven itself.

Phase-In Accounting Modules

For the same reasons, begin with no more than two or three accounting modules and add the others only after the first ones are operational. For example, you can start with inventory, accounts receivable, and general ledger. Once these run smoothly, add accounts payable and payroll. To bring up a full accounting system at one time might prove to be too much for you and your staff. Gradually gaining experience with the accounting modules one by one, and allowing the time for your company to get used to them, shows good judgment. The experience gained with these first sub-systems will make it easier to adapt the others later. Also, the accounting modules brought up first provide the operational framework and build the data base for the succeeding ones.

Phasing in the accounting modules over time simply means to approach the computer installation with cautious optimism. Difficulties that arise while you are trying to do too much tend to compound even the smallest problems. Place your vendor on standby status and call for help when you really need it. Normally, the vendor should be showing your staff how to correct the problems rather than doing the work for you.

From the day the computer arrives, you should make every effort to become self-sufficient. Some companies allow up to a year for the full implementation process, while others have taken even longer. It seems to make life simple for everyone if no particular final installation date is set, and management allows just whatever time it takes. But you should remember that the longer the installation process, the longer you go without receiving the full return on your computer investment.

The Acceptance Test

At some point the vendor will be asking you for the final acceptance test, usually noted in your contract with him. His final payment may depend on this last test. Your signing off the acceptance test declares that the system is installed satisfactorily and that it meets its promised specifications. These tests sometimes show that no part of the system, hardware or software, is at fault, but that the users do not fully understand how the system works. Thus an important part of this final step is to be sure the computer operators can in fact run the system properly. Nonetheless, if you find some portions of the system unacceptable, review them with your vendor, along with whatever corrective steps are necessary.

INSTALLATION CHECKLIST

A system installation checklist is provided that summarizes the main points of this chapter. Spaces are included to show the start and finish dates, and the office staff responsibility. You may want to modify the checklist to adapt it to your own installation requirements.

THE JOB IS NEVER DONE

Even after the computer is fully installed and working properly, you can expect to be continually involved with the system. Because of the computer's profound effect on your organization, you should stay active with it for at least the first year. Don't expect the system to meet all the objectives you originally had in mind. To accomplish all of these things takes time—sometimes years. However, when a computer is installed, management usually sees things differently after the system is fully integrated into the business. You will probably find that how you originally conceptualized using the computer is somewhat different from the reality of having it in your business.

Installation and Preparation Checklist			
	Personnel Assigned	Start Date	Finish Date
Physical Installation			
Off-Site Preparation:			
Hardware Assembled, Tested			
Operating Software Installed			
Application Software Installed			
On-Site Preparation:			
Hardware Re-Assembled, Tested			
Application Working Diskettes			
Accounting Package Initialized			
Preliminary Package Tests			
Accounting Data Conversion			
Establish Account Codes:			
Chart of Accounts			
Customers			
Vendors			
Inventory Items			
Employees			
Other _____			
Enter Master File Data:			
General Ledger			
Accounts Receivable			
Accounts Payable			
Inventory Description			
Payroll			
Enter Transaction Data:			
General Ledger			
Accounts Receivable			
Accounts Payable			
Inventory			
Payroll			
Test System with Live Data			
Test Data Backup Procedures			
Conversion to the Computer			
Documentation Changes			
Final Acceptance Test			
Cutover Date			

Figure 17-1   System Installation Checklist

For instance, you may find little practical use for the reports you originally thought would be informative. Or you may have to add some reporting capabilities that were not part of the original application software. You may find a dramatic improvement in the speed of processing information in some areas of your business, while other areas may be slightly out of step with the computer operation. It usually takes several months of working with the computer and continually making adjustments to it. The process of being alert to these conditions and making changes is the "fine tuning" of the system. Be careful about making changes that can affect your warranty, and if you need to make software modifications it is best to group a number of small changes as one project.

Buying and installing a computer can be exciting and rewarding to your company. When used properly, computers almost always give management insight on new ways to improve the business. The real power and benefits of a computer become apparent only after it is installed and you have used it for a while. If you buy the computer and install it according to the guidelines in this book, you can be certain that only a few other kinds of investments will yield as high or higher a return on the time, effort, and money expended. Computers are here to stay and they will continue to transform the world of business.

Glossary

Acceptance Test   The final test, usually outlined in the customer's purchase contract, that determines if the system is installed correctly and meets performance specifications.

Address   A number the computer uses to designate a particular main memory location. The computer "finds" each specific piece of information by "looking" at an address.

Application Program   Computer software; a set of programs to perform a particular business function, such as inventory or word processing. A programmer can write a custom application program, or it can be purchased as packaged software.

ASCII   An abbreviation for American Standard Code for Information Exchange. The ASCII code, which many manufacturers adhere to, is used to represent 128 letters, numbers, and symbols in a way the computer can "understand."

Audit Trail Internal controls in an accounting package that automatically record the origin and type of each transaction entered. Audit trails facilitate tracing errors to their original source.

Backup An identical copy of data and/or programs stored on a diskette, magenetic tape, or hard disk cartridge to protect against possible loss. Also the process of creating the copy.

Backup Hardware A duplicate hardware unit, either a peripheral or an entire computer, to protect against service interruption if a device fails in the original unit.

Batch Processing A way of handling data to be entered in the computer as discrete groups at separate times. Batch processing does not immediately update the information in the disk file. Opposite of interactive processing.

Bit A contraction of the words "binary digit." The smallest unit of information the computer can move, read, and understand. Each bit is like a switch in either the On or Off position, represented by "1" or "0."

Boot Up Slang for loading the operating system software into the computer's main memory. The computer may automatically do this when turned on.

Bug A slang expression for a programming error that prevents a computer program from running as intended.

Bundled Often refers to application software that comes with a computer system at no extra charge.

Bus A row of uniform electrical contacts inside the computer. These contacts provide connections between the internal components of the computer when printed circuit boards are inserted.

Byte The amount of memory space occupied by one character of information, such as a letter or a number. Each byte is made up of eight bits. Computer main memory and mass storage are measured in bytes.

CAI Computer Assisted Instruction, using the computer itself. Special programs written to tutor the user in a self-paced study of almost any subject, including how to use the computer.

Cassette A permanent container for magnetic tape or hard disk that can be inserted into a computer's drive unit.

Character A single letter of the alphabet, a single numeric digit, a special symbol (such as #, $, &, @, +, etc.), or a blank space as found between words in text.

Chip The heart of the computer. A thumbnail sized square made of silicon containing thousands of electronic circuits. The chip and its immediate connectors are called an integrated circuit.

Computer Dealer Generally, a retail store carrying a number of brands of computers and packaged software for business-related tasks. Dealer is also used to designate most other kinds of suppliers of computer products to the final consumer.

Computer Program A set of precise instructions directing the computer to perform specific functions in a logical and predetermined manner.

Computer System Or "system"; the entire hardware and software setup used to perform tasks for a business.

Console The video screen and keyboard from which the computer operator uses or controls the computer. A multi-user computer may have one master terminal designated as the "system console."

CP/M The name of a family of general purpose operating systems for microcomputers. Trademarked in 1976 by Digital Research, Inc. (Pacific Grove, California), it stands for Control Program for Microcomputers.

CPS Characters per second. A speed rating for printers or data transmission.

CPU Central processing unit. A group of electronic circuit boards containing the arithmetic, logic, main memory, and control functions of the computer, housed in a metal or plastic enclosure. It also contains back panel connectors for other devices, and the main power switch.

CRT Cathode Ray Tube. A TV-like screen and a keyboard for displaying and entering information. Sometimes called (incorrectly) a monitor, which is a screen only.

Custom Software Computer programs written to a client's particular specifications. An expensive alternative to packaged software.

Data Base An organized collection of related information items, such as customer records or employee information, to be processed by application software or a data base management program.

Data Base Management A "general purpose" application program that allows the user to tell the computer what data is to be entered, stored, and reported. Has the effect of writing a custom program but with a much shorter setup time.

Data Conversion The one-time task of transferring business data from the present system to the computer. Often means gathering, editing, entering, and verifying accounting information from ledgers and other documents.

Data File Any number of records, each with the same set of data items. If stored in a computer, the contents of a telephone book would be called a data file, and each name, address, and phone number are data items that together make up a record.

Data File Inquiry An application software feature that allows calling to the video screen any item or record in a data file. Also called on-line inquiry, or information retrieval.

Data Item The smallest unit of meaningful information, such as a customer's last name, telephone number, or amount of last payment. A sub-section of a record, in which each data item is made up of one or more characters.

Default   The way a hardware or software variable feature automatically occurs unless deliberately changed by the user. For example, a word processing program may default to single spacing or one inch page margins unless changed by the operator.

Degradation   Loss of computer speed or response time due to heavy usage of the CPU by concurrent multiple users.

Disk Drive   An information storage and retrieval device using a rotating magnetic disk similar to a small phonograph record. Provides permanent mass storage of data and programs.

Diskette   Often called a floppy disk. A flexible, oxide-particle-covered circle of plastic with a square protective jacket that is inserted in a disk drive. A magnetic recording technique is used and the data is stored in a digital format.

Documentation   The printed instruction material needed to use a computer or application software. An owner's manual.

DOS   Disk Operating System; a set of computer programs that resides on a floppy or hard disk. The term is used interchangeably with operating system or system software.

Dot Matrix Printer   A type of printer using tiny wires striking an inked ribbon to make dot patterns that form letters and characters. Relatively inexpensive and has a faster print speed than letter quality printers.

Dual Processor   A computer having both eight- and sixteen-bit processors built into its CPU, with the advantage of running both kinds of software.

Eight-Bit CPU   A microprocessor chip that handles data eight bits at a time. The 8080, 8085, and Z80 chips are eight-bit processors.

Electronic Spreadsheet   A software package that turns the video screen into a "ruled pad" with rows and columns. Numbers, formulas, and descriptions can be entered and manipulated to quickly find the results of changing variables.

Expandable Computer   A computer system designed to allow adding more external devices, such as disk drives or terminals; or more internal circuitry, such as RAM memory, color graphics, or data communications.

Field   One logical piece of information in a data record, such as name, address, or zip code. Same as data item.

File Lockout   A one-user-at-a-time software feature in multi-user systems that prevents users from accidentally destroying each other's files should they be accessed at the same time.

Floppy Disks   Another name for diskettes. Popular sizes are 8-inch, 5-¼-inch, and 3½-inch. (See "Diskette".)

Hard Copy   A permanent copy of information or data printed on paper or other tangible media.

IEEE Interface   A standard type of parallel connector for cables used to attach a printer or hard disk to a computer.

Information Retrieval   The ability of the computer to "look up" and display specific information from quantities of stored data.

Input   To enter data into the computer.

Integrated Circuits   A name for the very small enclosures that hold micro-computer chips. A typical computer will contain many integrated circuits attached to printed circuit boards inside the CPU.

Integrated Package   An accounting package in which all of the modules work together as a unit. For example, upon entry a single transaction sets off a series of conditions that affects one or more modules.

Interactive Processing   A "conversational" style of using a computer, in which the user and computer respond to each other in turn. In contrast to batch processing.

Interface   The electronic and software connection between the computer's CPU and its peripherals.

K   An abbreviation for a thousand bytes (or characters) of computer memory. More precisely, each K is 1,024 positions, and a 64K computer actually has 65,536 positions of main memory.

Keyboard   A data entry device similar to the array of keys found on a type-writer and a calculator. A detachable keyboard is connected to the computer by a flexible cable like a telephone cord.

Letter Quality Printer   A type of printer that makes fully-formed characters by impressions of a molded hammer-key like those on a typewriter. Best for pro-ducing high-quality printed documents.

License   Express permission from a software developer to use a computer program, but with certain restrictions. The license constitutes a right to use the program rather than direct ownership.

LPM   Lines Per Minute. A speed rating for printers.

Machine Language   A highly detailed set of program instructions that the computer "executes." English-like instructions (or code) are written by a program-mer, and are later translated into "machine language" by compilers or interpreters.

Magnetic Tape   A recording medium, similar to an audio cassette tape, used to store data and programs, but which can be read only by a computer. Used primarily for data backup purposes.

Main Memory   The storage and processing area inside the CPU, as opposed to external memory on tape or disks. (See "Memory.")

Main Processing Unit   Also called the Central Processing Unit (CPU). The cabinet or enclosure that contains a group of electronic circuit boards holding the microprocessor chips.

Mainframe   The largest of three classes of computers, used primarily by large corporations and government agencies. (The other two are mini- and micro-computers.)

Mass Storage Device   A means of storing data in permanent form outside the computer's main memory. The most common device is a floppy or hard disk drive.

Master Files   Business data that changes little from day to day once it is stored in the computer, such as customer names and addresses and general ledger chart of account descriptions.

MB   Megabyte, or one million bytes of information. Also, 1,000 K.

Mega-   Prefix standing for 1 million.

Memory   The part of the central processing unit that holds programs and data as they are processed. Size is measured in K, or kilobytes (1,024 characters). ROM and RAM are two types of internal memory.

Menu   A list of program functions on the video screen, usually numbered, from which the operator makes choices and proceeds to the next level.

MHz   Megahertz, a technical specification for processor speed in cycles per second. The higher the number the faster the processing speed. Most small computers operate in the four MHz to twelve Mhz speed range.

Microcomputer   A small, low-priced computer based on a microprocessor chip. The smallest of three classes of computers.

Microprocessor Chip   The heart of the computer, formed on a single integrated circuit chip about one-quarter inch square. It contains the arithmetic, logic, and control units, and may have the equivalent of over 100,000 transistors.

Minicomputer   A small business computer of greater sophistication and cost than a microcomputer. Generally classed between a microcomputer and the large mainframe computers.

Modem   Contraction for modulator/demodulator. A device that enables computers to communicate over ordinary telephone lines by translating the computer's digital signal into an analog signal and back again.

Monitor   A cathode ray tube, similar to a television set, attached to a computer as an output display device.

MS-DOS   An operating system developed in 1981 by Microsoft, Inc. (Bellevue, Washington), originally for the IBM Personal Computer. It's called PC-DOS when used on the IBM, and is available for other brands of computers.

MTBF   Abbreviation for Mean Time Between Failures. A manufacturer's statistical estimate of how long a hardware device will run without failure.

MTTR   Abbreviation for Mean Time To Repair. A service department's statistical estimate of how long it takes to restore operation from the time of reported malfunction.

Multi-User Computer A computer that can handle more than one user, each running a computer program from separate terminals. Normally, all users have access to all data files and programs. When the system has multiple separate computers it is called a networking system.

Multi-Tasking A single or multi-user computer that is capable of running more than one program at a time.

Networking Connecting several different computers or CPUs by a common hard-wire linkage. Most networking systems allow the users to share peripherals.

Node One computer or work station in a network.

Object Program Also called "object code." The actual instructions the machine follows when converted from a program written in a programming language (which is called its "source code").

OEM Original Equipment Manufacturer. Now a misnomer, since an OEM typically assembles components made by others into a system it sells under its own name. Sometimes an OEM buys finished hardware and only adds its own software packages.

Off-Line Not directly connected to the computer system. Data may be entered directly onto a diskette by a separate machine and entered into the computer at later time.

On-Line Editing The automatic verification of data as it is entered into the computer but before it is processed or passed to the disk files.

On-Line Processing The opposite of off-line. The user interacts directly with the computer as it processes information.

On-Line Storage Having immediate access to information stored on a disk, rather than having to first insert the disk in the drive unit.

On-Site Customer's office or location of the computer.

Operating System A set of essential programs that resides in the computer's main memory when it is running. Sometimes called "system software," the operating system mainly directs the computer's internal functions.

Output The resulting information from the computer's processing. It may be sent to any output device, such as a printer, terminal, or disk.

Packaged Software Generalized application programs for a variety of business tasks. The software comes ready to use without any further programming.

Parallel Interface A particular type of connector between a computer and a peripheral device. The Centronics or IEEE-488 are parallel interfaces.

Parallel Method A way of converting a manual accounting system to a computer by running both systems concurrently using the same data.

Password A computer security technique. The user gains access to the computer and/or data files by entering a secret code known only to the user and the system manager.

Peripheral An external input/output device connected to the CPU, such as a printer, disk drive, terminal, or modem.

Personal Computer A small computer used by only one person. A computer used within the domain of one's job.

Phase-In Method A way of computerizing an accounting system by separating it into components, which are converted one at a time.

Pin Assignments The location and particular use for each pin (or wire) within a multi-wire connector, such as an RS-232 interface cable.

Port A connector on the back panel of the computer for attaching a cable from a peripheral device, such as a printer or a modem.

Printer An output device that produces printed copy on paper.

Programming Language A software "tool" for programmers to develop application programs. All programs are written with symbols in a language that is translated into machine code for the computer to execute.

Prompt A word or symbol displayed by the computer program on the video screen asking for specific information, such as a command or data item.

RAM Random Access Memory. The main memory in the CPU for data and instructions. Measured in K (kilobytes) of memory, it is erased each time power is turned off or a new program runs.

Random Access The ability of a disk drive head to locate and "read" specific information stored anywhere on the disk, rather than having to search through every file or record sequentially.

Read What the mass storage device does when its "playback" head retrieves a piece of information from a tape or disk. It "reads" the data and transfers it to the main memory.

Real-Time When the computer updates its files almost instantaneously in response to a request or a transaction, it is said to run in "real time." As opposed to batch processing.

Record One or more data items related in a meaningful way, such as a name, address, telephone, ship-to address, etc. for one customer, make up a record.

Record Layout The fixed arrangement of data items in a record. Also called its "format."

Response Time The lapse of time between entering data on a terminal and the answer back from the CPU, usually a few seconds.

RFP Request For Proposal. A set of written specifications for a computer system from a prospective buyer to a prospective vendor. It mainly describes hardware and software requirements, and the terms and conditions of the sale.

RS-232 A standard designation for a serial interface, or connection, between the computer and a peripheral device.

S-100 Bus A row of 100 gold-plated electrical connectors that is a standard receptacle for printed circuit boards to be placed inside a computer.

Serial Interface A type of connector between a computer and a peripheral device, such as a printer or a modem. An "RS-232" is one type of serial interface.

Service Bureau A company that provides programming or data processing services, but does not normally sell hardware.

Single Board Computer A computer with all its internal circuitry for main memory and other CPU functions on one major printed circuit board.

Single User Computer A small business or personal computer designed to run only one program for one user at a time.

Sixteen-Bit CPU A microprocessor chip that processes sixteen bits (two bytes) of data at a time. The 8086 and 8088 are sixteen-bit microprocessor chips.

Software The programs a computer runs, which consist of instructions stored in a digital format usually on magnetic media.

Software House A firm that writes custom software to the user's specifications. Generally means the same as systems house.

Source Code What the computer programmer writes when he or she creates an application program. Written in a programming language and then translated into machine code for the computer.

System Crash A major mishap in which the magnetic recordings on the disk files become unreadable by the computer. This is often caused by electrical interference or hardware failure.

System Software Another term for the operating system, a set of programs that direct the internal functions of the computer.

Systems Analysis A detailed study to find the best computer system, including the software, for a particular business. Also, an effort to solve a particular business problem.

Technical Support A highly qualified person available from the computer dealer to answer questions and solve problems concerning hardware and software.

Telecommunication Using telephone lines and other communication devices to send and receive messages or files between computers.

Terminal The video screen and keyboard as a unit. Used to enter and display data, and to control the computer's operations.

Timesharing Usually used in reference to a large mainframe system, a term for many people at different locations using the computer via telephone lines.

Transaction Files Stored data that change frequently as a result of business activities, such as sales orders.

Turnkey System A complete computer system sold ready to use. ("You just turn the key.")

Unbundled Software sold separately from the hardware it runs on.

UNIX A sophisticated, multi-user operating system developed by Bell Laboratories originally for minicomputers, but versions are now available for microcomputers.

Utility Program A program or routine within an operating system that performs specific "housekeeping" tasks such as copying disk files.

VDT Video Display Terminal. The same as a CRT.

Vendor An organization that sells one or more components of a computer system and/or software.

Video Screen A television-like display device.

Winchester Disk A type of hard disk drive that is sealed inside an enclosure to protect it from environmental hazards.

Word Processing Combines a computer with a typewriter to electronically create, store, manipulate, and print various documents.

Work Stations The main devices for entering and retrieving data, as well as controlling the computer. Each consists of a video display screen and a keyboard. Same as terminal.

Write To record information onto a storage medium such as tape or a diskette for later retrieval. Drive units use a "read/write" head.

Index